WORKSHOP MANUAL

SCOOTERS
1959 - 1965

Two-stroke 175cc

Four-stroke 250cc
(Including electric start)

Includes the following publications:

* Instruction Manual *

* Service Sheets Manual *

* Illustrated Parts Manual *

A Floyd Clymer Publication – Published 2021 by VelocePress.com

INTRODUCTION

Welcome to the world of digital publishing ~ the book you now hold in your hand was printed using the latest state of the art digital technology. The advent of print-on-demand has forever changed the publishing process, never has information been so accessible and it is our hope that this book serves your informational needs for years to come. If this is your first exposure to digital publishing, we hope that you are pleased with the results. Many more titles of interest to the classic automobile and motorcycle enthusiast, collector and restorer are available via our website at www.VelocePress.com. We hope that you find this title as interesting as we do.

NOTE FROM THE PUBLISHER

The information presented is true and complete to the best of our knowledge. All recommendations are made without any guarantees on the part of the author or the publisher, who also disclaim all liability incurred with the use of this information.

TRADEMARKS

We recognize that some words, model names and designations, for example, mentioned herein are the property of the trademark holder. We use them for identification purposes only. This is not an official publication.

INFORMATION ON THE USE OF THIS PUBLICATION

This manual is an invaluable resource for those interested in performing their own maintenance. However, in today's information age we are constantly subject to changes in common practice, new technology, availability of improved materials and increased awareness of chemical toxicity. As such, it is advised that the user consult with an experienced professional prior to undertaking any procedure described herein. While every care has been taken to ensure correctness of information, it is obviously not possible to guarantee complete freedom from errors or omissions or to accept liability arising from such errors or omissions. Therefore, any individual that uses the information contained within, or elects to perform or participate in do-it-yourself repairs or modifications acknowledges that there is a risk factor involved and that the publisher or its associates cannot be held responsible for personal injury or property damage resulting from the use of the information or the outcome of such procedures.

WARNING!

One final word of advice, this publication is intended to be used as a reference guide, and when in doubt the reader should consult with a qualified technician.

PAGE NUMBERS

Please note that the page numbers relate to the individual manuals. The number to the bottom of the final page is the total number of pages in the manual.

TRIUMPH TIGRESS & BSA SUNBEAM SCOOTER 1959 to 1965

This manual is a compilation of three factory publications including the owner's instruction manual, the parts/spares manual and a set of service sheets. These publications cover all three variations of the 175cc two-stroke and the 250cc four-stroke and electric start models manufactured from 1959 to 1965. Neither BSA or Triumph ever published a workshop manual for these models, however, the combination of these three publications provide the most comprehensive maintenance and repair information that was ever available, and it is an adequate substitution for a workshop manual.

MANUALS & TECHNICAL PUBLICATIONS

Maintenance, repair and service information was issued under both the BSA and Triumph name. However, as the machines were identical in all aspects, any technical documentation can be applied to either manufacturer without hesitation.

SERVICE SHEETS: Beginning in December 1959, both BSA and Triumph began publishing repair, overhaul and technical information in the form of individual (dealer only) 'Service Sheets' numbered 1001 through 1013 plus 1050 through 1054. It should be noted that it was never intended that these service sheets would be distributed to the general public. However, they were eventually combined into a single publication (with the exception of sheet numbers 1053 & 1054) and released under both the BSA and Triumph names, the contents being identical in either case.

INSTRUCTION MANUAL: Both BSA and Triumph published an identical 'Instruction Manual' the only difference being the name on the front cover. These publications were somewhat more detailed than typical 'owner's manuals' as they included overhaul information in addition to general maintenance and adjustments. As these instruction manuals were included with each new scooter purchased, there were a number of 'editions' published during the lifetime of the model, however, the contents remained basically unchanged. When combined with the 'Service Sheets' they are a reasonable substitute for a workshop manual.

PARTS or SPARES MANUAL: The parts manuals are also identical and include exploded component diagrams that are extremely helpful in the rebuilding or restoration process, particularly when used in conjunction with the Service Sheets and the Instruction Manual.

ADDITIONAL DATA: There is an addendum to the rear of this manual that contains a number of communications that were sent from the UK factory to their US distributors. These documents are somewhat rare and they may be of help in assisting in the maintenance of one of these machines.

DESIGN & GENERAL SPECIFICATIONS

Designed by Edward Turner (Triumph) and sold under both BSA and Triumph brand names to take advantage of established distribution networks, this badge engineering was one of the last uses of the Sunbeam name. The differences between the BSA Sunbeam and Triumph Tigress were entirely cosmetic - the former in polychromatic green paint, also two-tone red and cream, with a BSA badge; the latter in a shell blue or mimosa and ivory (two-tone) with a Triumph badge.

Introduced in late 1959, the scooter was available with a 250 cc four-stroke twin (10 hp), or 175 cc two-stroke single cylinder engine (7.5 hp). Both engines were forced-air-cooled. The two-stroke was a development of the BSA Bantam engine but the four-stroke was a completely new parallel-twin with a gear drive to the gearbox. The contact-breaker fed two separate ignition coils, each of which connected directly to its own spark plug without the need for a distributor. Drive to the rear wheel was by a fully enclosed chain in an oil bath. Both versions had four, foot-operated gears. Some of the 250 twins were fitted with an electric starter and a 12 volt (not 6 volt) electrical system, they were identified as either B2S (Sunbeam) or TW2S (Triumph). The 250 cc four-stroke model was discontinued in 1964 and the 175 cc two-stroke model in 1965.

BSA SUNBEAM
SCOOTER SERVICE SHEETS

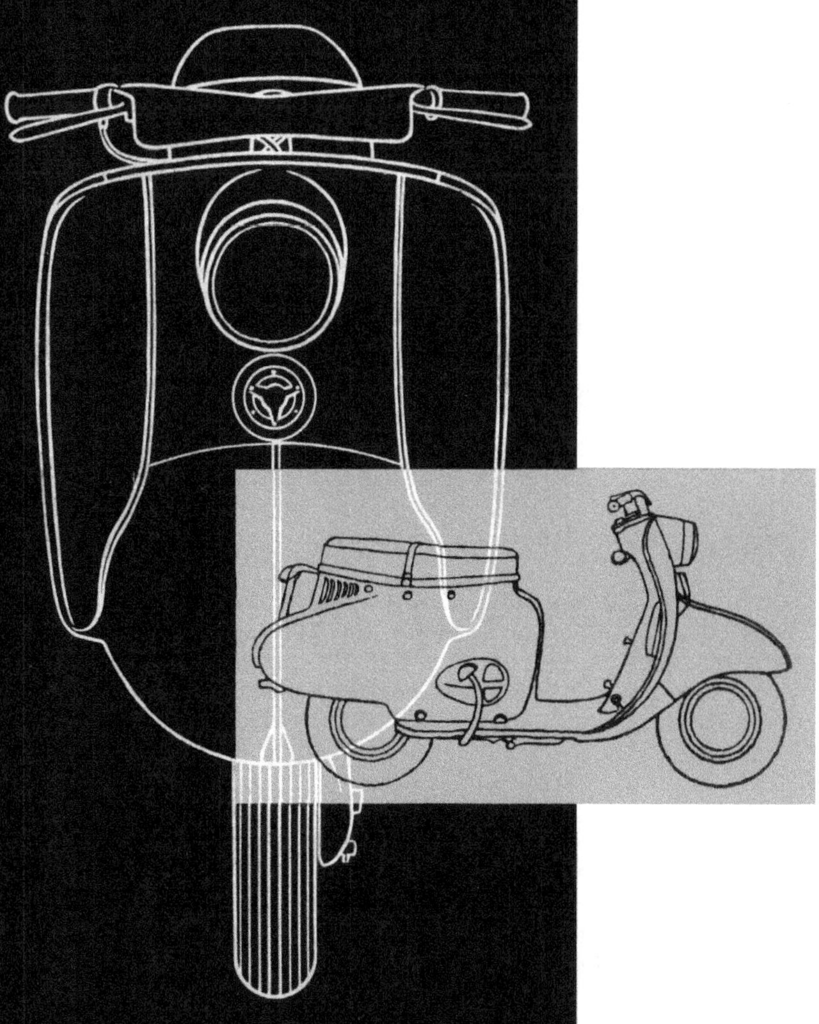

Scooter Service Sheet

1001

Printed December 1959.

250 c.c. O.H.V. TWIN CYLINDER SCOOTER
REMOVING THE SIDE VALANCES

Removing the Side Valances

To remove the side valances for maintenance on the engine unit, take off the dual seat by removing the two ¼ in. nuts and bolts coupling the "C" shaped hinges to the dual seat brackets. Take out the three 3/16 in. bolts, two at the front of the valances and one at the rear bottom end, and remove the two ¼ in. diameter nuts and bolts which secure the number plate.

When a spare wheel and rear carrier are fitted the number plate is on the rear carrier and need not be removed from the carrier.

Break the connectors to the rear lamp. These will normally be found underneath the rubber tool tray, but when a rear carrier and spare wheel are fitted the connectors will be well outside the valances and will be obvious.

When a spare wheel is fitted, undo the two nuts, slacken off the two bolts at each side of the dual seat that support the rear carrier, lift the carrier and take off the spare wheel. Then take out the two bolts at the sides of the dual seat and remove the carrier complete with number plate. Remove the two 5/16 in. bolts at the middle rear of the valances which also hold the spare wheel brackets.

The valances will now only be held by two bolts at each side, one domed slotted bolt immediately below the dual seat and one round head bolt at the bottom edge immediately above the pillion passenger's footboards. On the right-hand side of the machine the dual seat catch knob must also be removed. The valances are now ready to be taken away complete with the plastic beadings.

Reassembly of the valances is the complete reverse of dismantling. They should therefore be located first by refitting the two domed head slotted bolts immediately below the dual seat and the round head bolts above the pillion passenger's footboards, but these two bolts should be left slack to facilitate refitting the bolts around the edges of the valances. It is a wise precaution to locate all the bolts through the beading before tightening.

SCOOTER SERVICE SHEET

1002

Printed December 1959.

250 c.c. O.H.V. TWIN CYLINDER SCOOTER

DISMANTLING FOR DECARBONISING

The term decarbonising means the removal of all carbon deposits from the combustion chambers, piston crowns and ports. It is generally recognised as including attention to valves, guides and springs. Before commencing to decarbonise, it is desirable to have the following equipment available in case of need, in addition to the toolkit.

1. Top overhaul gasket set number 00-3120.
2. Inlet valves number 76-60(2).
3. Exhaust valves number 76-61(2).
4. Valve springs number 76-63(4) & 76-69(4).
5. Valve guides number 76-15(4).
6. Valve spring compressor number 61-5001.
7. Valve grinding tool (suction type). 61-5035
8. Valve grinding paste.
9. Scrapers for removing carbon.
10. Set of feeler gauges.
11. Supply of clean engine oil.

In order to carry out the work of decarbonising some dismantling is necessary and these instructions are for the guidance of owners wishing to undertake this job themselves. Care should be taken to avoid damage to nuts, bolts and other fixings by the use of incorrect tools, and as parts are removed the fixing bolts should be replaced and the nuts just started so that they are not lost and to facilitate reassembly.

Before the engine can be dismantled it is necessary first to remove the dual seat and side valances. The seat is held by two bolts and nuts securing "C" shaped brackets, and the side valances are secured by eleven bolts, all of which must be removed together with the dual seat catch knob.

Detach the sparking plug leads and remove the cylinder head cowl and rocker cover. The cowl is held by two nuts, one at each end of the cylinder head, and the cover by two nuts on top. Note that removal of the cowl does not release the exhaust pipe flanges and that it is necessary to take off two further nuts securing these flanges before the exhaust pipes can be moved away from the cylinder head.

There is no need to disturb the connection between the carburetter and its manifold. All that is necessary is to take off the two nuts securing the manifold to the cylinder head and the carburetter can then be moved sufficiently to one side to allow dismantling to proceed.

Slacken off the lower union of the rocker oil feed pipe and unscrew the upper union completely to allow the pipe to swing out of the way.

Remove the sparking plugs and take off the seven cylinder head nuts. These nuts will require a small cranked ring spanner to remove.

The cylinder head can now be taken from the block for decarbonising. This will reveal the cylinder head joint face gasket which should be removed and examined. Replacement is generally desirable.

Removal of carbon is best done using a simple scraper, but it is important to avoid damage to the soft aluminium cylinder head and piston crowns. Any marks on the joint faces will give rise to gas leakage and may lead to further damage by burning after the engine is reassembled. To facilitate attention to the pistons they should be turned to top dead centre (i.e., as far as they will come) and this position can be achieved by engaging top gear and rotating the rear wheel.

Having removed all traces of carbon, carefully clean all parts with a slightly oiled rag, being sure to move the pistons down the cylinders to enable carbon to be wiped from the top of the cylinder bores where it will have gathered above the top piston rings.

The opportunity should now be taken to examine the valves, and for this to be done they must be removed using Service Tool number 61-5001. The rockers need not be dismantled.

Be very careful not to lose the split collets which will be released when the valve spring has been compressed. It is a wise precaution to remove all the valves before continuing with any other work and to put them together with their respective collets and caps carefully on a shelf or in a box, indicating from which positions in the cylinder head they were removed.

Service Sheet No. 1002 (contd.)

Scrape all carbon from the inside of the ports, (i.e., the passages in the cylinder head which allow the entry and exit of gases.) Take care to avoid damage to the seats. (These are the angular faces in the cylinder head, which, when mated with similar seats on the valves, provide a gas-tight seal.) Clean up the valves by careful use of fine emery cloth.

Unless the engine has covered a considerable mileage, it is unlikely that anything but a simple grinding-in operation will be necessary to restore the valve seats to perfect condition. Valve grinding is done by smearing a small quantity of grinding paste (obtainable from any Dealer) on the valve faces, re-inserting them into their guides and rotating backwards and forwards. The valve should be moved round to a new position after every few movements. This should not be overdone, or in time valve pocketing, with consequent lack of efficiency, will develop.

If considerable pitting of the seats is evident they must be recut and the valves either reground or replaced. This is best left to a Dealer, who will have the necessary service tools.

Before reassembling, clean off all traces of paste and smear the parts with clean engine oil.

Reassembling is undertaken in the reverse order, but note should be taken that it is a wise precaution to replace valve springs when decarbonising. They are not expensive and replacement will help to maintain the efficiency and performance of the engine.

The part numbers of the valve springs are 76-69, 76-63, inner and outer respectively. When refitting valves particular care should be taken to ensure that the collets are correctly seated.

The cylinder head holding down nuts should always be tightened in the order shown in Fig. 1, and each nut must be pulled down a little at a time to avoid distorting the head.

Fig. 1.
Cylinder Head Nut Tightening.

Scooter Service Sheet | **1003**

Printed December 1959.

250 c.c. O.H.V. TWIN CYLINDER SCOOTER

REMOVAL OF THE ENGINE, GEARBOX AND FINAL DRIVE NUT

When the engine and transmission are removed for overhaul they must be taken out as a complete unit comprising the engine, gearbox and final drive.

Remove the side valances as described in Service Sheet No. 1001.

Drain off all the oil by removing the lowest Phillips head screw and the filler plug on the primary and the rear drive housings, the two ¼ in. bolts at the rear of the gearbox, and the drain plug in the base of the sump.

Raise the rear wheel clear of the ground. For this purpose a block or small wooden trestle as Fig. 2 is necessary and assistance will be required to lift the machine and place the block underneath the rear cross channel on the frame.

Remove the rear wheel by taking off the three hub nuts, which have a normal right-hand thread; these nuts are countersunk both sides and can be fitted either way. Now take off the air ducting around the cylinder head; it is secured by two small nuts on ¼ in. diameter studs which also secure the exhaust pipes. After these nuts are removed take out the one ¼ in. diameter bolt which secures the carburetter air pipe; this is on the top cross member between the two vertical pillars of the frame, and is immediately below the petrol tank. Disconnect the sparking plug leads. Now prise off the lug securing the air duct on the left-hand stud and lift the air ducting complete with the carburetter air pipe clear and place on one side.

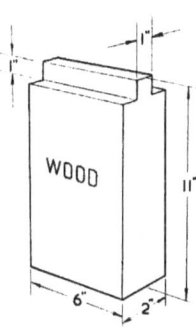

Fig. 2.

Next remove the exhaust pipes by taking off the remaining ¼ in. nuts from the studs nearest the rear wheel, and slacken off the clips securing the exhaust pipes to the silencer and the two bolts at the top of the silencer. This will enable the silencer to be swung away from the pipes and the exhaust pipes can then be taken off the studs securing them to the cylinder. The right-hand side exhaust pipe also carries the spring which tensions the kickstarter chain. The spring will therefore have to be unhooked from the exhaust pipe and the chain link before the right-hand pipe can be placed on one side.

Disconnect the speedometer drive from the rear hub by unscrewing the union nut (Fig. 3). The speedometer drive cable is the upper of the two cables which run to the rear wheel, the lower one being the brake cable. Also disconnect the rear brake cable by taking out the split pin and clevis pin which secure the cable end to the brake lever on the rear hub.

Remove the two black and yellow wires which run from the distributor to the left-hand and right-hand ignition coils by taking off the two nuts on top of the coils. Note that the longer of the two cables (black and yellow) goes to the right-hand coil.

With a suitable tool such as a screwdriver or a hammer shaft, press in the clutch lever on the engine, slip the nipple out of the lever, pull the outer casing out of the lug and place the spring on one side. Push the cable down under the frame out of the way.

Service Sheet No. 1003 (contd.)

Make sure that the petrol tap is turned off and uncouple the banjo union at the carburetter end of the petrol pipe. Be careful not to lose the two fibre washers or the small gauze filter which is fitted inside the banjo union.

The petrol tap rod is supported by a bracket which is secured to the nearside rocker cover stud; remove the ¼ in. nut on this stud lift the bracket off the stud and swing it to one side. Replace the nut loosely on the stud to retain the fibre and steel washers.

Fig. 3.
Speeedometer cable connection

On the right-hand side of the machine will be seen the gearchange lever, fitted to the quadrant spindle; take off the nut securing the lever to the spindle end and prise the lever off the squared end of the spindle. Now depress the kickstarter lever and disconnect the chain from the lever by removing the spring link. The kickstarter sprocket and the chain can be removed after the unit has been taken out of the frame, but the sprocket can be removed at this stage if necessary, it is fitted on to a taper shaft which is keyed. Remove the nut securing the sprocket, and with an open-ended spanner behind the sprocket and against the adjacent Phillips head screw, tap the end of the spanner sharply so as to jerk the sprocket from the taper on the shaft.

It will now be necessary to turn to the left-hand side of the machine, and here will be seen the curved support arm on the rear drive unit. This support arm must be removed before the unit can be taken out of the frame, since it passes round the left-hand vertical column of the frame. Unscrew the three nuts at the rear of the curved arm which secure it to the rear drive and remove the hollow bolt at the front end of the curved support arm, (this is the bolt which also carries a grease nipple). Take off the large diameter steel washer which is pegged. Now disconnect the lower end of the rear suspension damper unit, and swing the damper unit up and out of the way. Raise the rear drive and gently prise off the curved support arm. Lifting the rear drive unit will allow sufficient clearance for the support arm to pass over the pillion passenger's footboard.

The three bolts which secure the rear end of the support arm should now be taken away since they are liable to foul the frame as the unit is being removed.

Remove the rear mudguard by taking out the four ¼ in. diameter nuts and bolts, two at the front on the cross member between the two vertical tubes of the frame and two at the rear which also carry the silencer and petrol tank support bracket.

Unscrew the two ⅜ in. nuts on the bolts attaching the engine unit to the two vertical frame tubes at the rear of the frame. On the left-hand tube it will also be necessary to take out the two ¼ in. bolts securing the quarter portion of the clip. Drive the bolts partially through but still allow them to support the engine. Now remove the front engine plates by taking off the nuts on the two crankcase studs and remove the two 5/16 in. bolts and nuts which secure the "L" shaped engine plates to the chassis cross member. When the bolts securing the plates to the cross member have been removed slide the plates off to left and right from the studs. The engine will now be supported only by the two ⅜ in. bolts through the rear brackets.

Disconnect the generator cables by breaking the connectors which will be found underneath the floor boards. This operation will be easier to carry out if each connector is broken individually.

The unit is now ready to be taken out of the frame, and it is quite easy to do so providing the correct procedure is adopted, which is to drive out the two bolts holding the engine to the vertical frame tubes, tilt the unit forward so that the lugs on the engine clear the lugs on the frame and then tilt it sideways towards the left-hand side, at the same time lifting it out. This will enable the rear drive to pass between the two vertical tubes.

Complete dismantling of the engine, gearbox and final drive unit is described on Service Sheet No. 1004.

Scooter Service Sheet

1004

Printed December 1959.

250 c.c. O.H.V. TWIN CYLINDER SCOOTER

COMPLETE DISMANTLING OF THE ENGINE, GEARBOX AND FINAL DRIVE NUT

If the oil has not already been drained from the unit it should be done at this stage. To drain the final drive take out the Phillips head screw immediately below the oil level plug and remove the oil level plug as well. The primary drive is on the left-hand side of the unit and carries the clutch lever and the contact breaker unit; to drain, remove the Phillips screw immediately below the rear or final drive bearing and again remove the oil level and filler plug to allow the oil to flow.

To drain the gearbox, remove the two hexagon bolts, one above the other, at the rear of the gearbox just behind the gearchange assembly. The sump is drained by removing the plug on the right-hand side bottom corner of the sump; this is the rectangular container under the engine.

Dismantling should only be undertaken by someone with mechanical experience, otherwise serious harm could result to the unit. If in doubt place the job in the hands of the Dealer.

Before cleaning off any accumulation of oil or dust look for obvious signs of oil leakage. The points where this occurs usually show as very clean spots whereas the rest of the unit, though oily, will also be dirty with an accumulation of road dust.

Where the unit is heavily coated with dust and oil it is as well to wash it comparatively clean before dismantling.

During the actual dismantling care should be taken to look for signs which show that a particular part requires replacement. In the case of bearings they should be clean and polished, if there are any score marks or signs showing that the metal has "picked up" the bearing or bush should be replaced. Ball or roller bearings should spin quite freely without excessive play, and if there are signs of lumpiness or grit in them it is an indication that the balls or rollers or the races are pitted and here again the parts should be replaced.

It is good policy to use only sound and unworn spanners and in certain cases it is essential that an appropriate service tool is handy. Detailed below are those service tools which are used for dismantling the unit. Although one or two operations can be done without them, such as removal of the valve springs and contact breaker, (these are covered by service tool number 61–5001 and 5005 respectively), the use of the tools will facilitate the work.

Service tools are as follows:—

61–5001	Valve spring compressor.
61–5002	Extractor for generator and flywheel.
61–5005	Extractor for contact breaker cam and auto advance unit.
61–5007	Extractor for clutch.
61–5019	Extractor for speedometer drive.
61–5022	Crankshaft holder.
61–5025	Universal extractor (for primary drive and timing pinions).

Service Sheet No. 1004 (contd.)

Dismantling Drive Side of Unit

With the spanner provided in the toolkit remove the two sparking plugs, take off the two ¼ in. nuts holding the rocker box cover, remove the steel washers and fibre washers and remove the cover. Examine the cover gasket to decide whether or not it can still be used. If the gasket is damaged in any way, as for example, if parts of it have adhered to the cylinder head, or if it is compressed too thin, it is advisable to use a new one.

Slacken off the two union screws holding the oil feed pipe to the rocker box and crankcase, and remove the pipe, leaving the unions screwed into both the crankcase and cylinder head.

Remove the seven nuts and washers which hold the cylinder head to the block. Four of these are at the rear inside the rocker box and three at the front adjacent to the sparking plugs. The smaller ring spanner provided in the toolkit is the most suitable tool to use on these nuts. Take off the cylinder head and in this case, although the gasket may appear to be in good condition, since it is a comparatively cheap and certainly an important item, it is advisable to use a new one when reassembling.

There may be no need to dismantle the rocker assembly but in case this operation is described at a later stage.

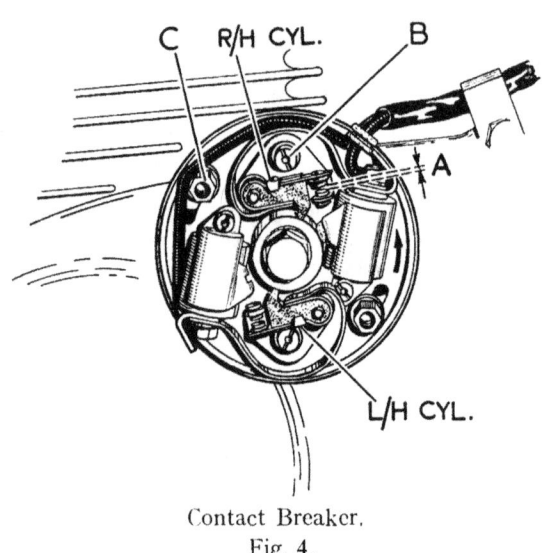

Contact Breaker.
Fig. 4.

A standard type of screwdriver can be used to take off the contact breaker cover by removing the two 3/16 in. screws, following which the cover can be placed to one side after the rubber grommet holding the leads has been slid out of the "U" shaped slot in the cover. Unscrew the two long hexagon nuts (C) Fig. 4, which are slightly to the left and right of the contact breaker plate and take off the plate complete with the leads after disconnecting the black and white lead from the left-hand ignition coil and the black and yellow lead from the right-hand coil.

The contact breaker cam and automatic advance and retard unit is retained by the centre bolt which is now visible. Slacken off the bolt and if tool number 61-5005 is not available tap the bolt sideways to release the unit from the tapered shaft. If the tool is available take out the bolt, insert the tool and withdraw the unit by screwing the tool in clockwise.

Take off the plain steel bush from the bearing support arm spindle and the plain steel thrust washer behind the bush, noting that the washer is fitted with the chamfered side towards the primary drive cover.

The primary drive cover itself is held in position by seven Phillips head screws and one ¼ in. nut and a 5/16 in. nut and bolt at the front. This bolt also carries the starter motor support bracket when a starter is fitted.

Service Sheet No. 1004 (contd.)

When all the screws, nuts and bolts are removed, the primary drive cover can be taken off, the joint being broken by gently tapping the cover with a rawhide mallet or a hammer shaft but great care must be taken or the cover may be cracked or distorted.

The clutch push rod will come away with the cover. The condition of the phosphor bronze pad on the push rod should be carefully noted and if it shows signs of having worn or the metal having "picked up", the push rod should be replaced. Make sure that the small rubber "O" ring on the push rod shaft is in good condition, and if necessary replace it to prevent leakage of oil through the push rod bore. The final drive support arm bearing is a press fit into the primary drive cover and if it is to be removed the cover should be heated in boiling water, and the bearing driven out with a suitable punch through the hole in the housing. The replacement must be fitted while the cover is still hot. (This method should be employed whenever a bearing is to be removed from an aluminium case.) The contact breaker drive is simply a sliding fit in the bronze bush in the rear primary drive case.

Removing Clutch Unit
Fig. 5.

Before removing the clutch, flatten the tab washer on the larger primary driven gear and slacken off the centre nut. This operation will be facilitated if the unit is placed in gear by operating the gearchange spindle and the brake applied with a suitable length of tube over the brake lever.

Now unscrew the three clutch pressure spring nuts. To avoid tilting the plate and locking the nuts give each nut approximately one full turn at a time. When all the nuts are off take off the springs and place the pressure plate on one side. Then replace the spring and nut on one of the studs to keep the unit intact during dismantling. Flatten the star shaped tab washer under the clutch centre nut and remove the nut, again locking the unit in the manner just described. Great care must be taken to avoid damaging the clutch spring studs for they can very easily be bent if the spanner slips. When the nut is off remove the star washer and, using service tool number 61-5007, draw off the clutch centre and clutch complete as in Fig. 5.

The clutch housing and gear is a push fit over the bearing and can be taken off without an extractor. It should be noted that there is a thrust washer between the end of the clutch sleeve and the splined clutch centre, and this washer has the chamfered face outwards towards the clutch.

The driving and driven plates should be carefully examined. If the steel driving plates are badly scored they should be replaced and if the bonded driven plates have the segments worn thin these also should be replaced. (The sequence of assembly is first a driven plate with a bonded lining against the rear pressure plate, than a plain steel driving plate and so on alternately.

Service Sheet No. 1004 (contd.)

The plain steel clutch housing bearing sleeve can be slid off the mainshaft. Note that it is fitted with the larger diameter towards the engine.

Having previously flattened the tab washer and slackened off the nut on the large primary driven gear, this gear can now be drawn off the gearbox mainshaft using service tool number 61–5025 fitted with the short extractor legs 61–1732 (Fig. 6). The final removal of the gear should be carried out with care, and if possible with the key in the gearbox mainshaft at 12 o'clock position since if the key is loose and drops down behind the oil seal it may cause damage.

Unscrew the six ¼ in. nuts holding the primary drive inner cover to the crankcase and remove the washers. The joint can be broken by tapping gently with a rawhide mallet or something similar. The inner cover also carries the crankshaft main bearing housing and if this bearing is to be changed owing to noticeable roughness or up-and-down play it will be necessary to flatten the tab washers on the four retaining bolts, remove the bolts and take off the bearing plate. The bearing itself can then be removed from the inner drive cover by heating the case in boiling water and then tapping gently out on to a wooden bench. The replacement should be fitted while the cover is still hot and the replacement bearing is cold. There is also an oil seal in the cover, which is fitted from the inside, (i.e., the clutch side with the lip towards the bearing.)

Removing Primary Gear
Fig. 6.

Behind the primary drive inner cover there is a rubber "O" ring pressed on to the boss on the outside of the outer chain cover. If this "O" ring has become soft or enlarged then a replacement should be fitted on reassembly.

It will now be possible to remove the outer chain cover by taking out the nine Phillips head screws, but careful note should be made of their respective positions and lengths. Before final removal of the cover take out the chain adjuster screw by unscrewing the locknut and removing the screw completely.

Again break the joint by tapping gently with a rawhide mallet and remove the cover. This may come away complete with the slipper pad and its fulcrum pin, or the pad may remain in the rear portion of the swinging arm case. It should be noted that the pad must be quite free on the bearing pin.

In the outer chain cover will be found a ball bearing at the rear and an oil seal at the front. The ball bearing can be removed by heating the case in boiling water and then tapping gently on to a bench. The oil seal is fitted from the outside of the case, with the lip pointing inwards. When replacing care should be taken to ensure that it is fitted squarely in the hole and is not tilted to one side. The Woodruff key in the gearbox mainshaft should now be removed carefully to avoid damage to the key or to the shaft.

Service Sheet No. 1004 (contd.)

Flatten the tab washer on the rear cush drive unit and unscrew the nut, locking the assembly by applying the rear brake. The nut has a normal right-hand thread. The gearbox sprocket nut has no tab washer and is also unscrewed in a normal anti-clockwise direction. Here again it will be necessary to lock the unit by applying the rear brake, or alternatively by applying a substantial tool between the rear hub studs and locking against the bench.

Now remove the single countersunk screw which retains the brake drum on the stub axle and slide the drum off. Using a rawhide mallet or copper hammer, gently tap the stub axle through the cush drive towards the wheel side. The cush drive can then be taken out of the chain and the gearbox sprocket together with chain can be taken off the splined gearbox mainshaft.

Behind the cush drive and rear sprocket assembly are the speedometer drive and thrust washer, the latter being between the speedometer drive and the rear sprocket, and inside the inner chain cover is a bearing retained by a lock ring having a normal right-hand thread. To remove this bearing it will be necessary first to extract the speedometer drive using service tool number 61-5019. When this is taken out it will be seen that there is a pressure pad let into the case at the opposite end of the speedometer drive.

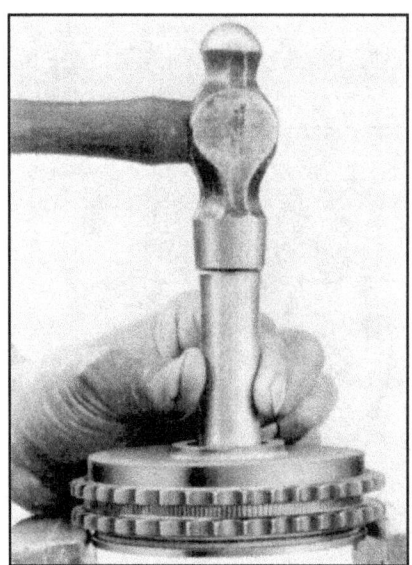

Parting the Cush drive
Fig. 7.

After the bearing lock ring has been removed, the case should be heated in boiling water and the bearing dropped out in the manner previously described, and the replacement, if necessary, fitted while the case is still hot. Note that the speedometer drive is fitted with the flange outwards, (i.e., towards the cush drive and rear sprocket unit). The plain steel washer can be fitted either way round.

If the cush drive is to be dismantled for fitting new rubbers the spider should be pressed out of the sprocket using a wooden plug or similar tool on the centre splined portion and supporting the sprocket on one of the double row of teeth, as in Fig. 7. Do not attempt to prise the spider out with a screwdriver under the flange as this may cause the flange to break away.

The cush drive comprises twelve rubbers, which are fitted between the spider and sprocket vanes. On some early models all twelve rubbers were soft; later models employ six soft and six hard rubbers, the hard ones being fitted immediately to the left of the vanes looking inside the rear sprocket, as in Fig. 8. These hard rubbers are usually painted white.

Take off the rear brake shoes by pressing the lower shoe down and at the same time twisting it off the brake cam and fulcrum pin. The inner chain cover can now be taken off the pivot stub. Note the rubber "O" ring on the stub.

The phosphor bronze bush in the front end of the cover is a press fit and the usual method of extraction should be employed if it is worn and therefore to be replaced.

Service Sheet No. 1004 (contd.)

An oil seal is fitted in the cover from the brake shoe side, again with the lip of the oil seal facing inwards towards the bearing. If a replacement is to be fitted the old seal can be prised out with a screwdriver but care should always be taken when fitting a new oil seal to see that it is inserted squarely into the hole, and great care should be taken to avoid any damage to the feather edge of the seal.

The brake cam spindle can be removed by taking off the nut behind the brake arm, and drawing the cam out towards the hub side. If, however, the cam is quite free in the housing and there is no apparent excessive wear on the cam face there is no need to disturb it. The fulcrum pin is secured by a nut on the inside of the cover; here again there is no need to disturb it unless there is obvious damage. The two location dowels in the cover should be undamaged and a good fit in their holes.

Dismantling Timing Side of Unit

Dismantling of the left-hand or primary drive side is now completed and attention can be given to the right-hand side of the unit.

If the fan cowl has not already been removed, unscrew the three small Phillips head screws and the one plain screw at the top right-hand front which also carried the throttle cable clip. Unscrew and remove the nut securing the kick-starter sprocket and remove the sprocket complete with the chain and spring. Take out the Woodruff key, being careful not to damage the key or the slot in the shaft.

Cush Drive Rubber Assembly
Fig. 8.

The large extension nut securing the flywheel and fan can now be removed by screwing in a normal anti-clockwise direction, using an 11/16 in. Whitworth ring spanner. The crankshaft, however, must be prevented from turning by holding the opposite side with service tool number 61-5022.

With the flywheel centre nut removed, the flywheel can be extracted with service tool number 61-5002. This will expose the stator unit secured to the crankcase by three 5/16 in. nuts and washers, which should be unscrewed using a tubular spanner to avoid damage to the

Service Sheet No. 1004 (contd.)

stator unit. With the nuts and washers removed the stator can be drawn off the three studs by simply pulling it away and threading the leads through the rubber grommet in the back of the case. The three distance pieces on the studs should be taken away to avoid being lost in subsequent dismantling. Carefully prise out the Woodruff key from the mainshaft, again taking care to avoid damage to the key or the slot in the shaft.

If the machine is fitted with a starter motor, the two 5/16 in. bolts securing the motor to the back of the timing gear cover should be removed and the starter taken away. In the case of models without starter a blanking plate is fitted in lieu of starter and this plate need not be disturbed.

Slightly to the left of the starter sprocket is a projection having two flats; this is the cam plate plunger housing. Using a spanner which is a good fit on the two flats, unscrew the housing in a normal anti-clockwise direction and remove it complete with the plunger and spring.

The gearbox end cover can now be removed after the five Phillips head screws have been taken out; again the joint will have to be broken by tapping gently with a rawhide mallet.

Removal of the end cover will expose the outer portion of the cam plate and the selector quadrant together with its scissor spring, the spring being retained in the inner cover by a large hexagon-headed bolt. Unscrew this large bolt and draw it out noting that as it is drawn through the spring it will remove the star washer which is fitted between the bolt and the case. The selector quadrant can then be taken out quite easily if a thin strip of steel such as a table knife is slipped between the two plungers and the cam plate. (See Fig. 9). The other end of the quadrant spindle is simply a push fit into the back of the case.

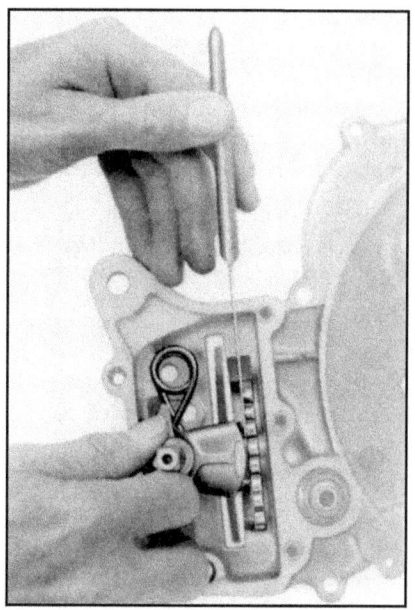

Removing Selector Quadrant

Fig. 9.

The two plungers should be undamaged on their chamfered ends and quite free to move in the housing, and should not be disturbed if they are satisfactory.

The next operation is to remove the timing and gearbox cover which is in one piece.

Take out the five large countersunk screws holding the timing cover around the crankshaft and the five Phillips head screws on the gearbox cover portion. (Two of these are inside the gearbox portion on the left-hand side of the selector quadrant.) Do not disturb the slotted screw on the timing cover portion; this retains the kickstarter stop plate. See Fig. 10.

With all screws removed the cover can now be withdrawn, bringing with it the gearbox mainshaft, cam plate, selector forks, layshaft and gear cluster. See Fig. 11.

Service Sheet No. 1004 (contd.)

Gearbox and Timing Cover Screws.
Fig. 10.

As the assembly is drawn out it may be that the thrust washer which is fitted to the mainshaft will drop into the case. Look for this washer and if it does drop replace it temporarily on the gearbox mainshaft so that its location is remembered. It will be necessary during this operation to hold the cam plate centrally to avoid fouling either the upper or lower portions of the gearbox case.

In some cases the selector fork spindle may remain in the gearbox. It is simply a push fit into the gearbox and the cover.

At this stage it should be noted that there is a possibility of the top front engine mounting stud dropping out of the crankcase if it is an easy fit in the case, and since it is essential that this stud is in position before the gearbox and timing cover and the primary drive inner covers are fitted the point should be borne in mind for reassembly. It is therefore, a wise precaution to replace the two nuts on to this stud so that it is retained in position.

The only parts now left in the gearbox are the pinion sleeve and the main bearing. The pinion sleeve can be driven through the bearing into the gearbox and this will release the gearbox sprocket distance piece which fits over the pinion sleeve on the outside of the gearbox.

The pivot stub for the chaincase swinging arm unit is fixed to the gearbox by four bolts and two locking plates that are turned up over the bolts. It is most unlikely that the stub will have to be replaced but it has to be removed to allow replacement of the gearbox mainshaft bearing if examination proves this to be necessary.

Remove the stub by turning back the locking plates and taking out the four bolts, but obviously if the mainshaft bearing has to be removed it is better to do this when the complete unit has been stripped. The usual method of removal and replacement is employed but it must be tapped from the outside of the gearbox and replaced from the inside. The same applies to the layshaft phosphor bronze bearing.

Gear Cluster.
Fig. 11.

Service Sheet No. 1004 (contd.)

Dismantling the Gear Cluster

Take out the selector fork spindle, which is a push fit into the cover, and remove the two selector forks. The mainshaft and layshaft can then be removed from the bearings in the outer cover, and this will only leave the cam plate and its pivot pin in the outer cover. The cam plate can be removed by taking out the split pin and drawing out the pivot pin from the side. The kickstarter spindle and ratchet slide on to the end of the layshaft. The ratchet pawl should be examined to see that it is in good condition and that the small plunger and spring underneath the pawl are not sticking. If the pawl is worn or damaged it should be replaced. The ratchet teeth inside the low gear and kickstarter pinion should also be examined to make sure that it is fit for further use.

The mainshaft phosphor bronze bush in the outer cover is an interference fit and is also pegged on the face to prevent it revolving. Replace this bush only if wear is apparent.

The 20T sliding dog pinion can be slid off the mainshaft splines leaving the small 16T pinion, which is a press fit on the shaft, retaining in position the 25T pinion. The mainshaft 16T and 25T pinions are selectively assembled during manufacture and if any one of these parts has to be replaced the complete assembly under part number 76-3174 must be obtained.

Similarly, the 25T layshaft pinion is retained on the shaft by the 17T pinion, also a tight press fit, and this assembly is always supplied complete. The part number is 76-3018.

Removal of the Timing Gear

To remove the timing gear it will be necessary to hold the crankshaft using service tool 61-5022.

Flatten the tab washer on the large timing or camshaft pinion and unscrew the nut in a normal anti-clockwise direction; the camshaft pinion is then extracted from the shaft using service tool 61-5025 fitted with legs 61-1732 (short legs). See Fig. 12.

Removing Camshaft Pinion
Fig. 12.

The large crankshaft pinion nut is again unscrewed in an anti-clockwise direction. There is no tab washer and the tool required is a normal 11/16 in. Whitworth spanner. To withdraw the pinion special long bolts must be used with extractor number 61-5025. These are numbered 61-5006.

It will be noted that both pinions are marked to facilitate reassembly and that the crankshaft pinion nut has a register which goes against the pinion. There is also a dowel in the crankshaft which locates the small crankshaft pinion.

Service Sheet No. 1004 (contd.)

Removal of the camshaft pinion will expose the oil pump link which is driven by an eccentric on the camshaft and is retained in position by a phosphor bronze plate held by two large countersunk screws. These screws can be removed with a normal type screwdriver, after which the phosphor bronze plate can be taken off and the distance piece removed showing the eccentric and linkage assembly.

To remove the link, flatten the tab washer underneath the screw head on the oil pump plunger, take out the bolt and then slide the link out of the fork end. It can then be taken off the camshaft together with the eccentric.

There is a Woodruff key in the end of the camshaft and if this is undamaged and a good fit it need not be disturbed for removal of the camshaft, which can be slid out of the crankcase from either end.

This unit uses a timed camshaft breather which is simply a hole drilled straight through the camshaft, lining up with holes drilled through the centre camshaft bearing. The breather is therefore open at every half revolution of the camshaft.

To remove the camshaft turn the block upside down so that the cam followers drop away from the shaft and then slide the camshaft out. The unit can then be turned the right way up and the cam followers dropped down into the crankcase.

Turn the unit upside down again and remove the twelve Phillips head screws retaining the sump cover. The cover can then be taken away together with the baffle plate and the oil pump filter, which is fitted over the oil pipe between the baffle plate and the sump cover.

The oil pipe is an interference fit into the crankcase and should not be disturbed if it is undamaged.

Gaskets are fitted between the crankcase and the baffle plate and between the baffle plate and the sump cover. The engine breather cover, which is to the bottom rear of the cylinder block, can be removed together with the fibre gasket by taking out the small 3/16 in. Phillips head screw. The only attention required in this case will be to clean it of any dirt or accumulation of sludge.

Removal of the Oil Pump

Unscrew the slotted plug which will be seen on the crankcase joint face; this has a normal right-hand thread. With the plug removed the remaining parts of the pump can be taken out, using a piece of thin wire bent to a hook at the end. First lift out the spring, if this has not come away with the screw plug, then drop out the first steel ball; next lift out the long plunger noting that the small hole with the countersunk face is uppermost. Then another spring and another steel ball with finally a thin washer, again having a countersunk face or ball seating which is uppermost, (i.e., next to the ball). When these parts are removed it only leaves the plunger which is connected to the link and the phosphor bronze plunger bush which should not be disturbed.

Service Sheet No. 1004 (contd.)

Removal of the Connecting Rods and Pistons

With the crankcase and cylinder block upside down on the bench flatten the tab washers underneath the connecting rod cap bolt nuts and unscrew the nuts. Take off the tab washers and lift off the big end caps. These are numbered and the caps must be mated with the corresponding numbers on the connecting rods. If the bolts are a tight fit in the caps they should be gently tapped through with the handle of a mallet.

Each connecting rod complete with piston should then be drawn upwards through the cylinder bore and taken out from the top of the cylinder. Each piston should be immediately marked on the inside face to show which bore it was taken from and which way it was fitted; a good plan is to mark the inside of the skirt with the letter "L" for the left-hand cylinder, putting the mark on the back of the skirt to denote which way round the piston was fitted. A note should be made of which way the number on the connecting rod was fitted, or alternatively, mark the web of the rod in a similar manner to the piston to indicate which cylinder it came from and which way round it was fitted. Do not in any circumstances mix the big end nuts and bolts; the nuts should be placed immediately on the bolts from which they were taken to facilitate reassembly. If the wrong nut is fitted to a bolt it will affect its position and may make it difficult to secure by the tab washers.

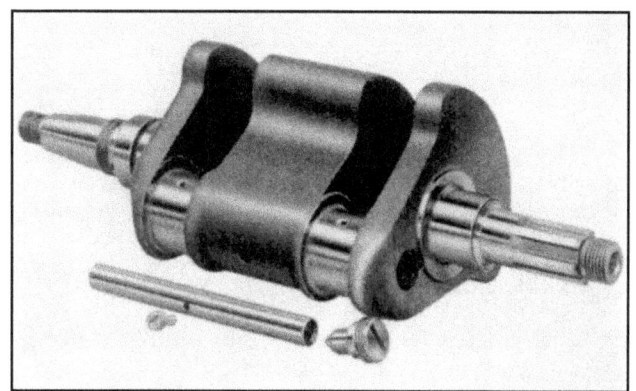

Crankshaft Sludge Trap
Fig. 13.

With the removal of the connecting rods and pistons the crankshaft can be drawn out from the left-hand side of the cylinder block.

The big end bearings should be bright and free from any score marks. If there is any sign of seizure then the bearing shells should be replaced; in the same manner the crankpins on the crankshaft should be clean and bright. Pistons should be carefully examined to see that the rings are free in their grooves and that they are not carboned up or broken. If there is any suspicion that the rings are worn they should be removed and gaps checked with the ring inside the cylinder bore. The gaps should be between .006 in. and .010 in.

If the unit has covered a considerable mileage there may be a certain amount of sludge built up in the crankshaft sludge trap, in which case it is advisable for it to be cleaned out. Procedure is to take out the slotted plug on the drive side end of the crankshaft and the grub screw in the centre of the crankshaft and then to draw out the sludge trap. (See Fig. 13). The passage ways should be cleaned very thoroughly in petrol or by using a suitable degreasing plant.

When reassembling the sludge trap insert the trap into the shaft, then the small centre grub screw and finally the large screw. Both the screws must then be centre-punched after final tightening. This is most important.

Service Sheet No. 1004 (contd.)

The only parts now left are the fixed items such as studs and the crankshaft bush. This is a press fit into the timing side and again the block should be heated in hot water or a suitable degreasing vat, if the old bush is worn or scored and therefore to be replaced. Note that the replacement is fitted from inside the crankcase and that there is a locating peg through the steel face of the bush into the case.

Any stud can be removed (although this is not normally necessary) by screwing on two of the appropriate nuts, locking them, and then unscrewing the stud with a spanner on the lower of the two nuts. A new stud can be replaced in similar manner, this time using the spanner on the top of the two nuts. When the replacement stud has been screwed home, simply unlock the two nuts and take off, but care must be taken not to overstrain a stud when fitting. Note that in general a screw thread into the crankcase is B.S.F. whereas the thread for the nuts is usually C.E.I. In some cases, however, a Whitworth thread is used into an aluminium case, but it is always the coarser of the two threads on a stud which goes into the case. If there is any doubt as to which end of the stud to insert, check the threads with one of the nuts which fits that particular stud. Another guide is that it is usually the longer length of thread which enters the case.

SCOOTER SERVICE SHEET   1005

Printed January 1960

250 c.c. O.H.V. TWIN CYLINDER SCOOTER
RE-ASSEMBLY OF THE ENGINE, GEARBOX AND FINAL DRIVE UNIT

Before commencing re-assembly make sure that all the necessary gaskets, tab washers and woodruff keys are available to replace any that have been damaged during dismantling.

Another essential is to ensure absolute cleanliness of all parts.

It is assumed that any bushes or bearings which needed replacement have already been fitted to the block; no further mention will be made of these except in special cases.

First the oil pump must be assembled into the crankcase; the parts are fitted from the base, where the sump is bolted to the crankcase block.

Insert the one thin steel washer with the chamfered hole towards the base—this provides the seating for the first steel ball. Insert the ball, then the spring and the spring seat so that the counterbore engages correctly over the spring and the chamfered hole is facing the crankcase base to provide the seating for the second steel ball. Insert the second ball, the second spring and finally the screwed plug, making sure that it engages over the spring. Screw it right home and see that it is below the crankcase face. Centre punch the edge of the screw and the face to secure. Insert the plunger with the fork end uppermost and the tapped hole towards the back of the case.

Fig. 14. Oil pump.

Now insert the camshaft, making sure that the woodruff key is in position for the pump drive, place the eccentric over the camshaft, then the connecting link over the eccentric, followed by the distance piece and finally the elongated locking plate which is secured by two countersunk screws. Centre punch the edge of the screws and the plate to secure.

Swing the connecting link down into the fork of the oil pump plunger, and insert the small hexagon bolt with the tab washer underneath the head of the bolt. Lock the bolt securely and turn the tab washer underneath the head of the bolt. Lock the bolt securely and turn the tab washer over on to the flat of the bolt and the flat of the oil pump plunger.

At this stage it is as well to check the action of the oil pump by filling the sump with clean oil. Place the dip tube in the oil, screw the nut on the camshaft and operate the pump by turning with a spanner in a clockwise direction. High speed will not be necessary and if the pump is satisfactory oil will be drawn up and ejected through the oilways of the crankshaft main bearing bush. If the oil pump fails to function then the assembly procedure has been incorrectly carried out.

We now come to one of the bearings which requires special mention; this is the gearbox mainshaft and pinion sleeve bearing and it is a special sealed bearing, the seal being outwards, and the rear swinging arm bearing plate must be refitted before this bearing can be inserted through the gearbox.

Refit the swinging arm bearing plate, which is secured by the four hexagon headed bolts and two locking plates, turn the locking plates up on to all four bolts after final tightening, press the sealed bearing in, seal side first, through the gearbox, making sure that it seats right home against the swinging arm plate. Now press the pinion sleeve through the gearbox and into the bearing and make sure that it is right home, otherwise when the gearbox cluster is assembled it may tighten up. After pressing the pinion sleeve right home insert the distance piece over the outside of the pinion sleeve and into the rear swinging arm bearing plate.

Apply clean engine oil to the crankshaft timing side bearing and insert the crankshaft from the left hand side, making sure that it is absolutely clean and free from any traces of grit or dust. Be sure that the dowel is in position on the timing side to locate the timing gear.

Place the timing gear over the crankshaft so that the keyway is in line with the dowel and the timing mark on the pinion is on the outside. In this case there is no tab washer used under the nut, but the nut has a special register which faces towards the pinion. Using service tool 61-5022 hold the crankshaft and tighten the nut on the pinion.

Now remove the nut which was placed on the camshaft for the purpose of testing the pump, insert the thrust washer over the camshaft and against the elongated brass plate, then refit the camshaft pinion with the timing mark on the outside and meshed with the timing mark on the crankshaft pinion. The easiest way to do this is to mesh the camshaft gear with the crankshaft gear and then to turn the camshaft gently to line its keyway up with the keyway in the pinion. When both are in line gently tap the pinion home, place the tab washer in position so that the centre key or tab is in the keyway on the shaft, screw on the nut and tighten, finally turning over the tab washer on to one of the flats on the nut.

It will be assumed that the carbon has been removed from the pistons, that the rings have been checked for gap, and that the pistons have been replaced on their connecting rods the correct way round according to the markings placed inside the skirt when dismantling.

Fig. 15. Timing pinions.

Apply a coating of clean engine oil to the piston skirt and rings and to the crank journals, remove the cap from one of the rods, placing the cap and the nuts in such a position as to facilitate assembly and ensure correct mating of cap, bolts and nuts as mentioned in Service Sheet No. 1004 dealing with dismantling. With service tool 61-5004 compress the rings on the piston, having first positioned the ring gaps equidistant round the piston. Lubricate the cylinder wall and insert the big end of the connecting rod down through the cylinder, being careful not to scratch the cylinder bore, slide the piston into the bore and at the same time direct the big end over the crankshaft. When the big end of the connecting rod is in position replace the cap ensuring that the numbers on the cap mate up with the numbers on the rod, place new special tab washers over the bolts and screw on the nuts until they grip the tab washers, then turn down the two tabs which are opposite each other on to the cap of the connecting rod. Tighten the nuts down with a torque wrench which has been set to 15 lb./ft., finally turning up the single tab on to one of the flats on the nut and repeat this operation for the other cylinder.

Smear the base of the crankcase with good quality jointing compound and place a new paper washer in position. Apply compound to the washer and then fit the baffle plate with the lips of the cross slits inwards towards the cylinder. Place the oil filter over the dip tube or feed pipe, apply compound to the base of the sump cover, place the cover in position over the crankcase and insert the 12 Phillips head screws. (Each screw should have a shakeproof washer underneath the head). Tighten all the screws down finger tight then finally secure with a screwdriver working diagonally across the cover. Do not completely tighten one screw at a time but increase pressure gradually. Make sure that the sump plug and fibre washer are in position in the base of the sump.

It is now advisable to assemble the gear cluster and the simplest method of carrying this out is to assemble the cluster on to the cover plate.

Pick up the plate and insert the cam plate through the slot in the cover plate so that the larger portion with the cam tracks is towards the inside of the gearbox, insert the pivot pin so that the hole in the pin lines up with the hole in the cam plate and insert a new split pin, opening out the ends.

Now take the 29 tooth ratchet pinion, 'A' (Fig. 16), place the thin steel washer 'B' inside and then fit the kick starter spindle complete with its pawl into the ratchet pinion. Slide the kick starter spindle through the cover, engaging the pawl under the stop plate with the stop against the plate.

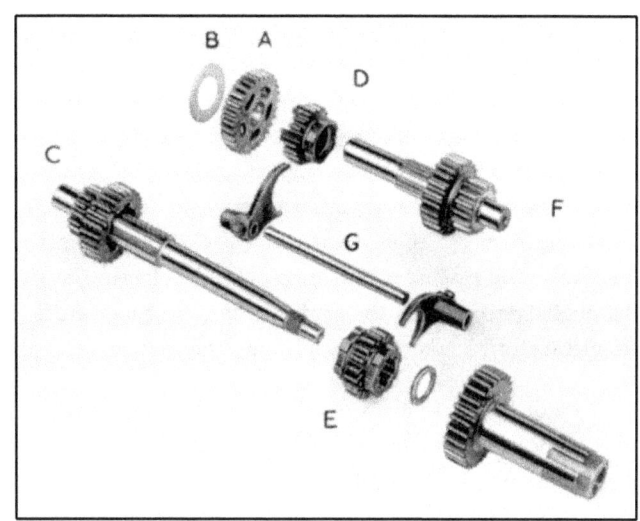

Fig. 16. Gear cluster.

If, for any reason, the stop plate has been removed from the cover make sure that it is re-fitted the correct way round, which is with the leading edge which is slightly chamfered against the stop on the spindle. If it is fitted the wrong way round it is liable to prevent the spindle from going right home in the case.

Fit the main shaft 'C' complete with the fixed 16 tooth pinion and the free 25 tooth pinion but leaving off the sliding 20 tooth pinion and the selector fork. Pick up the 20 tooth sliding lay shaft pinion 'D', and fit the selector fork to it so that in its final position the boss will point towards the change lever side of the box. Place the pair in position over the ratchet pinion and engage the fork roller in the small cam track on the cam plate, that is the track nearest to the cover. Slide the main shaft sliding pinion 'E', complete with fork over the shaft and engage the roller in the longer cam track on the cam plate, which in this case is the track away from the cover. Slide the layshaft 'F', through the 20 tooth pinion twisting slightly to engage the splines and press right home. Now pick up the selector fork shaft 'G', pass it through the two selector forks and engage in the hole in the gearbox cover.

Apply jointing compound to the face of the gearbox and the mating face of the cover (place thrust washer between the splined end of the mainshaft and the pinion sleeve), and slide the mainshaft through the pinion sleeve, at the same time engaging the selector fork shaft and the lay shaft at the back of the box. This operation will be simplified if the cam plate is held in the central position. When the shafts are correctly located press right home and insert all the screws. If difficulty is experienced it is usually an indication that the pinion sleeve has not been pressed fully home into the mainshaft bearing at the back of the box.

Enter the five countersunk screws around the crankcase portion of the cover, Fig. C12A, Service Sheet **422**. One of these screws is longer than the rest and this is fitted at the top of the cover immediately above the stator screw or stud. Insert the three Phillips head screws between the stator housing and the gearbox and the two screws on the gearbox portion, one inside just above the cam plate pivot pin and the other at the bottom edge of the joint face. Care should be taken to see that the correct screw is used. A general guide as to the correct length is that as the screw is about to engage the thread there should be approximately $\frac{5}{16}''$ of the shank showing below the head of the screw.

The gear change selector quadrant should have both the plungers and the scissor spring already fitted, if the scissor spring is to be replaced it should be fitted as shown in Fig. 00. Pick up the large diameter bolt and pass it through the eye of the spring and place the star washer over the thread of the bolt. Insert the assembly into the gearbox, engaging the short end of the spindle in its hole, screw in the stud and secure. Some slight difficulty may be experienced in meshing the plungers but this can be facilitated by placing a thin strip of steel between the two plungers and the cam plate thus compressing both plungers. When the shaft of the gear quadrant is right home and the bolt is screwed up the strip of metal can be taken away, allowing the plungers to engage properly on the camplate.

Place the three distance pieces on the three stator plate studs, pass the leads of the stator through the rubber grommet in the back of the case and slide the stator over the studs so that the lead is in line with the hole in the back of the case. Replace the three nuts and spring washers tightening with a tubular spanner to avoid damage to the coils of the stator unit.

Apply jointing compound to the gearbox portion of the inner cover and to the face of the gearbox outer cover, tap the cover gently home over the shafts and insert the screws, taking the usual care to see that the correct screw is fitted into each hole.

Now pick up the kick starter sprocket and chain, place the return spring over the kick starter spindle with the long end dropping downwards, engage the sprocket over the keyway place on the washer and nut and secure, making sure that the key is in position.

Engage the short end of the return spring in the hole at the back of the sprocket, and then, with a hooked piece of wire over the long end of the spring, swing it round clockwise to place the long end behind the gearbox cover. The spring is then under tension. Swing the chain over the sprocket anti-clockwise, pick up the cam plate plunger, spring and housing and screw in, using a good spanner on the flats of the plunger housing.

Make sure that the flywheel key in the crankshaft is secure, place the flywheel and fan over the crankshaft engaging the key in the keyway and screw in the extended nut and washer. Hold the driving end of the crankshaft with service tool 61-5022 and secure the flywheel nut.

To complete the assembly on the fan side it is only necessary to fit the cowl, using a small $\frac{3}{16}''$ Phillips head screw and one slotted screw at the top front. This screw with its nut also secures the throttle cable clip.

The re-assembly of the rear transmission and swinging arm can now proceed. First make sure that the distance piece is in position over the outer end of the gearbox pinion sleeve. This distance piece will be inserted through the bearing which supports the rear swinging arm. Also replace the rubber 'O' ring over the outside of the bearing, making sure that it is in good condition and is a close fit on the housing.

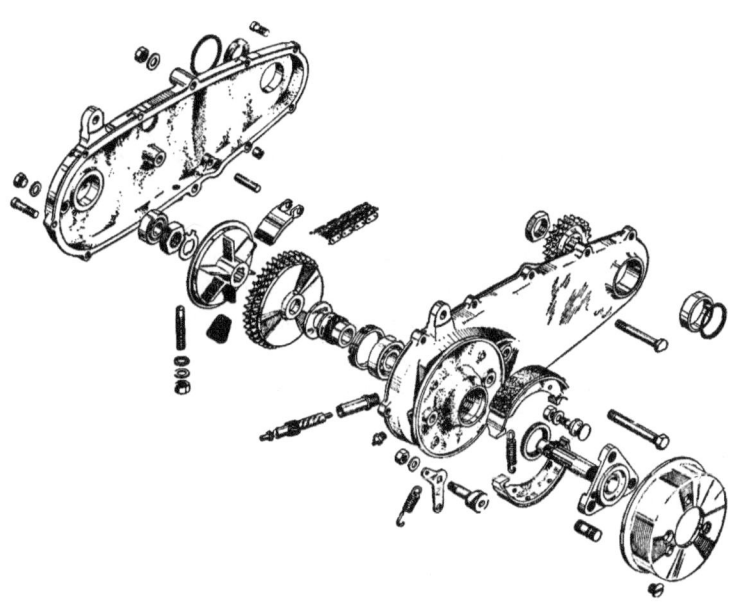

Fig. 17. Rear transmission assembly.

If the bearing in the rear end of the back half of the chaincase is to be renewed, heat the chaincase, press the new bearing in and, using service tool 61-5026, secure with the castellated lock ring which has a normal right hand thread.

The oil seal behind the main bearing is fitted from the brake drum side with the lip of the oil seal towards the bearing. Make sure that the pressure pad at the end of the speedometer drive is in position in the case, and replace the speedometer drive spindle and bush. This can be carried out by screwing on service tool No. 61-5019 and then driving in the bush using a rawhide mallet or hammer.

Pass the stub axle through the bearing, making sure that it is right home. Slide the speedometer drive worm wheel over the axle and then place on the plain steel thrust washer which can be fitted either way.

The rear sprocket and cush drive assembly has twelve rubbers. Six of these are now soft and six hard, but some of the earlier models employed twelve rubbers all of which were soft. The hard rubbers are fitted on the left hand side of each vane in the chainwheel or sprocket, the soft rubbers being on the right hand side. See Fig. 8, Service Sheet No. 1004. The vanes of the sprocket cover are then pressed between the rubbers in the chainwheel.

Having assembled the cush drive, place the chain over the sprocket and slide the sprocket over the splines of the stub axle. Fit a new splined tab washer, and then the locknut which should be secured tightly and locked with the tabs turned up over the nut. It will be necessary during this operation to lock the spindle by using a suitable bar through the studs on the outer side of the stub axle.

Place the gearbox sprocket in the other end of the chain and slide the rear half of the chaincase together with the sprocket and chain over the gearbox mainshaft, screw on the nut securing the gearbox sprocket and secure by centre punching between the inside diameter of the nut and the outside diameter of the shaft. Replace the rear chain tensioner or slipper pad over the pivot pin and engage the pin in the lower portion of the rear case with the slipper facing towards the rear hub. Make sure that it is free to move on the pin.

If the bearing in the rear end of the outer half of the chaincase is to be renewed the case should be heated before pressing in the replacement bearing.

Apply jointing compound to both faces of the rear chaincase. Replace the outer section and screw in the nine Phillips head screws, and the rear chain tensioner stud with its locknut, making sure that the locknut is well clear of the case. Adjust the pin until some resistance is felt, then release one full turn and secure the locknut against the lower edge of the case.

The rear brake shoes and drum should be re-fitted as described in Service Sheet No. 1011.

Press in the oil seal at the front outer end over the gearbox mainshaft. The lip of the seal should be inwards towards the gearbox and care should be taken to ensure that the seal is fitted squarely into the housing. Replace the other 'O' ring over the boss on the outside of the rear chaincase at the front end. Before fitting the primary drive case ensure that the upper front engine plate is in position.

If the crankshaft main bearing in the rear of the primary drive case is to be renewed it should now be pressed into the case from the crankshaft side. The circular steel retainer can then be fitted and secured by the four small bolts and tab washers. The hole in the tab washer for the bolt is offset so that the narrowest portion of the washer is towards the outside edge of the retainer, the longest portion dropping into the cut-away. After the four bolts have been secured, the tab washers should be turned up on to one flat of each bolt. The oil seal behind the main bearing is then fitted from inside the primary drive rear cover (i.e., on the clutch side), again with the lip of the oil seal facing towards the bearing.

The bush for the distributor drive spindle is a press fit into the case, being flush with the flat on the clutch side of the case. Apply jointing compound to the face of the crankcase and the rear face of the rear primary drive cover. Replace the cover over the studs around the crankshaft and the long stud at the top and replace the six nuts and shakeproof washers around the studs in the centre of the case, leaving the long top stud until the outer primary drive case is fitted. Now tuck a piece of clean rag between the rear of the primary drive case and the rear transmission underneath the gearbox mainshaft and insert the woodruff key into the mainshaft, making sure that it is a good fit, and press in the oil seal. Remove the piece or rag and refit the rear primary drive gear with the boss inwards, being careful not to dislodge the key since this would drop down into the rear transmission and would mean the removal of all this assembly to retrieve the key. Place the tab washer in position with the centre tab fitting the keyway and screw on the locknut tight enough to retain the pinion but leaving the final tightening until the remainder of the primary transmission is assembled. Now replace the collared clutch sleeve over the crankshaft at the front end of the primary drive case, the larger diameter of the sleeve seating inside the oil seal. Place the clutch housing and the primary drive gear (this is a composite component), over the mainshaft and sleeve, meshing the gear with the larger primary gear. Replace the chamfered distance piece inside the clutch housing over the crankshaft with the chamfer outwards towards the clutch plates.

The simplest way to assemble the remaining parts of the clutch is to assemble all the plates on to the clutch centre, which is the splined component with the three holes for the spring studs.

Fig. 18. Clutch assembly.

First slide on a plain steel plate up to the outer flange, then a lined plate, next a steel plate and so on alternately, finishing with the clutch pressure plate, which is the plate with the three studs, and inserting the studs through the housing. Now place one spring over a spring stud and screw on one of the spring lock nuts. This will retain the plates close together for the final assembly. Position the outer splines or teeth of the bonded plates in line with each other and slide the whole assembly over the crankshaft, engaging on the centre splines of the shaft and positioning the outer splines or teeth of the lined plates into the clutch housing at the same time. When the assembly is correctly located tap it gently home on to the shaft, replace the three-legged tab washer with the two thin legs into the holes in the clutch centre, and screw on the locknut. Be very careful not to slip with the spanner as this may damage one of the spring studs.

Having secured the clutch assembly, engage one of the gears, and apply the rear brake while tightening the nut on the large primary drive gear. Turn the tab washer up on to the flat of the nut to secure the nut.

Take off the spring and nut which was placed over one of the studs to hold the clutch assembly, insert the three nuts into the spring plate, place the springs over the studs and screw on the three nuts an equal amount at a time. Do not attempt to screw one nut down first as this will tilt the plate and make it very difficult to screw on the other nuts. Tighten the nuts down evenly until approximately one and a half threads are showing on the ends of the studs.

There should be no need to disturb the rear swinging arm support bearing which is projecting through the primary drive outer cover unless the bearing inside the support is to be changed. If this part is to be replaced the support arm bearing should be pressed out of the cover, the bearing extracted and the replacement fitted, finally pressing the bearing back into the cover, making sure that the small cut away is engaged over the dowel on the inside of the cover. It is always advisable to heat the case in hot water and to press the component in cold.

Replace the contact breaker drive spindle so that the tongue on the end of the spindle engages correctly in the slot in the end of the camshaft. Insert the clutch push rod through the outer cover from the inside with the phosphor bronze pressure pad on the inside, again make sure that the rubber 'O' ring on the push rod is in good condition. If the phosphor bronze pressure pad is worn thin or scored the push rod itself should be replaced.

Apply jointing compound to both the inner and outer cover faces, place the outer cover in position, replace the Phillips screws and the one $\frac{1}{4}"$ nut over the stud at the top of the cover together with one shakeproof washer and replace the $\frac{5}{16}"$ nut and bolt at the front end of the cover. This bolt also carries the starter motor support bracket when a starter motor is fitted.

Refit the automatic advance mechanism and cam so that the keyway in the end of the cam is at the bottom or at 6 o'clock. Replace the contact breaker so that the condenser with the black and white lead is on the left hand, and the nuts and washers are approximately central in the elongated slots. In this position the contact breaker points should be set just about to open. Reset ignition timing as described in Service Sheet No. 1007.

Before replacing the contact breaker cover see that the black and white lead is brought outside the left hand long nut and that the rubber grommet is correctly engaged in the U shaped slot in the cover. Slide the cover into position and secure by the two $\frac{3}{16}"$ screws.

Make sure that the cylinder bores are clean and that there is a liberal coating of clean engine oil, fit a new cylinder head gasket with the thin raised portion around each cylinder bore facing upwards.

Having previously assembled the valves and valve rockers in the cylinder head as described in Service Sheet No. 1006, prepare to replace together with the four push rods.

The simplest method of carrying this out is to apply a dab of grease to the cup of each push rod, then press each rod on to the ball end of the rocker arm. The grease will hold the rods in position while the head is being fitted over the studs. Slacken off the rocker adjusting screws, replace the seven cylinder head nuts and plain washers and tighten down evenly and securely.

Do not fully tighten one nut at a time as this might distort the cylinder head and result in leakage at the joint. See Fig. 1, Service Sheet No. 1002 for order of tightening.

When the cylinder head has been finally fitted reset the rocker adjusting screws in the following manner.

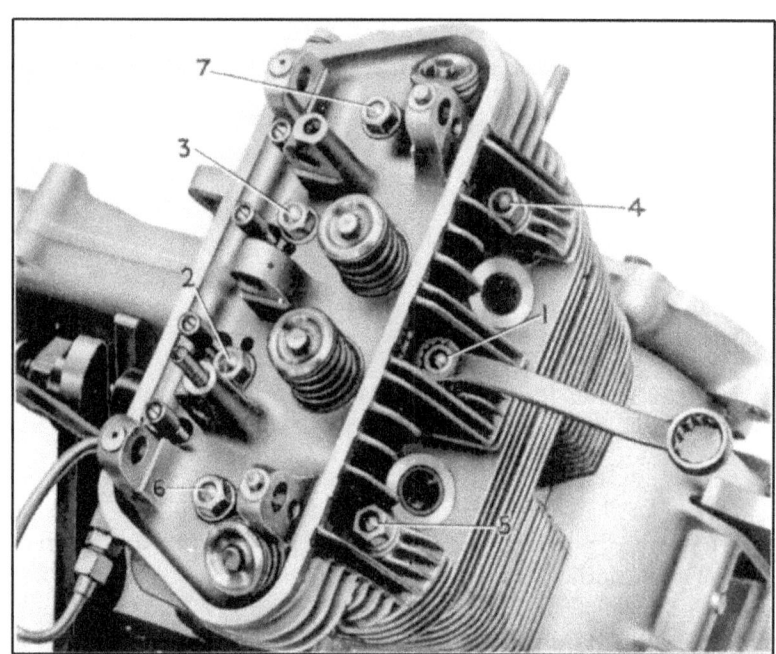

Fig. 19.

With the right hand exhaust valve fully open set the left hand exhaust valve clearance to ·005", then with the left hand exhaust valve fully open repeat the operation on the right hand exhaust valve. This procedure is the same for the inlet valves.

Replace the rocker box cover and gasket, making sure that the gasket is correctly located, and place on the two fibre washers, plain washers and the two nuts, but do not tighten these two nuts until the engine is finally set in the frame and the support bracket to the petrol pipe is replaced over the left hand stud.

Re-assembly of the unit is now completed and it is ready for re-fitting into the frame, but it will facilitate the replacement of oil if it is now added to the primary drive case, the gearbox and the rear transmission. Replenishment of the oil in the sump can be left until the unit is in the frame.

Printed in England by Buckler & Webb Ltd., Birmingham, 3

Scooter Service Sheet   1006

Printed January 1960

250 c.c. O.H.V. TWIN CYLINDER SCOOTER

ATTENTION TO VALVES

To remove a valve, compress the springs with Service Tool No. 61-5001. Take out the split collets and remove the valve spring cup and springs, and the valve will then drop down through its guide. Each valve is removed in the same way.

The valves must be cleaned thoroughly to remove carbon deposits. Fine emery cloth can be used sparingly but be careful not to remove metal.

Normally it will only be necessary to grind-in the valves to their seats lightly. To do this smear a small quantity of fine grinding paste on the face of the valve and return the valve to its seat. Grip the valve head with Service Tool No. 61-5035 and rotate, whilst maintaining a slight pressure. Raise the valve and turn it to a new position every few moments. Grinding should continue until both mating faces show a uniformly matt metallic surface all round.

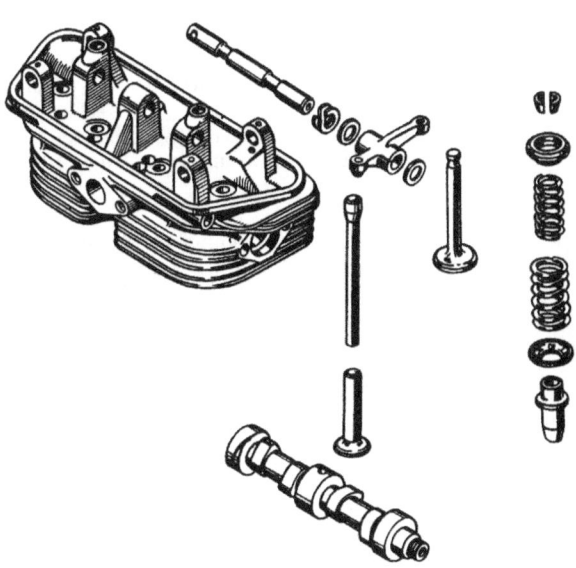

Camshaft and Valve Gear A.   Fig. 20

If the valve seats are badly pitted do not attempt to re-grind as this will only wear away the valves. Instead, the seats must be re-cut with Service Tool No. 61-5036 and the valve re-faced by a Dealer. If a valve guide is worn, as shown by excessive side clearance between stem and guide it can be pressed out from the combustion chamber side after the cylinder head has been heated in boiling water for 2 or 3 minutes. It is necessary first to remove the rocker before pressing out an exhaust valve guide and how to do this is explained in the next section. Press in the new guide from the rocker side, again with the cylinder head hot. After fitting a new guide the valve seat should be re-cut to ensure that it is concentric with the guide.

Re-assembly of the valves is in reverse order but do not forget to remove all traces of grinding compound and to smear the valve stems with clean engine oil.

Dismanting and re-assembling Valve Rockers and Shafts.

In normal circumstances there will be no need to disturb the valve rocker assembly. If it is necessary the operation is quite simple, but it must be noted that oil is pumped through passage ways drilled in the cylinder head and then up through the posts supporting the rocker shafts and through oilways in the shafts to lubricate valve rockers. It is, therefore, essential that the rocker shafts are re-assembled correctly, otherwise the oil supply to the rockers will be cut off.

The exhaust rockers are situated at left and right hand of the cylinder head with the inlet rockers in the middle. To take out an exhaust rocker shaft remove the small hexagon headed bolt from the sparking plug side rocker post and tap the shaft through towards the plug side. A small piece of tube must be fitted over the end of the shaft so that the steel ball which is pressed into the shaft to close the drilled oilway is not disturbed. As the shaft is drawn out it will be seen that there is an oilway drilled at 90° to its axis, this oilway mating up with the hole in the post.

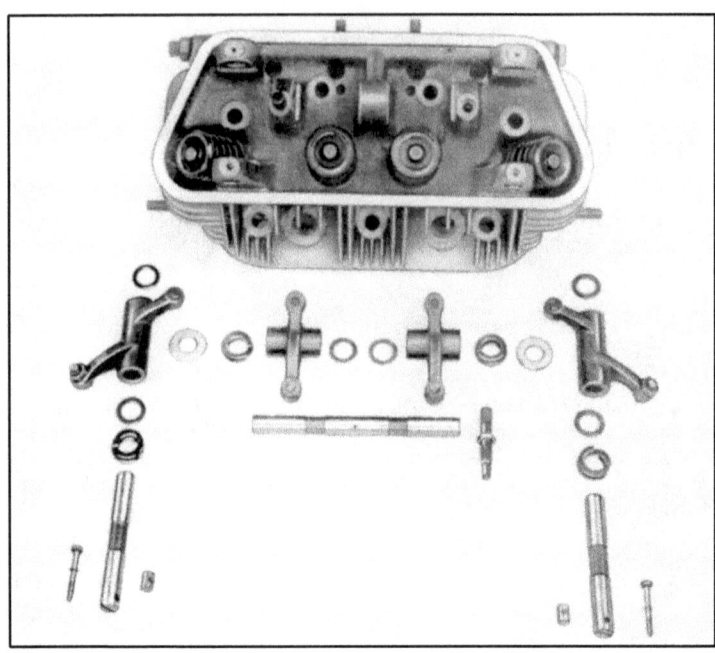

Valve Rocker Assembly.　Fig. 21

There is a thrust washer against each rocker post and on the plug side a spring washer between the end of the rocker and the thrust washer.

To remove the inlet valve rocker shaft and rockers, take out the hexagon headed stud on the left hand post and tap the shaft through towards the right hand side; there is no need to disturb the stud on the right hand post. There is a thick washer against each outside post, with a spring washer between thrust washer and rocker and a thin thrust washer between rocker and central post. There is a radial slot on the end of the shaft to line up with the stud on re-assembly. Again re-assemble in reverse order; partially insert the shaft, place a thick thrust washer against the outside post, then a spring washer followed by the first inlet rocker. Press the shaft through to the middle post, fit a thin thrust washer, then the second inlet rocker, the spring washer and finally a thick thrust washer against the outer post.

As a general rule there is no need to disturb the adjusting screws on the rockers except for setting the valve clearance on re-assembly, but it is as well to examine the ball ends of the screws. If these are chipped or damaged they will cause rapid wear on both the adjusting pin and the push rod and should therefore be replaced.

Scooter Service Sheet

1007

Printed January 1960

250 c.c. O.H.V. TWIN CYLINDER SCOOTER

REPLACING THE ENGINE, GEARBOX AND FINAL DRIVE UNIT IN THE FRAME

With the front engine studs in position, pick up the unit and holding it tilted slightly to the left pass the rear drive unit through the two vertical frame members. Bring the engine upright and slide it into position so that the two crankcase lugs slide into the mounting brackets on the two vertical frame pillars. Having placed the unit loosely in position, insert the rear right hand engine mounting bolt through the lug on the frame and the lug on the crankcase, then pass the left hand bolt through the mounting in a similar manner. Place the $\frac{1}{4}''$ clip over the main bolt and fit the two small $\frac{1}{4}''$ diameter bolts and nuts.

Pick up the L shaped front engine mounting plates and slide each one into position over the front engine studs so that the feet of the plates are turned outwards; refit the nuts and washers over the studs but do not tighten completely. Now replace the bolts through the chassis cross member and tighten down securely, finally tightening the nuts on the crankcase studs. At this stage the rear damper unit should be coupled at its upper end to the dual seat carrier.

Replace the curved bearing arm which passes outside the left hand vertical tube by sliding it over the main bearing bush, which has four holes equally spaced around its periphery. Insert the three long bolts which retain the rear end of the bearing arm, passing them through from the rear of the final drive case. Two of these bolts have flats on their heads which engage in flats on the back of the chaincase, the middle bolt having a hexagon head. Note that the lower bolt also carries the speedometer cable clip. Replace the large washer on the front end of the bearing arm, making sure that it is engaged over the dowel pin, and finally refit the hollow bolt which also carries a grease nipple.

Now pick up the speedometer cable and carefully engage the squared end of the inner cable in the speedometer drive and screw the cable union nut on to the drive bush. Re-connect the brake cable by passing the inner cable through the slot in the lug, fit the fork end of the cable over the lever, insert the clevis pin followed by the washer and finally the split pin. Do not omit to spread the ends of the split pin.

Re-connect the two low tension leads to the coils, the longer one going to the right hand coil. Refit the rear mudguard which is secured by four $\frac{1}{4}''$ diameter nuts and bolts, two on the cross members between the two vertical pillars and two at the rear on the bracket which carries the petrol tank and silencer.

The kick-starter chain can now be re-connected to the pedal by re-fitting the spring connecting link, making sure that the closed end of the spring is facing towards the rear of the machine. Replace the gearchange lever over the squared end of the gearchange spindle, fit the plain washer, spring washer and finally the nut. Make sure that the large plain washer is fitted over the square on the spindle, and is not trapped between the square and the other washer. Tighten the nut securely. Later models use a special nut only.

If the fabric distance piece is not already fitted to the carburetter flange studs it should now be re-fitted, together with the jointing washers and the manifold together with carburetter placed in position.

If the carburetter has been removed from the swan neck manifold make sure that the rubber "O" ring is in position inside the carburetter body. If this is omitted it is liable to cause air leaks and consequently weak mixture and overheating. Refit the two spring washers and $\frac{1}{4}''$ nuts on to the studs holding the inlet manifold and tighten evenly and securely. Do not in any circumstances tighten down one nut before the other as this is liable to distort the manifold face, and will again result in leakage.

Replace the petrol pipe on the float chamber, making sure that the gauze filter is inside the banjo union, and that the large fibre washer is between the union and the float chamber, with the small fibre washer between the head of the bolt and the outside face of the banjo union. Replace the petrol tap support bracket over the left hand rocker box stud and replace the $\frac{1}{4}''$ diameter nut. The fibre washer and steel washer should already be in position on the stud and underneath the bracket.

It is always advisable to use new exhaust pipe gaskets at the cylinder head joint. Refit the exhaust pipes on to the cylinder head and then swing the silencer down over the ends of the exhaust pipes and securely tighten the clips. Tighten the two bolts holding the silencer when the clips have been correctly fitted. The air ducting around the cylinder head, which also carries the pipe supplying air to the carburetter, can now be refitted by sliding it over the front exhaust pipe studs and securing in position with the small $\frac{1}{4}''$ nuts. The cool air pipe is secured to the strut across the frame immediately below the petrol tank, by one $\frac{1}{4}''$ nut and bolt with spring washer. Replace the H.T. lead on the plugs noting that the lead from the right hand coil is fitted to the right hand spark plug. Now slide the clutch cable through the slot in the lug on the primary drive cover, make sure that the outer casing is seating in the lug, fit the spring over the inner wire and with the aid of a hammer shaft, press in the clutch lever and slip the clutch nipple into the lever.

The rear wheel can now be refitted, care being taken to ensure that the valve is on the right hand side of the machine. The three conical wheel nuts can be fitted either way round but each nut should be tightened evenly; if one nut is tightened down too much it is liable to distort the wheel on its seating on the stub axle. Make sure that the nuts are securely tightened after the wheel is on the ground. Now re-connect the kick-starter chain tensioner spring, which is hooked on to the bracket on the right hand exhaust pipe, with the long flat connecting link hooked over the second chain roller from the kick-starter sprocket on the gearbox. When the sprocket is in the rest position this roller is the second from last tooth on the sprocket. The link must pass outside the gearchange lever. Re-connect the alternator cables to the couplings underneath the frame, making sure that the colours are correctly matched and that the rubber grommet is in position in the back of the flywheel case. Check the gearchange for operation and make sure that the two "C" shaped hinges are in position on the lugs of the dual seat carrier.

The small clip which supports the throttle cable must be connected to the air ducting around the flywheel by means of the $\frac{3}{16}''$ pin and nut at the top right hand side of the front.

Place the body panels in position, fitting the top and bottom screws. These are the round head screw beneath the dual seat, and the screw at the bottom immediately above the pillion passenger's footboards, but do not tighten either at this stage. Refit the bolts round the edges of the valances, these being the two $\frac{3}{16}''$ bolts at the front and one at the rear bottom end, then the two $\frac{5}{16}''$ bolts which also carry the spare wheel brackets (when fitted), and the $\frac{1}{4}''$ bolts at the top which support the number plate. When a spare wheel and carrier are fitted re-connect the rear carrier to the two lugs which project from the dual seat frame, refit the spare wheel, couple the lower end of the carrier in position on the spare wheel and secure the two wheel nuts. Make sure that the plastic beading is pressed well home before finally tightening the panel bolts.

Re-connect the "C" shaped hinges to the dual seat brackets by the two $\frac{1}{4}''$ bolts and screw on the dual seat catch knob.

Printed in England by Buckler & Webb Ltd., Birmingham, 3

Scooter Service Sheet

1008

Printed January 1960

250 c.c. O.H.V. TWIN CYLINDER SCOOTER

ADJUSTMENTS WHICH CAN BE CARRIED OUT WITHOUT EXTENSIVE DISMANTLING

It is essential for the efficient running of the machine that certain checks are carried out periodically, in accordance with the summary of routine maintenance laid down in the instruction manual.

On the left hand side of the machine is a nacelle with a wire mesh grill; this is held in position by one $\frac{3}{16}$" screw on the right hand side, the left hand side being retained by a small lip behind the valance. Take out the screw and remove by lifting the nacelle from the right hand side.

The circular contact breaker cover can now be seen situated to the right of the clutch operating lever. There is also a large hexagon plug which is the primary drive oil level and filler plug and slightly to the right is a hexagon bolt fitted with a grease nipple to provide a means of greasing the rear drive swinging arm bearing.

Contact Breaker.

The contact breaker gap (A Fig. 4 Service Sheet No. 1004) when fully open should be between ·014" and ·016".

To check the gap take out the two small screws which retain the circular contact breaker cover and turn the engine over carefully until one of the fibre heels is on the peak of the cam, and the points adjacent to this heel are fully open. This can be done either by placing the machine in gear and moving the rear wheel or by gently turning the engine by means of the kick-starter.

If gap A is incorrect when the points are fully open, slacken the small circular nut B which will be seen inside the C shaped coil of the spring, and the fixed contact point can then be moved in or out as necessary. This is the contact point nearest the small condenser. When the gap is correct, retighten the nut inside the C shaped spring and check again, re-adjusting if necessary.

Again turn the engine over until the other set of points is fully open and repeat the operation. When both sets of points have been checked replace the cover by sliding the rubber grommet into the U shaped slot, lift the black and white wire outside the left hand, long hexagon nut, to ensure that it does not foul the cam when the engine is running and replace the contact breaker cover screws.

Ignition Timing.

The normal ignition advance is 5° and the Scooter engine is very sensitive to ignition settings, only the smallest deviation from the correct setting being sufficient to cause overheating and rough running.

The best way to check the timing is to observe the vanes on the cooling fan. These are spaced 11° apart so that half the distance between two vanes is very near to 5°. The full procedure is, firstly, to rotate the engine until the nearside piston is on top dead centre of the compression stroke (i.e., both valves closed). Then turn the engine backwards through 5°, remembering that it is a "backward-running" engine, and the lower set of points (Fig. 4 Service Sheet No. 1004) should then be just breaking.

If the setting is incorrect slacken off the two long hexagon nuts C which secure the contact breaker back plate and rotate the plate until the points are just about to open. Then re-tighten the two hexagons and re-check the adjustment.

Note that turning the plate clockwise advances and anti-clockwise retards the timing. Also remember the importance of the contact breaker gap, for even a slight variation tends to alter the timing. (Opening the points advances the timing ; closing them retards the timing).

A rough check of the timing can be made by observing the position of the hexagon nuts C in the slots in the contact breaker plate. They should be approximately $\frac{1}{16}$" to the left of the centre of the slots and it will be seen that the timing can be roughly set by slackening off the hexagons, with the nearside piston on top dead centre of the compression stroke, ensuring that they are in the approximate centre of the slots and then re-tightening after turning the contact breaker plate approximately $\frac{1}{16}$" to the right.

Clutch.

Should it be necessary at any time to increase the spring tension on the clutch pressure plates, access to the spring nuts can be obtained through the primary drive oil level and filler plug. It should, however, be borne in mind that adjustment of the clutch springs should only be necessary after a very considerable mileage or if clutch slip is occurring, and before any alteration to the spring tension is made ascertain that the clutch cable is correctly adjusted, as indicated by approximately $\frac{1}{4}$" of free movement at the end of the clutch handlebar lever, as in Fig. 22. The inner cable must be quite free and not binding due to frayed wire or other causes.

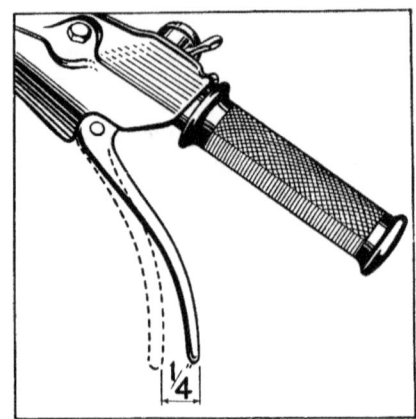

Fig. 22. Clutch control adjustment.

To adjust the clutch springs take out the oil level and filler plug and turn the engine gently until one of the three nuts can be seen through the hole, then with a forked screwdriver screw in the nut very slightly ; say a quarter to half a turn. Revolve the engine again until another nut shows and repeat the operation and again for the third nut, but great care must be taken to ensure that each nut is adjusted exactly the same amount, otherwise the plates will be distorted and clutch drag liable to occur.

Clutch slip can sometimes be detected by means of the kick-starter, for the slip can be felt if the pedal is depressed and the engine fails to turn over. It can also be detected when climbing hills under load by high revving of the engine with loss of pulling power.

Because either clutch slip or clutch drag (failure to free the drive completely) is occurring, do not jump to the conclusion that the clutch springs require adjustment. Instead make sure that the clutch cable itself is quite free in the outer casing and that it is not damaged in any way.

Checking Oil Level in Primary Drive.

This is done by leaning the machine over slightly towards the left hand side, when, if the level is correct, oil will start to run out of the filler plug hole. If the level is low then oil should be added up to the bottom edge of the hole and the plug replaced. For the correct grade of oil refer to the oil recommendation chart in your instruction book.

Adjusting Clutch and Throttle Control Cables.

Adjustment of both these cables may be necessary after a short initial mileage on the machine as outer casings are liable to contract. Adjusters are situated behind the headlamp and in front of the steering column, but do not attempt to carry out adjustment to either cable unless there is a definite need. There should be just perceptible play on the clutch lever when the machine is at rest to ensure that the clutch operates properly. If there is no play on the lever then the clutch is liable to slip when the machine is under load.

The throttle cable should only be adjusted if there is a time lag in the operation of the throttle, as indicated by a delay in response when the twist grip is turned towards the rider.

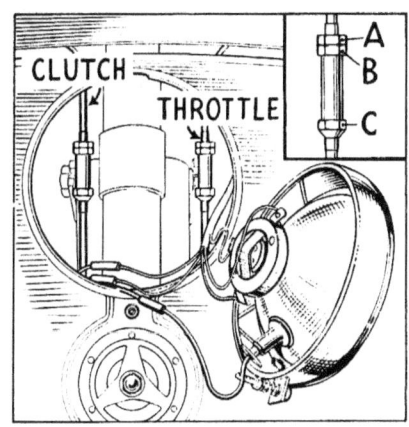

Fig. 23.
Adjusting the Clutch Cable (also Throttle)

To carry out adjustment take out the screw below the headlamp rim and lift the headlamp forward and upwards from the bottom, lifting it clear of the lip which retains the top edge. If it is necessary to place the lamp to one side it can be disconnected by twisting the black bakelite retainer anti-clockwise and by taking out the small parking light bulb which is a press fit into the reflector.

The clutch cable adjuster will be seen on the thicker of the two cables which carry adjusters, the thinner one being the throttle cable. If the clutch cable is too slack release the locknut, screw out the adjuster as required and re-tighten the locknut, but take care to see that there is slight movement on the clutch lever. The same procedure is adopted with the throttle cable if play has to be taken up.

If it is necessary to adjust the position of the throttle to provide a better tick-over, then this operation is carried out by means of an adjuster on the carburetter itself. This is described in the next section.

Before replacing the headlamp make sure that the cables are in the centre of the steering tube and not to the side of the steering column.

To replace the headlamp, engage the top edge of the rim over the lip on the front shield, press the lamp well home and screw in the screw at the base of the rim.

Throttle Control.

To adjust the throttle for tick-over, lift the dual seat to gain access to the screw on the right hand side of the carburetter. (14 Fig. 28). By screwing this in clockwise the throttle slide is raised to provide a faster tick-over or lowered to slow down the tick-over speed. The best throttle opening is that which gives an even but not too fast tick-over and is also suitable for starting the engine with the twist grip completely closed against the stop.

Front Brake Cable.

The front brake cable has an adjuster situated on the left hand side of the machine and on the front edge of the fork tubes. (See Fig. 24).

Fig. 24.

Care should be taken when adjusting to see that the brake does not bind. The handlebar lever should be quite free and should have a free movement of approximately $\frac{1}{4}''$ when measured at the tip of the lever.

To adjust, undo the locknut and screw the adjuster in or out as necessary, bearing in mind that screwing out will take up the slack in the cable and screwing in will provide more slack. Do not omit to re-tighten the locknut after the correct adjustment has been obtained.

Rear Brake.

The rear brake is foot-operated by cable connection and there is an adjuster situated to the rear and underneath the pillion passenger's left hand footboard. (Fig. 25). The adjustment is correct if the brake pedal is approximately $1\frac{1}{2}''$ from the footboard when the brake is applied. If the pedal comes too close to the footboard, undo the locknut on the adjuster and screw the adjuster out as necessary. Then re-tighten the locknut, and make certain that the brake is not binding.

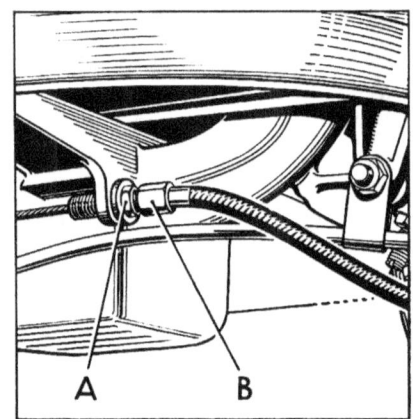

Fig. 25. Rear brake adjustment.

Changing the Wheel.

In the event of a puncture, the wheel affected will have to be removed for the puncture to be repaired, or for the wheel to be changed if a spare wheel is carried. The procedure for removal of the wheel will be described assuming that a spare wheel is carried on the machine.

Release the lightning fastener round the spare wheel cover, take off the two nuts securing the rear carrier and spare wheel and slacken the two bolts securing the rear carrier at each side of the dual seat. Lift up the carrier and take off the spare wheel, then remove the cover and place the spare on the ground next to the wheel to be changed.

Fig. 26. Changing a wheel.

In the case of the rear wheel, with the machine on the stand, slacken off the three wheel nuts so that they can finally be removed by hand, but do not remove the nuts completely. Now take the machine off the stand and lean it over towards the left hand side so that it is resting on the extreme end of the stand leg. (Fig. 26). This should be done gently to ensure that the machine does not fall over, although it will balance quite easily in this position. Now stand astride the rear of the machine and apply slight pressure so that the rear tyre is raised slightly off the ground. Take off the three wheel nuts and remove the wheel; pick up the spare wheel, place it in position with the deeper side of the wheel against the rear drive (that is with the valve on the right hand side or uppermost), screw on the three nuts until the counter-sink is gripping the wheel slightly and raise the machine upright. Place it on the stand and securely tighten the three nuts a little at a time. Do not tighten one nut completely since this is liable to tilt the wheel on the stub axle.

Always make sure that the three nuts are securely tightened.

In the case of the front wheel the procedure is the same but do not in any circumstances take the three wheel nuts off completely; simply slacken them off so that they can be finally removed with the fingers. Again, take the machine off the stand and lean it over towards the left hand side, resting on the edge of the stand leg. Then go round the machine to the right hand side, hold the handlebars and press slightly away so that the front tyre is slightly off the ground and pressure on the wheel is released. Take off the three nuts, pick up the spare wheel and place it in position on the hub, this time with the valve next to the hub or brake drum (that is on the left hand side of the machine), screw on the three nuts, again tightening each one a little at a time and when the wheel is gripped sufficiently to locate it raise the machine upright, place it on the stand and finally tighten the three wheel nuts securely.

Note that the front wheel is fitted with the valve on the left hand side and the rear wheel is fitted with the valve on the right hand side of the machine.

Valve Clearance Adjustment.

This is commonly known as tappet adjustment but the name does not properly apply in the case of the Scooter engine because the adjusting pins are mounted above the valves at the end of the valve rockers, and not on the tappets themselves.

A certain amount of clearance or lost motion in the valve operating mechanism is essential to ensure that the valve heads close properly on their seats and provide a gas-tight joint. The clearance of ·005″ for both inlet and exhaust valves is most critical and the Scooter engine is unlikely to run efficiently if there is any deviation from the standard settings.

The procedure for checking and adjusting (which can be carried out with the valances in position) is first to raise the dual seat and then to detach the sparking plug leads by placing the first two fingers of the right hand beneath the plug terminal and pulling upwards with the thumb against the rocker cover. Next remove the two nuts which hold the rocker cover in position, swing the petrol tap support bracket to one side and take off the steel and fibre washers from the two studs. The rocker cover can then be removed but care must be taken or the joint washer may be damaged.

Turn the engine by means of the kick-starter or by rotating the rear wheel with top gear engaged until Valve No. 1 (see diagram) is fully open. Valve No. 4 will then be in the correct position for checking its clearance. Check all the valves in this way in accordance with the table below by means of a ·005″ feeler gauge inserted between the end of the valve stem and the adjusting pin on the rocker.

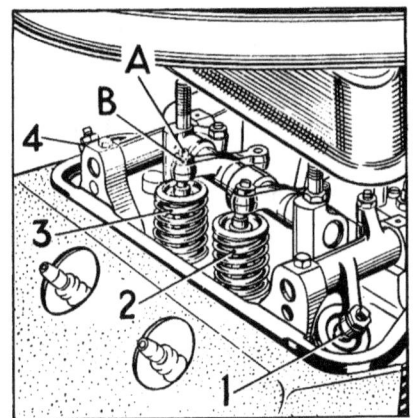

Fig. 27. Tappet adjustment.

How to set the valves for checking clearances.

When No. 1 Valve is fully open check No. 4 Valve.
„ „ 2 „   „   „   „   „ „ 3 „
„ „ 3 „   „   „   „   „ „ 2 „
„ „ 4 „   „   „   „   „ „ 1 „

Note that this operation must be carried out when the engine is cold.

When re-assembling make sure that the washer is in good condition before replacing the cover. Use a new one if in doubt. Carefully locate the cover over the two rocker box studs and press it gently down making sure that the washer has not been misplaced. Place the two fibre washers and then the steel washers in position over the studs, swing the petrol tap support bracket over the left hand side stud and screw on the two ¼″ nuts.

Both nuts should be tightened a little at a time to ensure that the cover is not distorted and it may also be necessary to support the petrol tap bracket to see that this is not twisted out of position for this will affect the opening and closing of the petrol tap.

Sparking Plugs.

It is essential for the efficient functioning of the engine that the sparking plugs are cleaned periodically at about 5,000 mile intervals and the gap between the plug terminals checked. Cleaning is best carried out by a garage having the proper equipment, the charge for this work being very moderate.

The plug gaps can be checked and reset by the owner-rider, however. To do this remove the plug leads and unscrew the plugs with the spanner provided in the tool kit. When lifting the plugs out be very careful not to drop the joint washers as they will be impossible to retrieve without removing all the valances and the ducting round the engine.

The plug electrodes should be bright black in appearance and not fouled with oil. If they are whitish in appearance it is an indication of weak mixture and the cause of this should be ascertained and be eliminated. In general it can be said that weak mixture can only be caused by a partial stoppage in the carburetter, usually in the main jet. Correct spark plug setting is ·018″—·020″ and the setting should always be corrected by bending the outside electrode; in no circumstances should the centre electrode be moved.

When replacing the plugs see that the copper jointing washers are in position, insert the plug very carefully through the hole in the shroud, screw in with the fingers and finally tighten with the plug spanner. When replacing the high tension leads and plug terminals make sure that the lead from the right hand coil is placed on the right hand side spark plug, and the one from the left hand coil on the left hand side spark plug.

Cleaning the Carburetter.

It is sometimes necessary to dismantle and to clean the carburetter to remove any foreign matter that may have found its way through the two filters, or to remove moisture which is certain to accumulate sooner or later. This is an operation which can be done without removing the valances, though the work will be simplified if it is carried out when the valances have been removed for some other operation.

Assuming that the operation is to be carried out without removing the valances first turn off the petrol at the tap. Remove the nut from the left hand side rocker box stud this being the one which retains the petrol tap bracket. Lift the bracket up and swing it to one side out of the way. Now, with a short screwdriver slacken off the screw (29 Fig. 28) on the left hand side of the carburetter which secures the banjo union on the end of the petrol pipe to the float chamber. Be very careful when lifting the screw out not to lose the fibre washers each side of the banjo union and not to damage or drop the cylindrical gauze filter inside the union.

Place the screw, washers and gauze filter carefully on one side.

Unscrew the two $\frac{1}{4}''$ nuts and washers securing the swan neck manifold to the cylinder head and carefully work the carburetter complete with manifold off the studs. It is sometimes considered easier to remove the manifold from the studs and to unscrew the banjo union afterwards but this is a matter of choice.

The carburetter can now be lifted up and out of the engine shields for removal of the float chamber, etc., for cleaning. In normal circumstances it is only necessary to remove the float chamber and possibly the pilot and main jets. (15 and 20, Fig. 28).

Unscrew the two small $\frac{3}{16}''$ pins (17, Fig. 28) one on each side of the

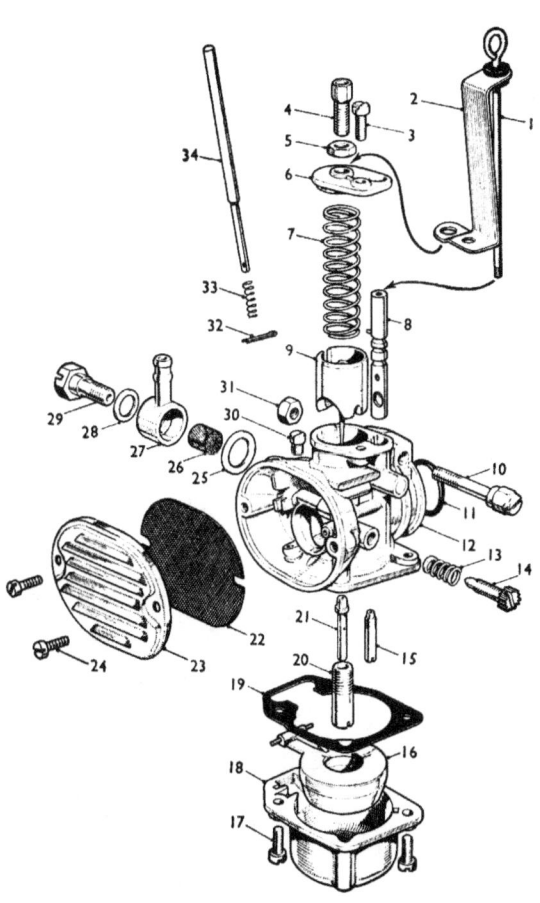

1. Starter Slide Control Rod.	18. Carburetter Bowl.
2. Bracket for Control Rod.	19. Gasket.
3. Cover Plate Screw.	20. Main Jet.
4. Cable Adjuster.	21. Emulsion Tube.
5. Locknut for Cable Adjuster.	22. Air Intake Gauze
6. Cover Plate.	23. Cover for Air Intake Gauze.
7. Spring, Main Slide.	24. Cover Screw (2)
8. Starter Slide.	25. Filter Elbow Washer.
9. Main Slide and Needle.	26. Filter Gauze.
10. Clamping Screw.	27. Filter Elbow.
11. "O" Ring.	28. Filter Plug Washer.
12. Carburetter Body.	29. Filter Plug.
13. Spring, Throttle Adjustment Screw.	30. Plugging Screw.
14. Throttle Adjustment Screw.	31. Clamping Screw Nut.
15. Slow-running Jet.	32. Split Pin.
16. Float.	33. Spring for Tickler.
17. Carburetter Bowl Screw (2).	34. Tickler Stem.

Fig. 28. The carburetter.

float chamber and remove the float chamber complete with the nylon float. Be very careful not to damage the paper gasket which will be found between the float chamber and the body of the carburetter.

The float can now be lifted out and the chamber cleaned thoroughly of any accumulation of water or foreign matter.

If the jets are to be removed, the screwdriver should be in good condition. Never use one which is badly worn and which can slip and possibly shave off a portion of the jet.

Unscrew the jets by means of the screwdriver (they have normal right-hand threads and are therefore unscrewed anti-clockwise), and blow out any foreign matter. Do not in any circumstances use a piece of wire to poke a jet out. The pilot jet (15) is situated at the corner of the body and the main jet (20) in the centre.

Having cleaned the jets they should be replaced, again taking extreme care not to shave a portion of the jet away by allowing the screwdriver to slip since any portion of metal may be jammed in the jet aperture.

If the paper gasket between the float chamber and the body of the carburetter has been damaged, it should be replaced with a new one. Place the gasket in position, see that the nylon float is correctly positioned in the float chamber and replace the chamber, screwing in the two small $\frac{3}{16}''$ screws. Make sure that these are tight before replacing the carburetter.

To reconnect the carburetter, place the screw with the small fibre washer against the smaller diameter of the banjo union, insert the cylindrical gauze filter, then place the larger fibre washer in position and screw up on to the float chamber, finally tightening with a screwdriver. Now work the carburetter down into the aperture and gently in position over the two studs. Again, care should be taken to see that the gaskets are in good condition. Replace the two $\frac{1}{4}''$ nuts and washers, tightening each one a little at a time so as not to distort the manifold joint face. Replace the petrol tap support bracket over the left hand side rocker box stud and replace the $\frac{1}{4}''$ nut.

Rear Chain Adjustment.

The total up and down movement of the rear chain should be $\frac{1}{4}''$. This can be checked by taking out the inspection plug situated half-way along the case towards the top.

When adjustment is necessary, slacken the locknut on the stud projecting from the lower edge of the case, and screw the stud in or out as required. Screwing in will tighten the chain and screwing out will slacken it.

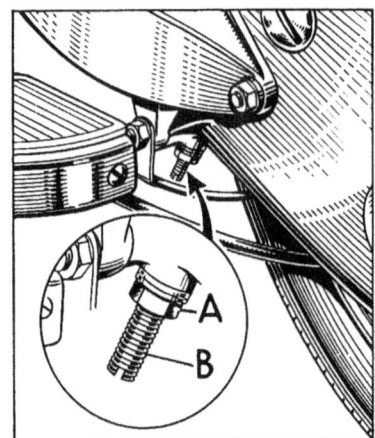

Fig. 29. Rear chain adjuster.

Scooter Service Sheet

1009

Printed Jan. 1960

250 c.c. O.H.V. TWIN CYLINDER SCOOTER

REMOVING AND REFITTING FRONT MUDGUARD AND LEGSHIELD ASSEMBLY AND STEERING HEAD TUBE

If the steering head tube is to be replaced, for example after accident damage, it is first of all necessary to remove the front mudguard and legshield assembly. Proceed as follows.

Remove the front forks as described in Sheet No. 1010. Disconnect and remove the battery or batteries, followed by the headlamp unit. Remove the single screw on either side of the instrument panel, which holds the panel to the legshield. The panel can remain loosely in position. Take out the four screws underneath the mudguard, which hold the headlamp cowl in position and remove the cowl. Disconnect the horn wires.

Remove the left and right hand chrome beadings, take out the screws holding the mudguard and mudguard extensions to the legshield and footboards and remove the mudguard and extensions. Remove the brake and gear change pedals and slacken off the foot board. After the bolts holding the legshield to the frame and foot board are taken out (those fastened to the frame are at the back of the shield just below the instrument panel) the shield can be removed.

Remove the earth wire from the frame and disconnect the head tube by taking off the four nuts from the studs that pass through the tube clips and driving the studs out of the clips. The legshield bracket will come away with the top stud. Draw the head tube complete with clips up and out of the frame tubes.

Re-assemble in reverse order, but do not tighten the top head tube stud until the legshield is bolted in position and take care that the beadings are in position before finally tightening the panels.

SCOOTER SERVICE SHEET

1010

Printed Jan. 1960

250 c.c. O.H.V. TWIN CYLINDER SCOOTER

DISMANTLING AND RE-ASSEMBLY OF THE FRONT FORK AND WHEEL

To withdraw the front fork from the steering column, sufficient clearance must be obtained at the front of the machine to allow the fork to be drawn out and downwards. This clearance can be obtained by placing the machine on a trestle with the wheel projecting over the end, or by placing blocks under the centre stand to give at least 6" clearance beneath the tyre.

If a windscreen is fitted, take off the two bolts and nuts which pass through the windscreen pillars and the handlebar cover, and remove the windscreen and the handlebar cover.

Disconnect the brake and clutch cables from both handlebar levers by pulling out the outer casing nipple and releasing the inner wire from the lever. Disconnect the front brake cable from the brake cam lever by pulling out the split pin and clevis pin, and then unscrew the brake cable adjuster from the aluminium sliding member.

Slacken off the two twist grip screws and take out the two small screws holding the dipper switch to the handlebar. Slacken the pinch bolt ' C ' (Fig. 32) in the handlebar clip.

Remove the front wheel by taking off the three wheel nuts. Now take off the two large hexagon nuts ' A ' (Fig. 32) on the top of the steering column, which have normal right-hand threads, and lift off the handlebar steering lock plate ' B ' (Fig. 31) and dust cover ' C '. Take careful note of the way in which the plate is fitted against the stop plate on the steering head tube. Carefully prise out the long key ' D ' from the column.

Now draw the fork down, at the same time holding a piece of clean rag to catch the balls which will be released from the lower race.

Complete Dismantling of the Fork

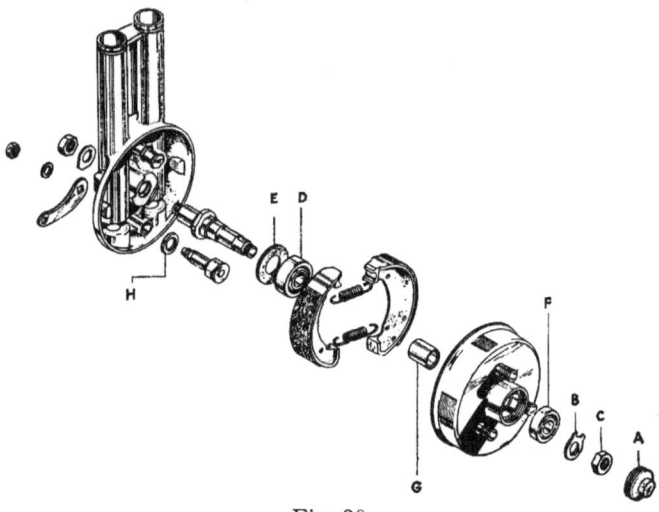

Fig. 30.
Front Hub (exploded)

Where the fork is to be completely dismantled, such as for replacement of one which has been damaged in an accident, proceed as follows.

Remove the cap 'A' (Fig. 30) on the hub; this has a left-hand thread and must therefore be unscrewed in a clockwise direction. It will be necessary to apply the brake by using a piece of tube over the brake cam lever.

The bearings are a press fit into the brake drum and on to the hub spindle, and in some cases it may be necessary to use an extractor to draw the drum and bearings off the spindle (tool No. 61-5033). Flatten the tab

Service Sheet No. 1010 (contd.)

washer 'B' which will be seen under the spindle nut 'C' and unscrew the nut in a normal anti-clockwise direction. Take off the tab washer and draw the brake drum complete with bearings off the spindle.

Examination of the drum will show that there is a large bearing 'D' on the inner end of the shell adjacent to an oil seal 'E' which has the lip facing towards the bearing. On the outer end of the shell is a smaller bearing 'F' and there is a distance piece 'G' between these two bearings.

Remove the brake shoes by prising them from the brake cam and the fulcrum pin, noting that the shoes are fitted with the narrow side towards the brake back plate and that there is a distance piece 'H' on the cam spindle between the shoes and the back plate.

To release the lower member from the fork, unscrew the two domed nuts 'E' (Fig. 29) at the lower end of the member. The front nut is removed with a spanner using a screwdriver to hold the slotted end of the damper rod. In the case of the rear or fork spring nut, no screwdriver will be necessary.

With the two domed nuts removed the lower member can be drawn off the two fork tubes. The two shouldered washers 'F', one on the spring stud and the other on the damper rod, may come away with the lower member, but in any case they should be removed and kept until ready for re-assembly. The spring can be removed by unscrewing the bolt and washer at the upper or crown end of the fork; this will release the spring complete with the bottom and the top scrolls.

To take out the damper, unscrew the disc valve 'G' in the end of the tube and draw the damper out complete with washer and nut at the top.

The dust cover can be removed by taking out the centre bolt and elongated plate which locates between the two fork tubes on the fork crown.

The brake cam lever can be released by unscrewing the nut on the lever and the cam can then be drawn through the lower member. The fulcrum pin is a press fit in the lower member and should not be removed.

If the hub spindle is to be removed it will be necessary to flatten the tab washer on the outer end of the spindle, unscrew the nut and then heat the aluminium sliding member in hot water before tapping the spindle through towards the brake drum side. Note that it is located by two flats.

Hub Bearings

The larger of the two bearings is fitted from inside the drum with the oil seal between the bearing and the brake shoes, the lip of the seal being towards the bearing. The smaller bearing is fitted from the outer end of the hub shell (i.e., the locknut end) with the distance piece between the two bearings.

Head Bearings

The bottom steering head cone is a press fit on to the fork steering column and the bottom cup is a press fit on to the outside of the steering head tube, the top cup being a press fit into the tube. There are 28 steel balls in each head race. A broad rubber band is employed on the lower race as a dust excluder.

When the head races are to be renewed (this is possible without removing the head tube or legshield from the frame), the bottom cup should be removed

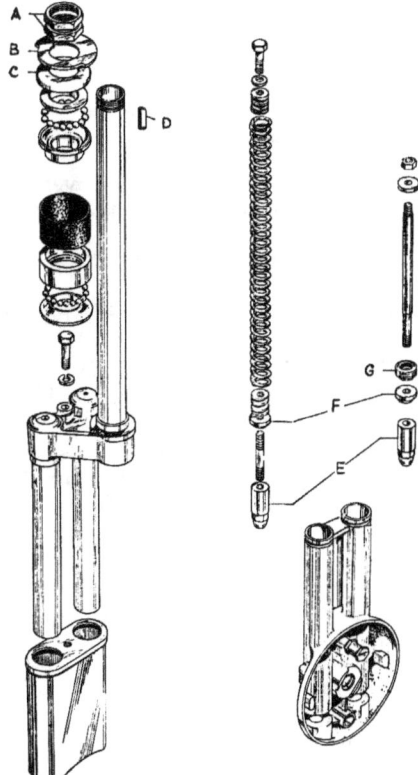

Fig. 31.
Front Fork (exploded)

Service Sheet No. 1010 (contd.)

from the head tube by tapping it with a suitable punch round the outside edge. The top cup can be removed by driving it from inside the tube, again using a suitable punch or drift. Replacements should be pressed on and into the tube; make sure that they are set squarely before being driven well home.

Front Fork re-assembly

Assuming that a new fork is being built into the machine, first slide the dust cover over the two fork tubes and secure with the centre bolt, washer and long steel plate. Pack the damper tube with as much " Jetlube " grease as it will hold (an old cycle pump will be found useful) slide the damper rod, nut and washer end first and screw in the disc valve at the lower end of the tube. Now slide the fork spring up the other tube, secure with the bolt and washer through the fork crown, and replace the two shouldered washers on the damper rod and spring stud so that the smaller diameters are at the bottom.

Screw service tool No. 61-5018 on to the end of the damper rod, but do not lock tightly, otherwise difficulty may be experienced in removing the tool. Guide the service tool through the lower member, at the same time guiding the fork spring through the other side. When the service tool is through, draw the damper rod and the stud on the end of the fork spring scroll through the lower member, so that the domed nuts may be fitted.

Remove the service tool from the damper rod and screw on the domed nut, holding the damper rod with the screwdriver through the nut, and then refit the other domed nut to the spring stud.

Pass the brake cam spindle through the distance piece with the chamfered side towards the head of the brake cam, place the brake lever on the outside and screw on the washer and nut. Pass the main spindle (if removed) through the lower member, having first heated the member in hot water, and locate it by means of the two flats. Replace the tab washer and screw on the locknut, turning the tab up on to the nut. Replace the brake shoes with the narrow portion of the shoe next to the aluminium lower member. This can be done by holding the shoes with the springs fitted in a V formation, then fitting them over the fulcrum pin and brake cam by pressing outwards and downwards against the lower member.

Slide the brake drum into position over the spindle, refit the tab washer and the locknut, turning the tab up on to the locknut when finally tightened.

The fork will now be ready for refitting to the steering head tube.

Grease both cups on the frame and apply 28 balls to the lower cup; make sure that the rubber dust excluder is on the bearing but high enough not to interfere with the fitting. Slide the fork column up through the bearing and then, supporting the fork, place 28 balls in the top bearing and refit the top cone and dust cover. Replace the long key in the fork column, slide the handlebar into position over the key and screw on the two top locknuts by first screwing the lower nut 'B' (Fig. 32) down until the steering head adjustment is correct; it should be free to revolve without any appreciable up or down movement. When the adjustment is correct, tighten the top locknut 'A' and retighten the clip 'C' on the handlebar.

With the races assembled, draw the rubber dust cover down on to the fork crown and replace the hub cap by screwing in anti-clockwise.

Slide the twist grip over the handlebar, replace the front brake and clutch cables and refit the dipper switch and horn button by screwing in the two small screws.

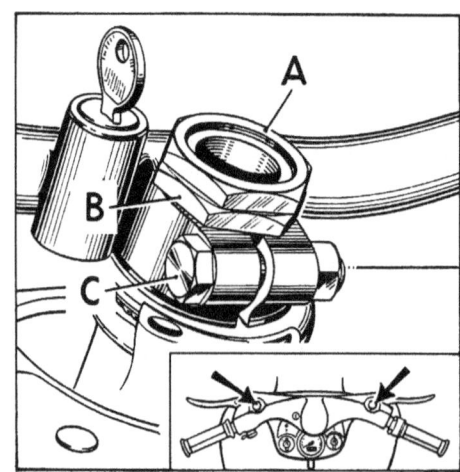

Fig. 32.
Steering Head Adjuster.

Service Sheet No. 1010 (contd.)

Make sure that all cables and controls pass down the front of the steering head and do not allow an acute bend above the instrument panel, as a cable in this condition may foul the stop plate. Connect the front brake by screwing the cable adjuster into the lower member and refit the clevis pin in the brake lever. Do not forget the split pin and do not omit to re-tighten the lock nut on the brake adjuster. Replace the wheel and check the wheel nuts when the tyre is on the ground.

Check that all controls are correct before replacing the handlebar cover and windscreen.

Scooter Service Sheet

1011
Printed Jan. 1960

250 c.c. O.H.V. TWIN CYLINDER SCOOTER

CHANGING BRAKE SHOES

After a very considerable mileage it will be necessary to replace the brake shoes, and this can be done without dismantling the hubs.

Rear Brake

To change the rear brake shoes first lift the machine off the stand so that the rear wheel is clear of the ground and place a small trestle or block of wood under the rear cross member of the frame.

Remove the rear wheel by taking off the three hub nuts and take out the single countersunk screw which holds the brake drum to the stub axle and draw off the drum.

With a screwdriver or similar tool unhook the springs from the shoes, taking careful note of the way in which they are fitted and remove the shoes. To refit, place the leading shoe in position on the fulcrum pin and cam, this being the shoe at the top looking from the right-hand side of the machine, and hook one spring into the hole nearest the brake cam.

Now obtain a piece of strong cord and tie it into a loop approximately 1" diameter; place the trailing shoe which is the lower one, in position, slip the loop of cord over the lower end of the spring and using a screwdriver as a lever through the other end of the loop expand the spring until the end can be pressed into the hole in the lower or trailing shoe. This will now hold the two shoes in position.

Pick up the remaining spring and hook it into the hole in the trailing shoe nearest the fulcrum pin, so that the loose end is uppermost, and, again placing the cord over the hook and using the screwdriver as a lever, expand the spring until the loose end can be hooked into the leading shoe. Now remove the cord.

As the rear brake cable may have been adjusted to compensate for wear on the brake linings, it will now be advisable to slacken off the cable by screwing the adjuster in before refitting the brake drum. After refitting the drum and screwing in the single countersunk head screw, replace the wheel, secure the three wheel nuts, spin the wheel to make sure that the brake is not binding and re-adjust the cable as necessary. Make sure that the locknut on the adjuster is tightened securely after the correct adjustment has been obtained.

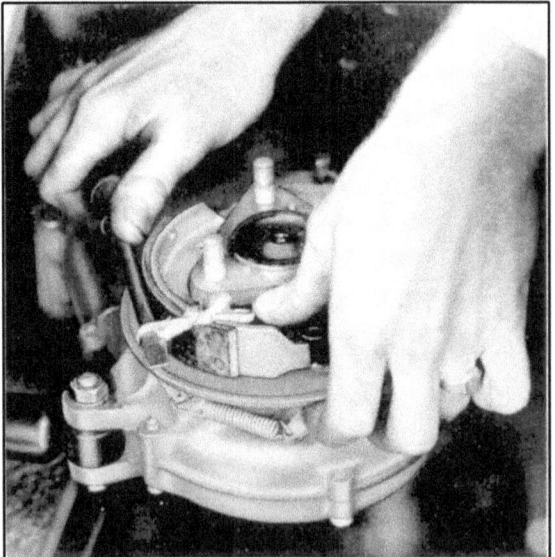

Fig. 33.
Fitting Rear Brake Shoe Spring.

Service Sheet No. 1011 (contd.)

Front Brake

The presence of the stub axle makes the procedure for the front brake somewhat different from that for the rear.

Raise the front of the machine so that the front wheel is clear of the ground by placing a block of wood approximately 2" thick underneath each leg of the centre stand. Remove the front wheel by taking off the three wheel nuts.

Apply the front brake and remove the hub cap by unscrewing in a clock-wise direction; it has a left hand thread.

Beneath the cap will be seen the wheel lock nut and a tab washer; flatten the tab on the washer and unscrew the locknut in the normal manner, which is anti-clockwise. Take off the nut and the tab washer and draw off the brake drum complete with bearings and oil seal. (Service tool No. 61-5033.)

Now, using two screwdrivers, prise the shoes up and away from the pivot bolt and brake cam.

To re-fit. Hold the two shoes with the springs fitted, open them to form a V and press them down and over the pivot pin and brake cam, making sure that they are fitted the correct way round, which is with the narrow portion against the brake back plate.

Slacken off the brake cable by screwing in the adjuster on the lower member, refit the brake drum with the tab washer and lock nut, turning over the tab washer after the nut has been secured. Screw in the hub cap by turning in an anti-clockwise direction and refit the wheel, finally resetting the brake cable adjustment. After spinning the wheel to ensure that the brake is not binding.

Always make sure when removing wheels that they are fitted the correct way round, which is the rear wheel with the valve on the right hand side of the machine and the front wheel with the valve on the left. If the wheels are incorrectly fitted the alignment will be affected.

Fig. 34
Front Brake Adjuster.

Scooter Service Sheet

1012

Printed Jan. 1960

250 c.c. O.H.V. TWIN CYLINDER SCOOTER
REMOVING AND REPLACING THE PETROL TANK

Removal

It is sometimes necessary to remove and clean a petrol tank where foreign matter such as dirt or water has got into the fuel. When this is necessary, turn off the petrol at the tap and then disconnect the lower end of the petrol pipe where it is coupled to the carburetter by taking out the screw, being careful not to lose the two fibre washers, or the gauze filter, which is fitted inside the banjo union. Remove the one $\frac{1}{4}$" nut which secures the petrol tap support arm to the left hand rocker box stud and swing the bracket clear of the stud. Slacken the bolts at the top of the silencer where it is secured to the petrol tank and silencer bracket and after releasing the clips securing the silencer to the exhaust pipes, swing the silencer clear of the pipes. The rear mudguard must also be removed. This is secured by two $\frac{1}{4}$" bolts and nuts to the cross member between the two vertical frame tubes and two bolts and nuts to the rear petrol tank and silencer bracket. Take out these bolts and remove the mudguard downwards and out. Take off the single nut and shakeproof washer which secure the rectifier to the frame and place the rectifier carefully out of the way.

The rear damper unit must be removed completely by taking out both the upper and lower pivot pins, one through the double brackets on the dual seat carrier and the lower one through the rear drive unit.

The petrol tank itself is secured by three shouldered bolts with nuts, two at the front and one at the rear. Take off the nuts, which also have spring washers and large plain washers, pull out the bolts, remove the rubber buffers, swing the rear bracket out of the way and drop the petrol tank down and out of the frame, taking care to see that the petrol pipe which is still attached does not hook itself round the frame cross members.

Replacement

The procedure for refitting the petrol tank is the reverse of removal, but first place the tank in position underneath the dual seat carrier so that the two lugs at the front are resting on the brackets between the two vertical members of the frame and the rear lug on the tank is resting on the bracket provided for supporting the petrol tank, the silencer and the mudguard.

When the tank is in position, see that the petrol pipe is free to be coupled to the carburetter, and place each of the plain $\frac{1}{4}$" thick rubber buffers between the lug on the tank and the lug on the frame. Now fit one of the special shouldered rubber buffers underneath the lugs on the frame, press the special shouldered bolt down through the petrol tank bracket, place the large diameter steel washer against the lower rubber buffer, then the spring washer, and screw on the nut. Repeat this for each of the three mounting points, leaving the nuts finger-tight until assembly of the three mounting points has been completed. Now secure the three mounting bolts and nuts until the nuts are tightened against the shoulders on the bolts. No difficulty will be experienced here providing that the special shouldered rubber washers have been correctly fitted with the shoulders inside the brackets provided on the frame and on the rear bracket. Now refit the mudguard by inserting the four $\frac{1}{4}$" diameter bolts and nuts, two at the front and two at the rear. Refit the exhaust pipes into the silencer and secure the clips, replace the rectifier on its bracket, making sure that the shakeproof washer is in position under the nut, replace the damper unit with the spring uppermost and finally reconnect the petrol pipe to the carburetter, taking care to see that the gauze filter is inside the banjo union, and that the small fibre washer is between the head of the screw and the outside face of the union with the larger diameter fibre washer between the banjo union and the float chamber of the carburetter.

SCOOTER SERVICE SHEET 1013

Printed Jan. 1960

250 c.c. O.H.V. TWIN CYLINDER SCOOTER

CHANGING SPEEDOMETER OR SPEEDOMETER CABLE

If it is necessary at any time to change the speedometer head or the cable, the following procedure should be adopted. When the cable is to be replaced, disconnect the cable at the rear brake drum underneath the swinging arm by unscrewing the outer casing union nut and pull the inner cable out of mesh with the drive. When only the head is to be changed it is only necessary to remove the cable clips to obtain sufficient slack in the cable for the instrument panel to be lifted up.

Take out the headlamp screw and lift the headlamp up off the lip on the top of the nacelle and disconnect the leads by turning the black bakelite ring in an anti-clockwise direction. Pull out the parking light bulb and place the rim and reflector on one side.

Now take out the two bolts holding the handlebar shroud and windscreen, when this is fitted, and lift the windscreen and shroud clear of the handlebars.

Slacken off the two screws holding the twist grip and remove the front brake and clutch cables from the levers on the handlebars by pulling out the outer casing and releasing the nipple from the lever. Take out the two screws holding the dipper switch and horn button to the left-hand side of the handlebar.

When all the cables are clear of the bars, slacken off the pinch-bolt on the handlebar and undo the two large nuts on the top of fork column. Lift the handlebars from the forks, then slide the twist grip off the end of the bar and place the handlebars to one side. Lift the steering stop plate off the fork column and take out the two screws at each side of the instrument panel these being just underneath the panel in the rear portion of the leg shield.

With a Phillips screwdriver take out the two small Phillips screws in the centre of the ignition and lighting switches and lift the two knobs off the switches. Then undo the two square nuts securing the switches to the panel and push the switches through to the underside of the panel.

The instrument panel can now be lifted up and by twisting slightly can be worked clear of the steering lock plate on the back of the steering head tube. It will only be necessary to obtain sufficient clearance to get at the speedometer cable union nut.

Unscrew the nut and pull the inner cable clear of the speedometer head.

When the cable is to be replaced, the old one should be drawn out and the replacement threaded through, then recoupled to the speedometer and reassembly can proceed.

If the speedometer head is to be changed, unscrew the nut holding the bracket on the underside of the speedometer head, take off the bracket together with the speedometer bulb and lift the speedometer head up through the top of the panel. The replacement head is then fitted in the reverse manner, but care should be taken to see that the bracket is positioned in such a way that the bulb will illuminate the speedometer through the small panel in the speedometer head.

Re-assembly

Having fitted the replacement speedometer head or the cable, refit the ignition switches by screwing on the square nuts, making sure that the switches are correctly located in the D shaped holes, and if any of the cables have been pulled through the steering aperture in the panel, make sure that they are replaced ready for the panel to be lowered into position. Now ease the panel down over the steering head stop plate

Service Sheet No. 1013 (contd.)

and into position, making sure that the two brackets on the underside of the panel lie between the rear portion of the leg shields and the front panel and that the panel fits over the top edge of the leg shields and is also clipping over the plastic beads round the outer edges of the leg shields. Insert the two screws underneath each side of the instrument panel and secure.

Place the steering stem stop plate over the stem, making sure that it is fitted the correct way up so that it engages properly on the stop plate on the back of the steering head. Place the handlebars in position over the steering column first sliding on the twist grip. Replace the two large nuts on top of the handlebars and adjust the head bearings, finally tightening the handlebar pinch-bolt.

Reconnect the front brake and clutch lever cables to the levers and refit the dipper switch and horn button by screwing in the two small screws. This operation will be facilitated if the lower screw is engaged in the hole slightly before refitting the top one.

Replace the lighting and ignition knobs over the flats on the switches and secure with the two Phillips screws with the dished washers underneath the heads of the screws.

See that all the cables are located down the front of the steering column and that there is not any excess loop in the cables which might foul the stop plate on the steering column.

Reconnect the bakelite headlight coupling by turning in a clockwise direction and press in the parking light bulb. Place the headlamp over the lip on the top of the nacelle and push it well home before securing with the screw at the base of the rim.

Check the operation of all the controls and refit the handlebar shroud and the wind shield. Finally recouple the speedometer cable at the rear wheel.

Scooter Service Sheet

1050

Printed December 1959

250 c.c. O.H.V. Twin Cylinder Scooter fitted with Lucas 5AF Alternator

Introduction and Testing Procedure

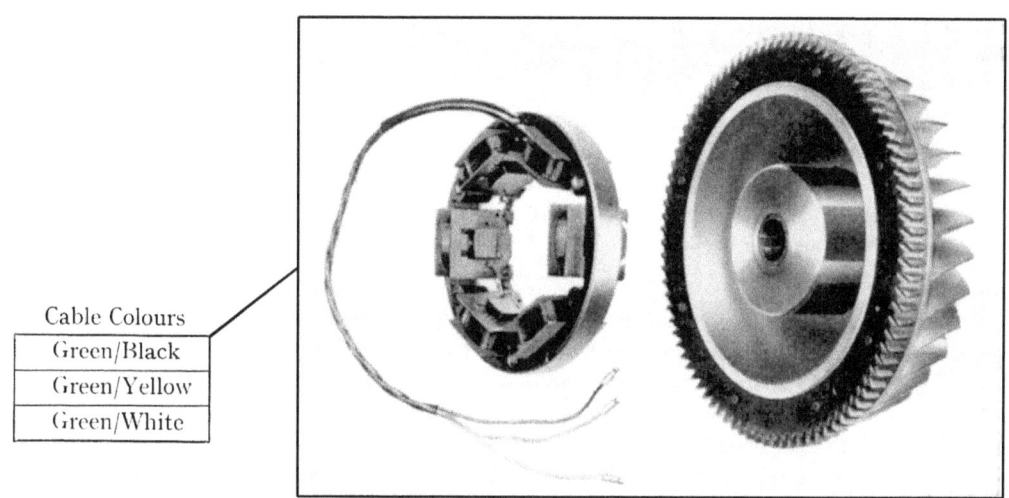

Cable Colours
| Green/Black |
| Green/Yellow |
| Green/White |

General Description

Designed specially for enclosed engines where fan cooling is necessary, the 5AF alternator consists of a conventional, RM13 type, wound stator for bolting to the engine crankcase but its RM15 type rotor is cast integral with the engine flywheel. This has cooling fins cast in its external surface while an inertia ring is screwed to its periphery. When the engine is fitted with an electric starting motor, a starter ring gear is substituted for the inertia ring. There is a 6 volt and 12 volt version of this unit. Two particular applications of the 5AF alternator concerns the 250 c.c. o.h.v. twin cylinder scooters, which include a de-luxe machine having a starting motor fitted with a starter ring gear. On the standard machine is fitted a 6 volt 5AF which incorporates an inertia ring, instead of the starter ring gear.

The 6 volt 5AF is rated at 60 watts, whilst the 12 volt unit is rated at 110 watts.

SERVICE SHEET No. 1050 (contd.)

Output Control

The standard circuit has the output wires from the generator connected by their snap connectors to similarly coloured wires on the wiring harness and provides the following output control.

Lighting Switch in "OFF" Position

The output is taken from one pair of coils by means of the Green/White and Green/Black wires, and the remaining coils (Green/White and Green/Yellow wires) are open-circuited.

Lighting in Switch "PILOT" Position

Output taken from one pair of coils by Green/White and Green/Black wires as before and the remaining coils are on open-circuit.

Lighting Switch in "HEAD" Position

All three pairs of coils are connected in parallel and the maximum output is obtained. **Note.—** To provide an increased charging rate with the lighting switch in the "OFF" position, some models will be found to have the wire joining terminals 5 and 6 of the headlamp switch removed. This means that no coils are shorted out in this switch position and the charging rate is slightly increased.

In circumstances where a considerable amount of low speed running is necessary or there are long periods of parking with the lights on, it is possible to increase the charging rate with the lighting switch in the "OFF" and "PILOT" positions by connecting the Green/Yellow alternator cable by its snap connector to the Green/Black harness cable and the Green/Black alternator cable to the Green/Yellow harness cable.

The Green/White cables should not be disturbed. These alternative connections considerably increase the charging rate in these switch positions, and the connections should be returned to standard for normal conditions of use or long runs.

Owing to the effects of the above modifications it is essential that the wiring circuit is returned to standard before checking the charging rates during fault finding.

Emergency Starting

With the ignition switch in the "EMG" position, the battery is not isolated from the alternator and will, in fact, receive a charge whilst the machine is being run.

This arrangement is also a safeguard against continuous running in the "EMG" position. The back pressure of the battery will increase as it is charged, until it is sufficiently strong to affect the working of the ignition system. When this happens misfiring will occur, resulting in poor engine performance. In view of this, always check that the machine is not being run with the ignition switch continually in the "EMG" position, before testing the system for other faults.

Motor Cycle Trials Events, etc.

When using the machine for trials riding, the alternator can be used continuously in the "EMG" position without a battery, providing the lead from the main harness to the battery negative terminal is earthed to the machine, but contact points are liable to become badly burned.

Test Procedure

As the lights and other equipment are operated on a normal D.C. circuit they can be checked by normal continuity tests with a battery and bulb.

The following equipment is required to satisfactorily test the charging circuit. The meters used should be accurate moving coil instruments.

- A.C. voltmeter scale 0–15 volts
- D.C. ammeter scale 0–15 amps.
- D.C. voltmeter scale 0–15 volts
- 1 ohm. load resistance
- 12 volt battery and 36 watt bulbs

SERVICE SHEET No. 1050 (contd.)

Checking D.C. Input to Battery

Test 1. Ammeter connected in series with main lead and battery.

Test 2. Disconnect main lead from battery. Connect 1 ohm resistor in place of battery. Feed ignition coil separately from battery. Turn ignition switch to IGN position.

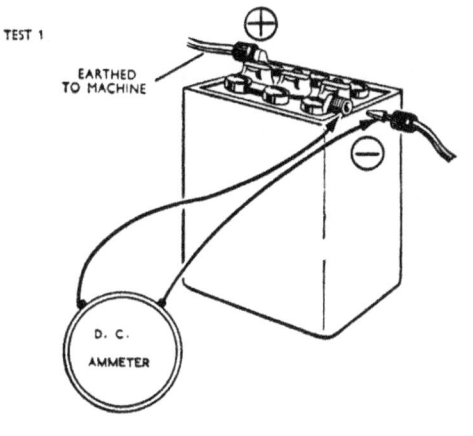

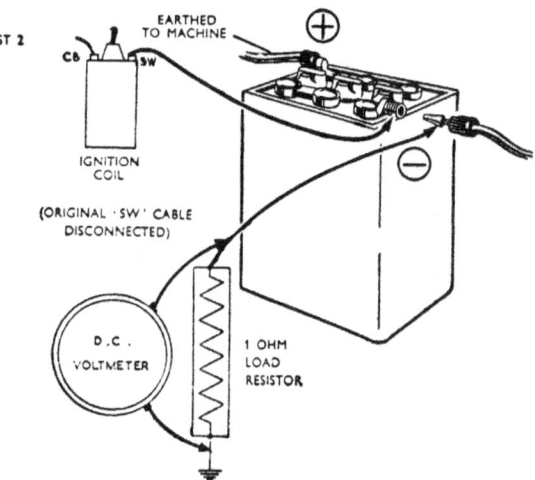

If battery is in poor condition or low state of charge use Test 2.

Test	Switch Position	Reading Amps. at 3,000 r.p.m.	
		6 Volt	12 Volt
1	OFF	1.75 (min.)	2.5 (min.)
	PILOT	0.75 (min.)	1.5 (min.)
	HEAD	0.5 (min.)	3.25 (min.)

Test	Switch Position	Reading Volts at 3,000 r.p.m.	
		6 Volt	12 Volt
2	OFF	1.75 (min.)	3.75 (min.)
	PILOT	1.75 (min.)	3.25 (min.)
	HEAD	3.25 (min.)	6.0 (min.)

Conclusions from these Tests

   Test 1. If meter readings are as stated, the charging circuit and alternator are satisfactory. No reading; check the generator.
   A low reading can be caused by a faulty battery.
   Proceed with Test 2. If readings still low check battery with hydrometer and discharge tester.

   Test 2. If meter readings are lower or higher than values stated, check the generator. No reading on meter, check the rectifier.

Important

   Inaccurate readings can be due to faulty wiring, bad connections at the snap connectors or poor earths. Make a quick visual check of all connections before proceeding with the tests.
   Remember it is no use carrying out Test 1 if the battery is faulty or in a low state of charge, if in doubt proceed with Test 2.

SERVICE SHEET No. 1050 (contd.)

Testing the Alternator on the Machine, using an A.C. Voltmeter and 1 Ohm Load Resistor

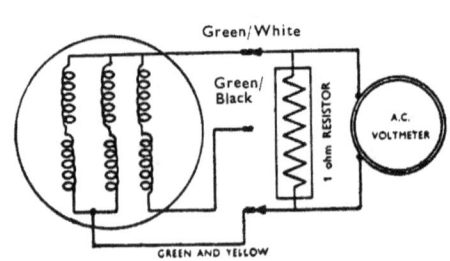

Test	Voltmeter and Resistor Connected Across	Reading Volts at 3,000 r.p.m.	
		6 Volt	12 Volt
1	Green/White and Green/Black	3.25 (min.)	3.5 (min.)
2	Green/White and Green/Yellow	6.25 (min.)	5.5 (min.)
3	Green/White and Green/Yellow (with Green/Black connected to Green/Yellow)	8.75 (min.)	7.0 (min.)
4	Any one lead and Generator Stator (Earth)	No Reading	No Reading

Conclusions from these Tests

Low reading on any group of coils indicates shorted turns.

Zero reading will indicate open-circuit coil.

If all coils read low, partial de-magnetisation of rotor may have occurred as a result of faulty rectifier. Check rectifier, and battery earth polarity before replacing rotor.

A reading between any one lead and the generator stator indicates an earthed coil. Replace stator or locate earth by isolating and testing individual coils.

Note

With the engine running at 3,000 r.p.m. (approx.) the output voltages are steady, and even if the engine is running a few r.p.m. faster or slower the values stated will be obtained from a good generator.

SERVICE SHEET No. 1050 (contd.)

Rectifier—Bench Testing

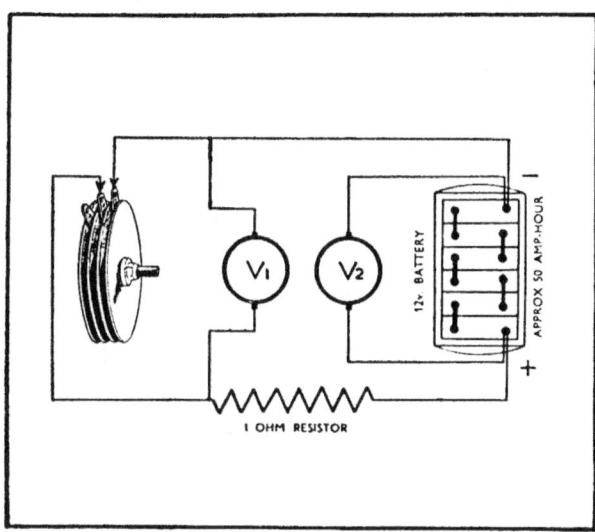

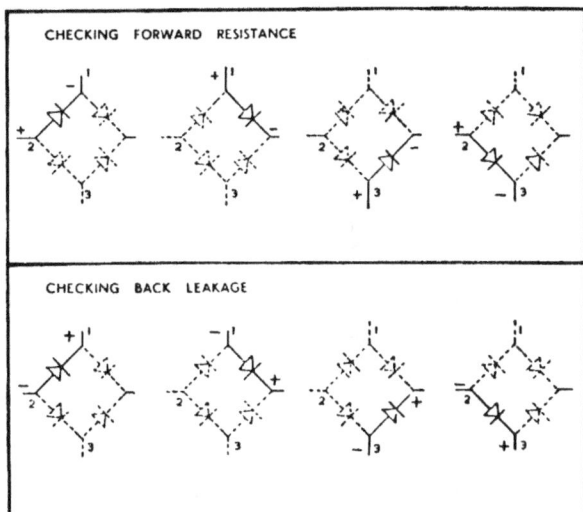

V1—will measure the volt drop across the rectifier plate.
V2—must be checked when testing the rectifier plate, to make certain the supply voltage is the recommended 12 volts on load.

It is essential that the supply is kept at 12 volts for these Tests.

Forward Resistance Test
Test 1. Connect test leads in turn across terminals 2 and 1, bolt and 1, bolt and 3, 2 and 3. Reading in all positions should not be greater than 2.5 volts. Keep the testing time as short as possible to avoid overheating the rectifier cell. **Note.**—If the latter type of rectifier, which has no terminal markings, is fitted, the same procedure is followed. The same voltage values also apply.

Back Leakage Test
Test 2. Proceed as for Test 1, and test each cell in turn, but reverse the test leads. Reading on V1 should not be less than 2 volts below the open-circuit reading on voltmeter No. 2, i.e., 10 volts.

Conclusions from these Tests
Test 1. If the voltage reading on V1 is more than 2.5 volts, on any cell, it is aged and the rectifier should be replaced.

Test 2. If the voltage reading on V1 is less than 10 volts, on any cell, the rectifier is shorted and should be replaced.

Important
Before fitting a replacement rectifier, check the following points:—
1. Check that battery is correctly connected, **Positive** to **Earth.**
2. Check rectifier visually for signs of damage.

Do not make any adjustment to the nut which holds the elements together on the through bolt. The efficiency of the rectifier depends upon the correct tension of this bolt. The tension on the bolt is set correctly before leaving the works, and cannot be adjusted correctly in service.

SERVICE SHEET No. 1050 (contd.)

Checking Rectifier in Position on Machine

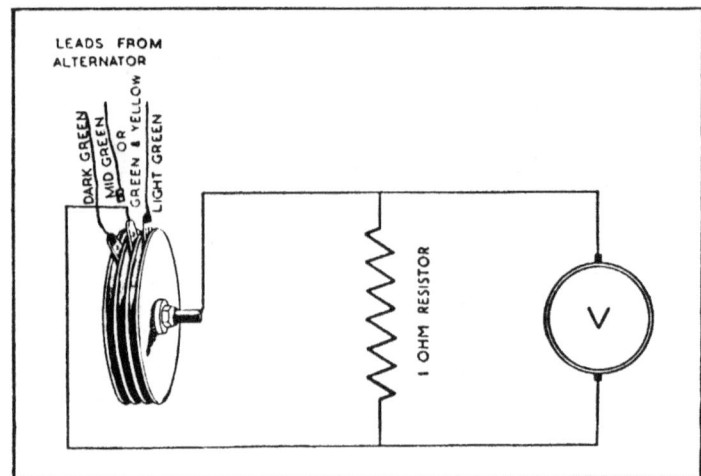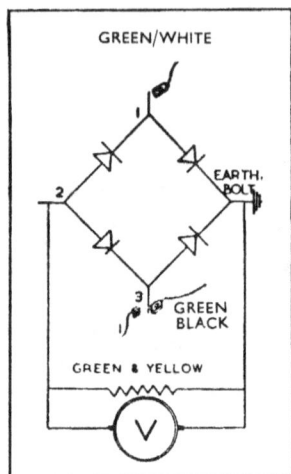

Voltmeter and Resistor Connected Across	Reading with Leads Connected as Shown
Terminal No. 2 (or centre terminal on latest type) and frame of machine	7.0 (min.) 6 volt 6.5 (min.) 12 volt

Procedure

Connect the alternator leads as detailed direct to the recifier terminals No. 1 and No. 3 with all the other cables dsconnected from the rectifier.

(**Note.**—On the latest type rectifiers the terminals are not numbered, so connect the alternator leads to the outer cranked terminals).

Connect the test leads which must have a D.C. voltmeter with 1 ohm load shunted across, between earth (frame of machine) and terminal No. 2 (centre terminal on latest type rectifier) when the values stated should be obtained with engine running at 3,000 r.p.m.

Conclusions from Tests

If the alternator passes its individual test, but it fails on this test it indicates that either the rectifier is faulty or it is not properly earthed.

Connecting the test leads to the centre bolt will eliminate the possiblity of faulty earth connection.

SERVICE SHEET No. 1050 (contd.)

Testing the External Wiring Circuit

Using D.C. Volmeter only
1. All cables, including battery, to be connected as normal.
2. Connect voltmeter Red test lead to earth.

Testing Charging Circuit through Ignition Switch
3. Connect Black test lead to No. 2 terminal on rectifier.
4. Switch ignition to IGN position.
5. Battery volts (i.e., six or twelve should register on voltmeter.
6. If there is a zero reading on voltmeter in the above condition, check circuit back through ignition switch and ammeter, etc., to the battery.

Testing Emergency Start Circuit
7. Connect Red test lead to earth.
8. Connect Black test lead to distributor C.B. terminal.
9. Open ignition contacts.
10. Switch ignition to EMG position.
11. Battery volts should register on the voltmeter.
12. Transfer Black test lead to alternator Green/Yellow lead.
13. Battery volts should register on voltmeter.

Note
These tests are to be carried out in the case of "No Charge" or "No Emergency Start" if previous tests have been carried out and all is in order.

It is important that both the ignition timing and the rotor timing is correct for efficient operation of Emergency Start.

Testing the 'Low,' 'Medium' and 'High' Charge Positions

Using D.C. Voltmeter only
1. Connect Red test lead to earth.
2. The set, including battery, connected as normal with the exception of the alternator Green/Yellow cable which should be disconnected at the snap connector under the saddle.
3. Connect Black test lead to Green/Yellow cable coming from headlamp (i.e., not coming from alternator).
4. With ignition switch in IGN position and lighting switch OFF.
5. A low voltage (i.e., 1—2) should register on voltmeter.
6. With lighting switch in PILOT, zero voltage should register on voltmeter.
7. With lighting switch in HEAD position a low voltage should register on voltage.

Note
Incorrect switching of these cables will cause incorrect charging rates, i.e., failure of Green/Yellow and Green/Black linking together in HEAD position will result in a low charge rate with headlight switched on.

In the case of incorrect switching it is necessary to check the wiring and the switch for correct connections, etc.

SERVICE SHEET No. 1050 (contd.)

Wiring Diagram 6 Volt Model

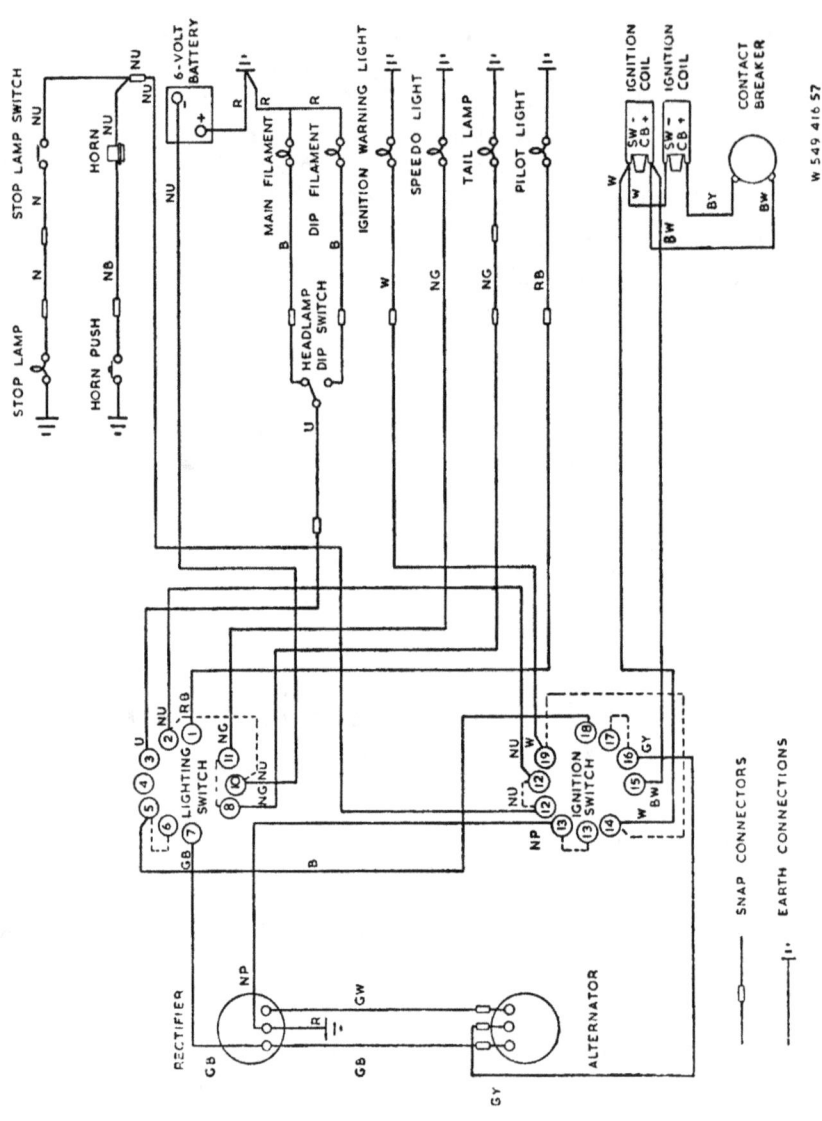

Colour Code

R—Red.	N—Brown.	U—Blue.	P—Purple.	L—Light.
B—Black	G—Green.	Y—Yellow.	W—White.	D—Dark.

SERVICE SHEET No. 1050 (contd.)

Wiring Diagram 12 Volt Model

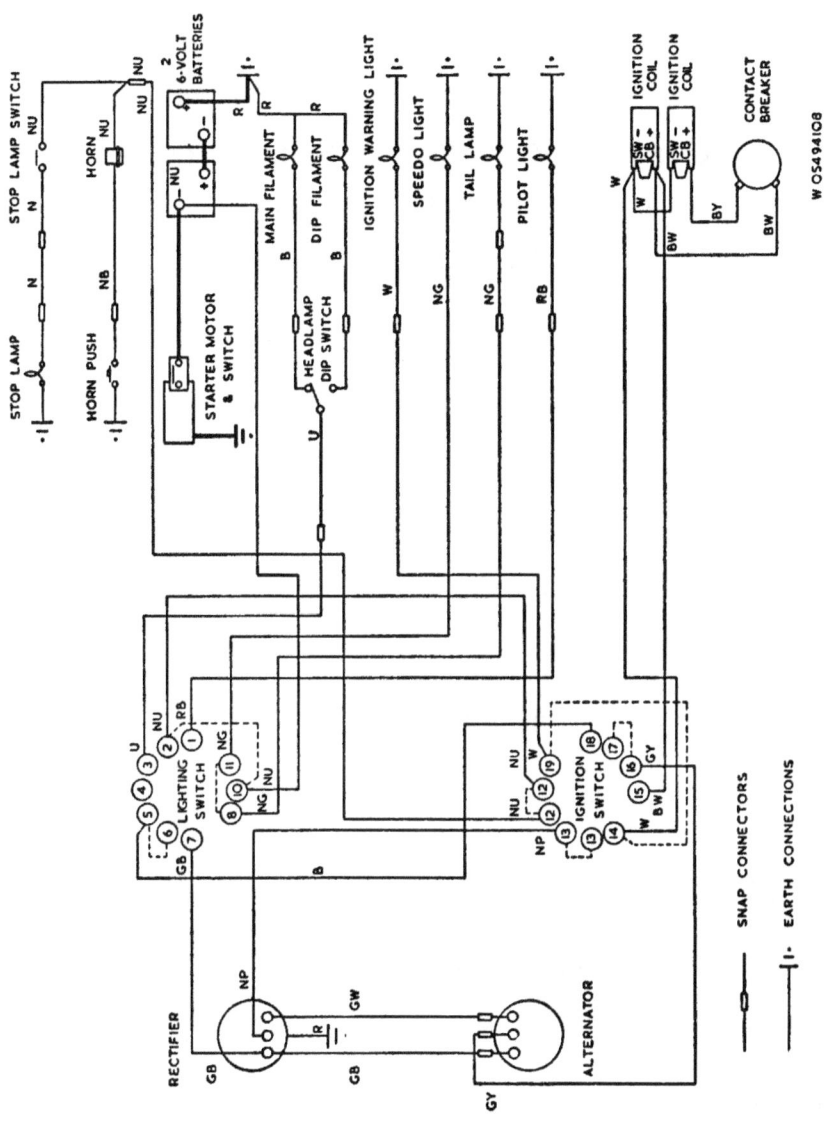

Colour Code

| R—Red. | N—Brown. | U—Blue. | P—Purple. | L—Light. |
| B—Black. | G—Green. | Y—Yellow. | W—White. | D—Dark. |

Scooter Service Sheet

1051
Printed March 1960

250 c.c. O.H.V. TWIN CYLINDER SCOOTER
THE LUCAS MODEL M3 PRE-ENGAGED STARTING MOTOR
WITH ROLLER-CLUTCH DRIVE

Introduction and Servicing

GENERAL

Model M3 manually pre-engaged starting motor is a four-pole two-brush earth return machine with series-connected field coils. A lever-operated drive assembly incorporating a roller-clutch is carried on a straight-splined extension of the armature shaft. The starter switch is mounted on the yoke and when the drive pinion is almost fully engaged with the flywheel ring, the contacts are arranged to close and connect the motor to the battery.

The drive and armature are spring-loaded to the out-of-mesh position.

Overspeed protection is afforded by the clutch to prevent rotation of the armature by the engine.

MAINTENANCE

Keep the supply terminal on the starter switch clean and tight. If the connection has become dirty, clean the contacting surfaces and lightly smear them with petroleum jelly. No periodic lubrication is necessary, but at a general overhaul the starter motor should be removed and given a thorough examination on the bench.

PERFORMANCE DATA

The following figures are based on the use of two fully charged, series-connected 6-volt batteries having a capacity of 12 amp.-hr. at the 10-hour rate.

    (a) Light running on 12 volts: 50 amp. at 6,500 - 7,500 r.p.m.

    (b) Lock torque: 5.3 lb.-ft. with 240 amp. at 6.5 terminal volts.

    (c) Torque at 1,000 r.p.m.: 2.75 lb.-ft. with 170 amp. at 8.1 terminal volts.

SERVICING

Testing in Position

Switch on the headlamps, operate the starter and watch for the following symptoms.

    (i) The lamp dims and the motor does not crank the engine.
        Remove the sparking plugs and check that the engine is not abnormally stiff.
        Check the battery by substitution.

    (ii) The lamp does not dim and the motor does not crank the engine.
        Check the starter switch terminal connection for tightness.

If the source of trouble cannot be readily located, remove the starting motor from the engine for examination by disconnecting the battery, removing the fixing bolts from the drive and bracket and lifting the starting motor free.

Service Sheet No. 1051 (cont.)

Bench Testing

(i) Measuring the Light Running Current.

With the starting motor clamped in a vice and using two fully charged, series-connected, 6-volt 12 amp.-hr. batteries, check the light running current and compare with the value given in paragraph on Performance Data. Look for excessive arcing at the commutator and, if necessary, remedy. Excessive arcing may be due to faults outlined in Fault Diagnosis 7 and 8.

(ii) Measuring Lock Torque and Lock Current.

Carry out a torque test and compare with the values given in paragraph on Performance Data. If a constant voltage supply is used, it is important to adjust this to be 6.5 volts at the starter terminal when testing.

(iii) Fault Diagnosis.

An indication of the nature of the fault, or faults, may be deduced from the results of the light running and lock torque tests.

Symptom	Probable Fault
1. Speed, torque and current consumption correct.	None.
2. Speed, torque and current consumption low.	High resistance in brushgear, e.g., faulty connections, dirty or burned commutator causing poor brush contact.
3. Speed and torque low, current consumption high.	Tight or worn bearings, bent shaft, insufficient end play, armature fouling a pole shoe, or cracked spigot on drive end bracket. Short-circuited armature, earthed armature or field coils.
4. Speed and current consumption high, torque low.	Short-circuited windings in the field coils.
5. Armature does not rotate, no current consumption.	Open-circuited armature or field coils. If the commutator is badly burned there may be poor contact between brushes and commutator.
6. Armature does not rotate, high current consumption.	Earth field coil or switch. Armature physically prevented from rotating.
7. Excessive brush movement causing arcing at commutator.	Low brush spring tension, worn or out-of-round commutator. " Thrown " or high segment on commutator.
8. Excessive arcing at the commutator.	Defective armature windings, sticking brushes or dirty commutator.

ENGAGEMENT LEVER ADJUSTMENT

With the switch firmly bolted to the yoke, fix and lock the engagement lever adjusting screw in such a position as to provide a clearance of 0.005" to 0.010" between the pinion face (when the drive is lightly pushed backwards to take up any slackness) and shaft jump ring when the lever reaches its ultimate engaged position.

Service Sheet No. 1051 (cont.)

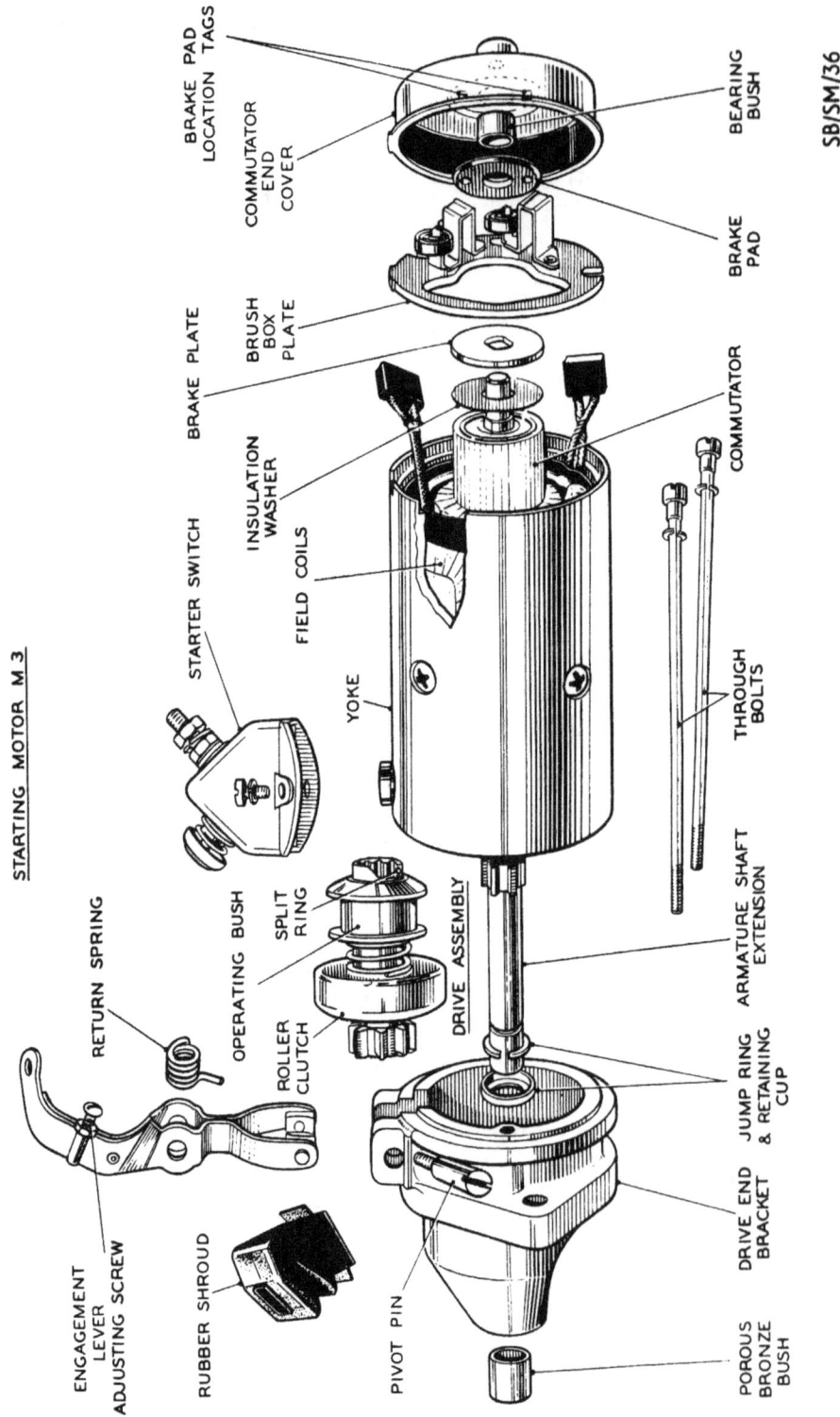

SCOOTER SERVICE SHEET

1052
Printed March 1960

250 c.c. O.H.V. TWIN CYLINDER SCOOTER
TWIN COIL IGNITION SYSTEMS — AND EMERGENCY STARTING

A description of the working principles of twin-coil ignition systems.

GENERAL

The 250 c.c. scooters have engines of the vertical twin-cylinder, four-stroke pattern. They are fitted with a Lucas alternator and coil ignition system incorporating two ignition coils and double contact-breaker units. The contact-breaker runs at half engine speed.

Under normal running conditions, lighting switch in the " IGN " position, a twin-coil ignition system functions in the same way as does the single coil ignition system in the " IGN " position, i.e., current from the battery feeds the primary of the ignition coils, producing the H.T. spark in the conventional manner. It is only under " emergency starting " conditions that the working principles of the twin-coil ignition set differ slightly from those of the single coil set. The system does, of course, work on the energy transfer principle which is now standard practice on all machines fitted with a Lucas alternator and coil ignition set.

N.B.—Before reading the following description of the working principles of the " EMG " start circuits, it should be remembered that they are being considered only in relation to true emergency starting conditions, i.e., the batteries in a healthy non-sulphated but fully discharged condition. For the sake of clarity, reference to mechanical considerations has been kept to a minimum, the functional descriptions being confined mainly to the electrical characteristics.

FUNCTIONAL DESCRIPTION OF TWIN COIL IGNITION SYSTEM WHEN EMERGENCY STARTING

The emergency ignition circuit on the twin coil system is so designed as to enable the engine to be started on one cylinder only, utilising one of the ignition coils and its associated contact breaker.

In the combination used (the L/H cylinder) the coil has two cables (each coloured black with white tracer) connected to its " CB " or " + " terminal to enable it to work on the energy transfer principle. One cable connects to the No. 1 contact breaker (lower pair of contacts for L/H cylinder) and the other to terminal " 15 " on the ignition switch.

The illustration shows the circuit used for emergency starting. With this circuit the No. 1 contact-breaker is arranged to open when the alternating current in the windings reaches a maximum in the direction shown by the large arrow. The circuit functions as follows :—

With the contacts closed the main return circuit to the alternator is then via one arm (element) of the rectifier bridge and the closed contacts. In effect the four output control windings have been short-circuited allowing a heavy current to build up and circulate through them.

At the instant of contact separation this built-up energy quickly discharges through an alternative circuit provided by the battery and primary winding of the No. 1 or " EMG " ignition coil. The rapid transfer of current from alternator to ignition coil primary results in H.T. being induced in the secondary winding and an efficient spark, at the plug.

The efficiency of the energy transfer is quite high because the alternative circuit through the battery, when the contacts are opened, is virtually a short-circuit path owing to the fact that the " flat " battery has little or no potential difference across it. Therefore very little energy is lost at this point.

However, due to the fact that the current surges do pass through the battery, and the fact that the two permanently connected charging coils are also in circuit, the battery begins to build up a potential difference across its terminals until, after several current pulses, assuming the engine has fired and is running on one

Service Sheet No. 1052 (cont.)

cylinder, it gradually effects a reduction in the amount of energy available for transfer to the ignition coil. This reduction in spark energy will cause misfiring to occur, which in the event of the rider omitting to return the ignition key from position " EMG " to " IGN ", serves as a reminder to do so. The contact points will be badly burnt if the rider prolongs running in the " EMG " position.

Another feature of the system is that coil No. 2 eventually comes into operation during emergency starting, so that after a few seconds of running on one cylinder, number two cylinder cuts-in and the engine functions as a normal twin-cylinder unit. The fact that it will operate on both cylinders after a few seconds does not detract from the statement, made in the previous paragraph, about the rising battery voltage causing misfiring to occur.

Although the No. 2 coil " SW " terminal is linked to the same feed cable as the " SW " terminal of No. 1 coil, it does not pass any of the energy transferred from the alternator, during the " energy transfer " pulse, as at this particular instant the No. 2 contact-breaker points are open, open-circuiting the No. 2 coil primary circuit. It is fed eventually, however, because the battery voltage or potential difference builds up due to the current from the alternator passing through it, causing the battery to assume a stronger polarity characteristic. Therefore, in between the No. 1 coil being fed by energy pulses from the alternator, the No. 2 coil will, when its associated contacts close, receive current direct from the battery which is gradually becoming charged. This results in the engine firing on both cylinders. It will not run at full power until switched to the " IGN " position, because the energy now available for the No. 1 coil is being reduced and misfiring will still occur.

Actually, during the stage when both coils are functioning, their primary windings are being fed in opposite directions. The No. 1 coil is receiving pulses from the alternator, via the battery, the insulated side of the circuit, through the primary from " SW " to " CB " and back to the alternator. The No. 2 coil is fed by a steady current direct from the battery, via earth, through No. 2 contacts to " CB ", through primary to " SW " and back to battery—VE.

FAULTS WHICH CAN AFFECT EMERGENCY STARTING PERFORMANCE

In the foregoing description of the functions of the emergency start circuit, it was stated that the energy transfer efficiency was high. It should give a starting performance, at " kick-start " speeds, equivalent to that of a conventional type of magneto. Provided, of course, the circuit connections and units are maintained in a good condition. If they are not attended to regularly and are allowed to deteriorate, then even emergency starting becomes hard work and its inherent advantages nullified. Any of the following faults can affect emergency starting performance, and they are the most likely to be encountered during normal service life.

(1) Incorrect timing of the engine.
(2) Faulty circuit connections.
(3) Dirty contacts or incorrect contact gap setting.
(4) Dirty plug or incorrect gap setting.
(5) Faulty rectifier.
(6) Dirty or corroded battery terminals.
(7) Sulphated battery.

Incorrect Timing of the Engine

It is very important that care is taken when timing, for ignition purposes, any machine which is fitted with an ignition system utilising " energy transfer " principles for emergency starting. To obtain the best possible performance it must be accurately set. Remember, it is not only the piston/spark timing relationship which is involved but also the " magneto " performance (spark energy) of the alternator.

This will be appreciated more fully when it is remembered that, as the rotor of the alternator is keyed to the engine crankshaft, which in turn is coupled through the connecting rod to the piston, any movement of the piston during the timing procedure will affect the position of the crankshaft and hence the magnetic timing position of the rotor.

Service Sheet No. 1052 (cont.)

In other words the maximum "magneto" performance of the alternator can only be obtained when the piston is accurately set to the timing position recommended, i.e., 5° before top dead centre.

Faulty Circuit Connections

Faulty or dirty connections anywhere in the alternator electrical circuit will obviously have a bad effect on performance. The points to watch for particularly are bad earth connections at the battery and rectifier. Both units are connected to the frame of the machine and a periodic check should be made to see that they are clean and tight. Remember that the battery "+VE" terminal is the one earthed to the frame of the machine.

Dirty Contacts or Incorrect Contact Gap Setting

The contact-breaker points should be periodically checked and cleaned if necessary, also the gap should be checked and maintained at its correct setting, i.e., 0.014" - 0.016". This applies to both contact-breaker units.

Dirty Plugs or Incorrect Gap Setting

Plug gaps should be periodically checked and if necessary adjusted to the required gap, i.e., .020"-.025". It is also very important that the external insulator is kept clean and dry. Plugs should be replaced if the electrodes are badly worn.

Faulty Rectifier

A rectifier can be faulty, due to ageing which is an inherent characteristic, even though its external appearance may suggest it is in good working order. There is only one way of finding out and that is by removing it from the machine and carrying out a bench test.

Rectifiers should be kept clean and dry and so fitted as to allow air to circulate freely through the plates for cooling purpose.

Dirty or Corroded Battery Terminals

Battery connections should be kept clean and tight, particularly the one made to the frame of the machine. It is also important to keep the top of the battery clean and dry.

Sulphated Battery

A sulphated battery is usually the result of lack of maintenance, i.e., failure to maintain the electrolyte at the specified level, and allowing the battery to remain for long periods in a partially charged or discharged condition. A regular check on each cell should be made to see if it requires "topping-up" and if necessary distilled water should be added to the electrolyte to bring it up to the correct level.

Service Sheet No. 1052 (cont.)

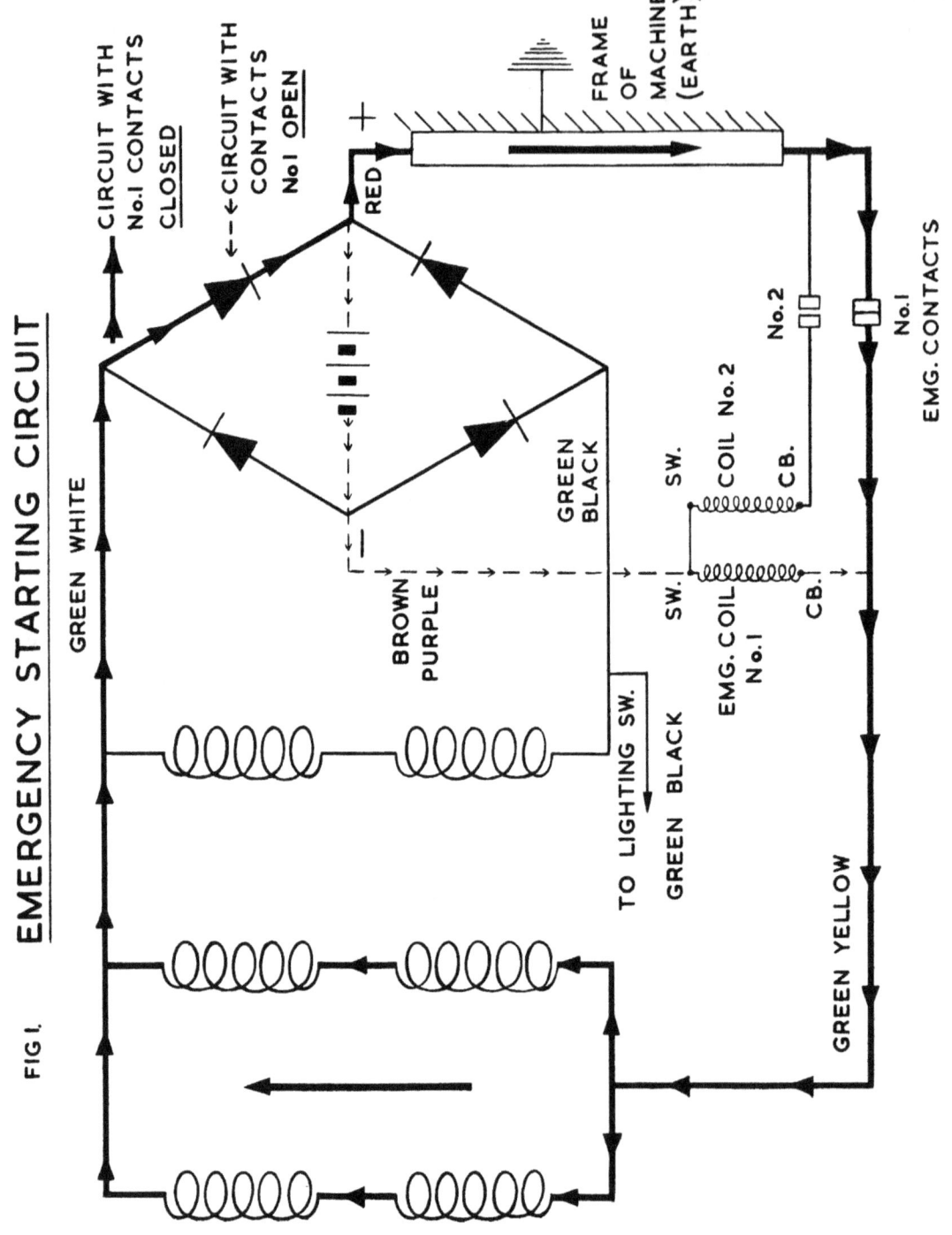

FIG 1. EMERGENCY STARTING CIRCUIT

Scooter Service Sheet

1054
Printed August, 1960

Reprinted January 1961.

SERVICE TOOLS

FOR

175 and 250 c.c. SCOOTERS

Scooter Service Sheet No. 1054 (contd.)

Taking out an Inlet Valve using Spring Compressor 61-5001 (250 c.c.).

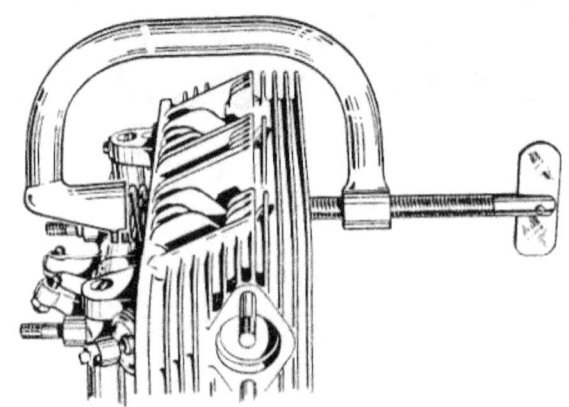

Pulling off the Flywheel with Extractor 61-5040 (175 or 250 c.c.). 61-5002 is similar but for 250 c.c. only.

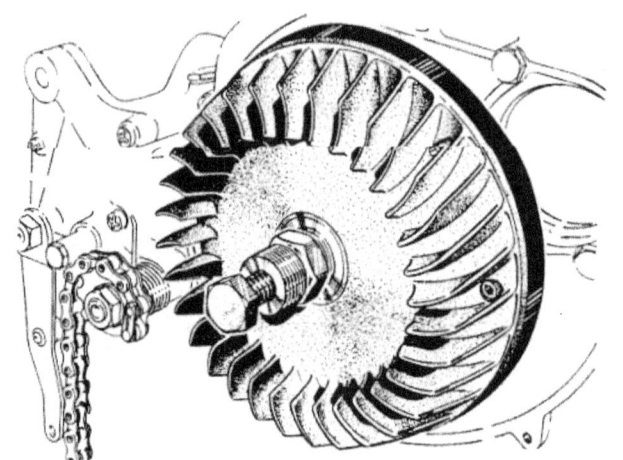

Replacing a Piston is made easier using Slipper 61-5004 (250 c.c.) or 61-5051 (175 c.c.).

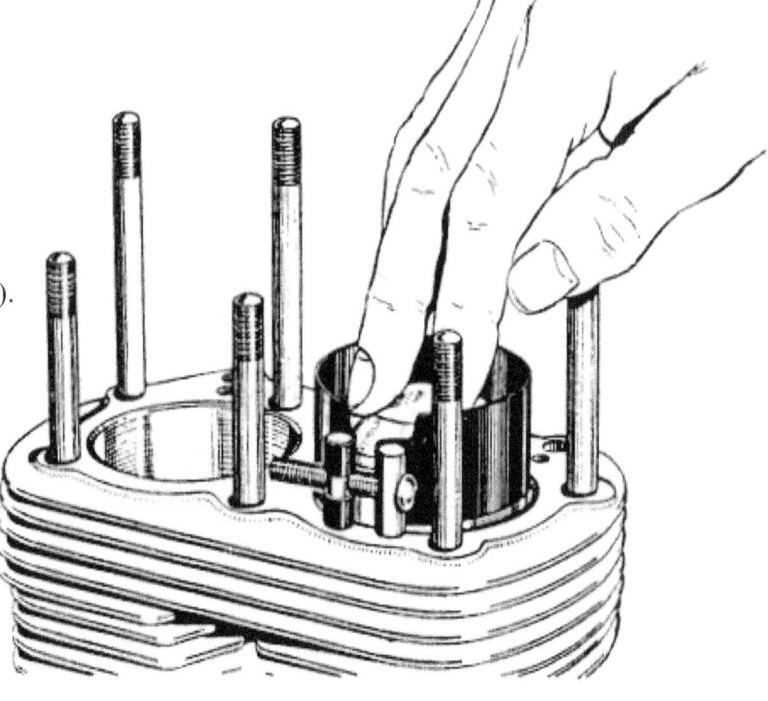

Scooter Service Sheet No. 1054 (contd.)

Removing the Auto Advance and Cam with Extractor 61-5005 (250c.c.).

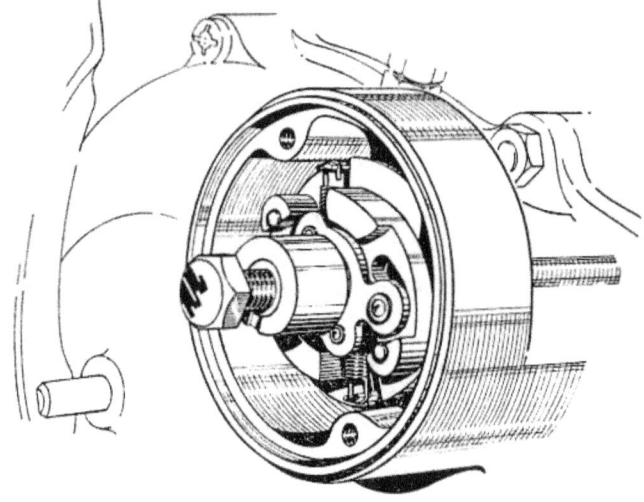

Pulling off the Crankshaft Pinion (250c.c.) with Extractor 61-5025. Similar to 61-5050 Primary Gear Extractor (175 c.c.).

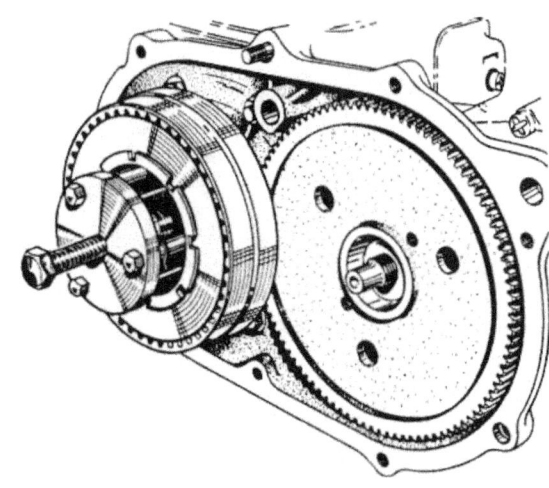

Removing the Clutch Centre with Extractor 61-5007 (175 and 250 c.c.).

Scooter Service Sheet No. 1054 (contd.)

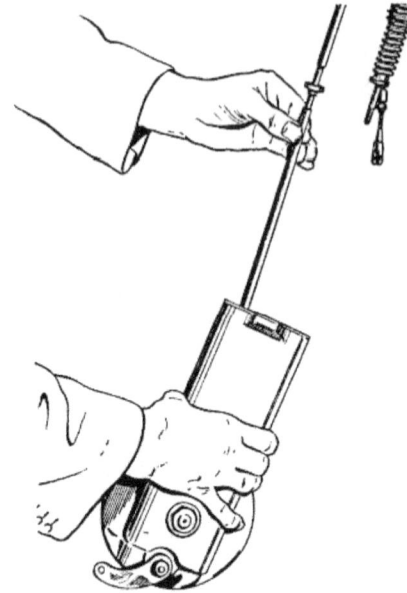

Feeding the Front Fork Damper Rod through the Sliding Member using tool number 61-5018 (175 and 250 c.c.).

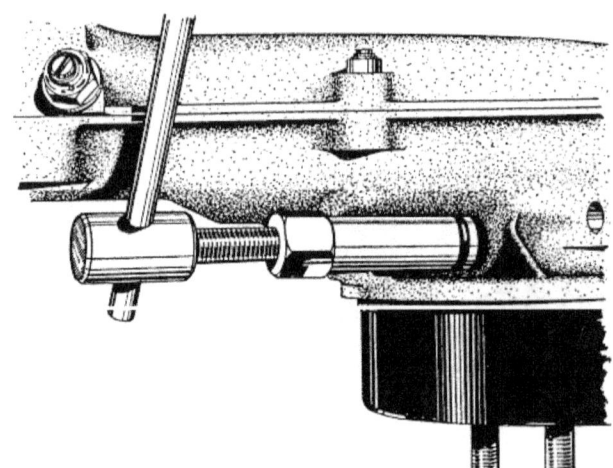

Drawing out the Speedometer Drive Bush with tool number 61-5019 (175 and 250 c.c.).

Holding the Crankshaft with tool number 61-5022 (175 and 250 c.c.).

Scooter Service Sheet No. 1054 (contd.)

Valve grinding with tool number 61-5035 (250 c.c.).

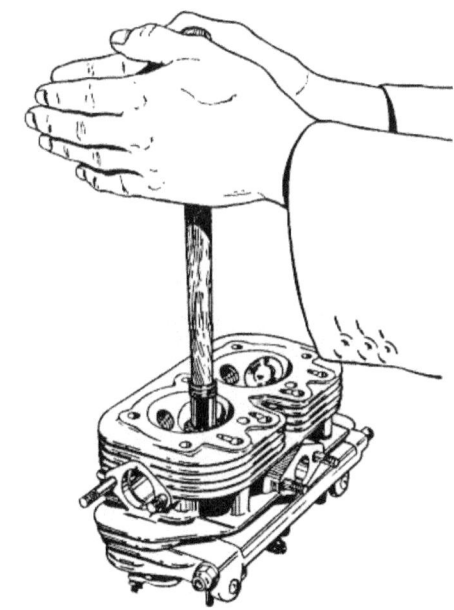

Unscrewing the Rear Spindle Bearing Lock Ring with tool number 61-5026 (175 and 250 c.c.).

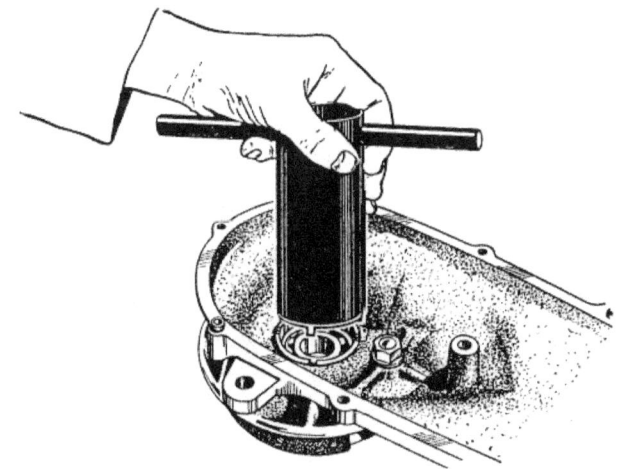

Pulling off the Front Brake Drum with Extractor number 61-5033 (175 and 250 c.c.).

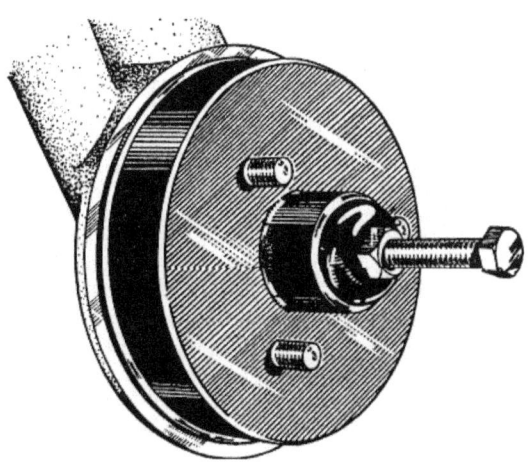

Scooter Service Sheet No. 1054 (contd.)

Driving in an Inlet Valve Guide using Punch 61-3382 (250 c.c.).

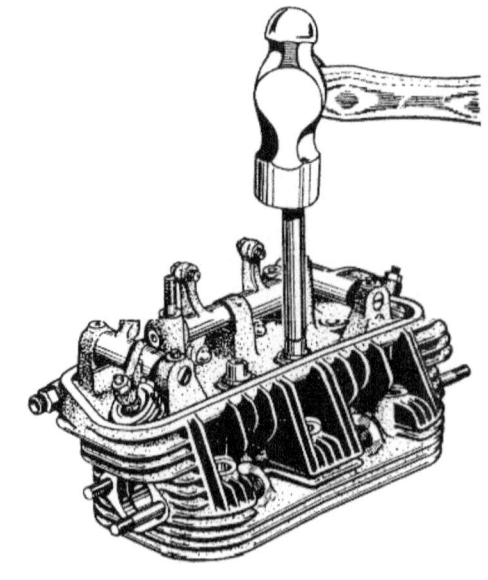

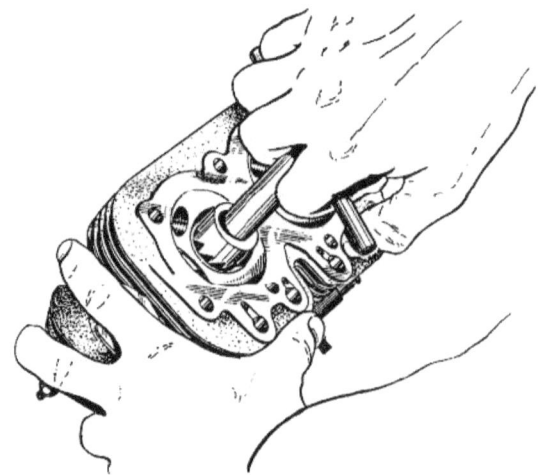

Re-cutting a Valve Seat with Cutter number 61-5036 (250 c.c.).

Engine Assembly jig number 61-5046 (175 and 250 c.c.).

Scooter Service Sheet No. 1054 (contd).

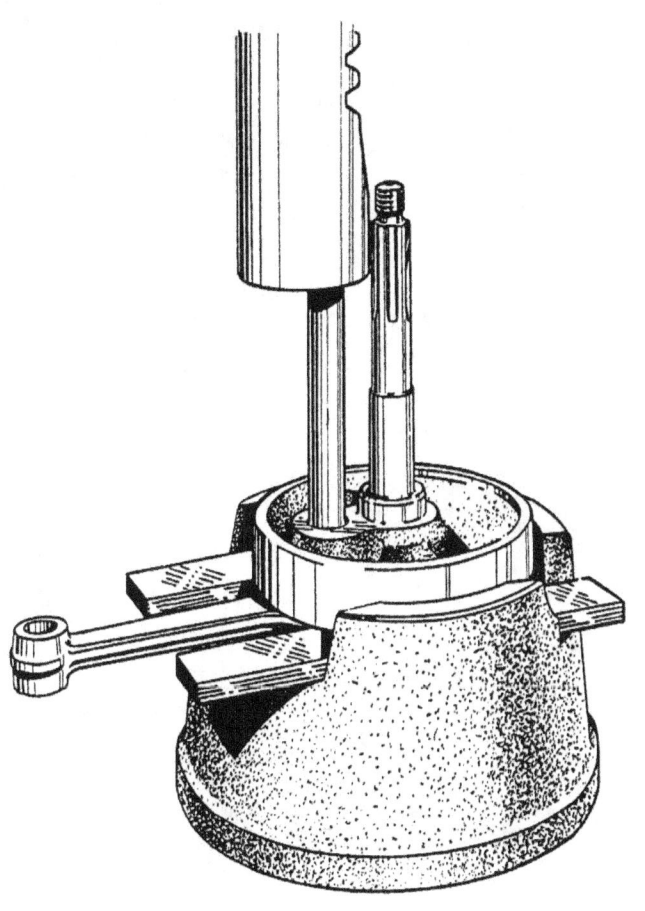

Assembling the Flywheels (175 c.c.) using Bolster 61-3207, Adapter 61-5047, Bridge 61-3210.

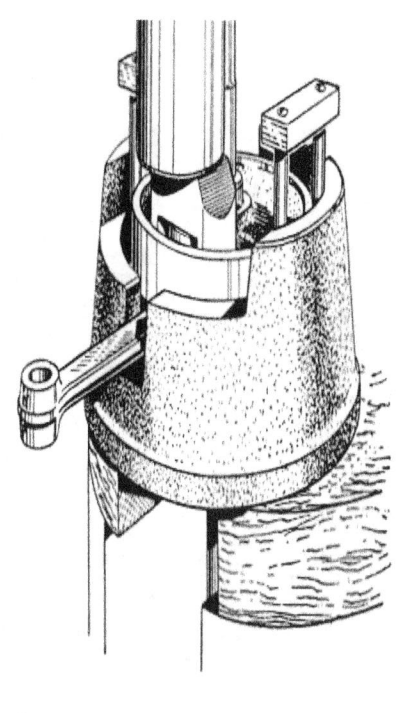

Parting the Flywheels (175 c.c.) using Bolster 61-3207, Stripping Bars 61-3208(2), Dismantling Punch 61-3209

The WAVERLEY SERIES OF ACCESSORIES

for TRIUMPH Tigress SCOOTERS

Part No.		£ s. d
76-9197	Windscreen with fittings	4 19 6
76-5507	Spare Wheel with tyre	5 9 0
76-9164	Spare Wheel cover	1 12 6
76-9169	Spare Wheel cover weather shield	9 6
76-9181	Rear Carrier (chrome plated) with fittings	3 15 6
76-9170	Pannier Carrier (enamelled), left-hand	1 17 6
76-9171	Pannier Carrier (enamelled), right-hand	1 17 6
76-9175	Pannier Bag, left or right-hand	2 11 1
		including P.T.
76-9166	Front Carrier with fittings (chrome plated) *not illustrated*	3 10 0
76-9157	Front Wheel Disc with bolt and circlip	1 4 6
76-9159	Rear Wheel Disc with bolt and circlip	1 4 6

Please quote Part Number when ordering

Triumph Engineering Company Ltd. SCOOTER DIVISION, Waverley Works, Birmingham, 10

Ref TSC 138/2½

SCOOTER

INSTRUCTION MANUAL

NOTES

Part One

THE CONTROLS
FILLING INSTRUCTIONS
MAINTENANCE REMINDERS

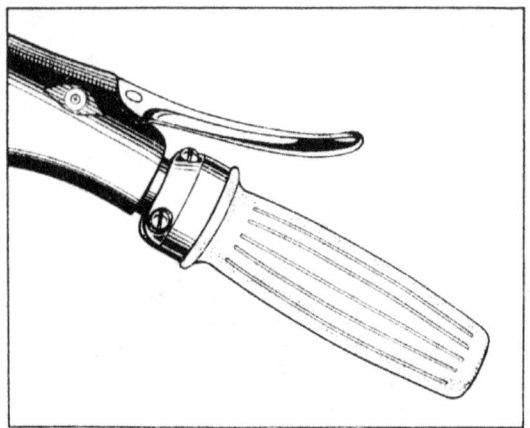

Fig. 1.

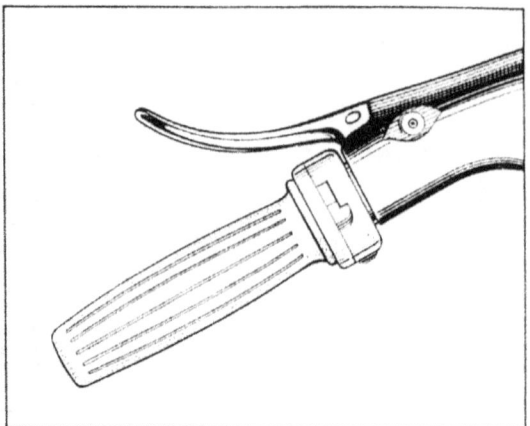

Fig. 2.

CONTROLS ON THE RIGHT HANDLEBAR

The twist grip operates the carburetter throttle. To open (i.e., to increase the engine speed) turn the grip towards the rider. To close the throttle turn in the opposite direction. The total movement from throttle closed to throttle fully open is a quarter of a turn. The lever mounted in front of the twist grip is for the front brake. To operate, squeeze the lever towards the bar.

CONTROLS ON THE LEFT HANDLEBAR

The lever in front of the grip is for operating the clutch. When it is squeezed towards the bar the clutch is disengaged, and the drive to the rear wheel is disconnected. The clutch is re-engaged when the lever is released. This lever is also used in conjunction with the foot gear change pedal (see Fig. 5) when changing gear. Mounted on top of the handlebar close to the grip is the headlamp dip-switch trigger, and combined with this is the horn button.

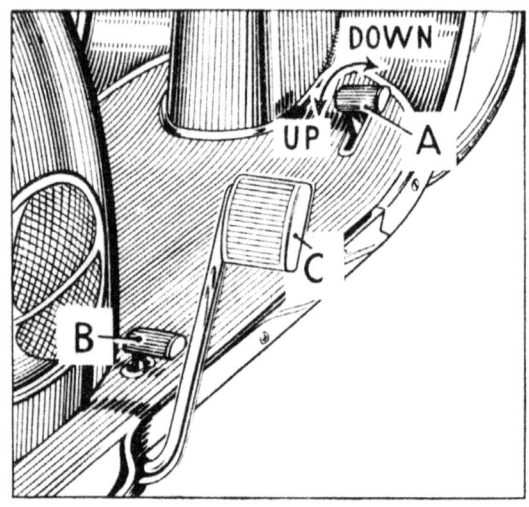

Fig. 5.

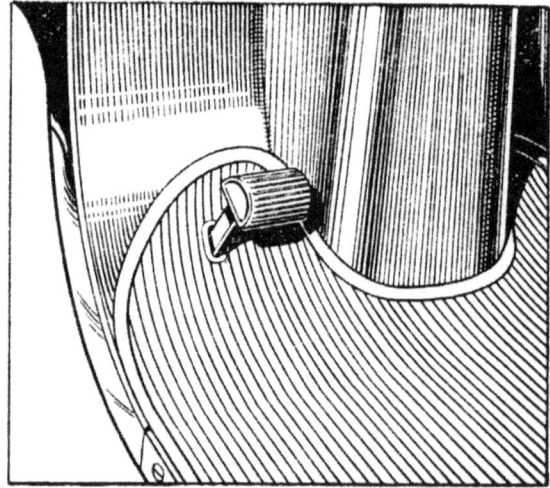

Fig. 6.

CONTROLS ON THE RIGHT HAND SIDE OF THE SCOOTER

A. **Gear Change Pedal.**
   Move forward to change down.
   Move to the rear to change up.
B. **Neutral Finder Pedal.**
   Depress to move gears to neutral (see page 7).
C. **The Kick Starter.**

CONTROL ON THE LEFT HAND SIDE OF THE SCOOTER

The only control on the left-hand side of the machine is the rear brake pedal which is toe-operated.

Note that this does not actuate both brakes; only the rear.

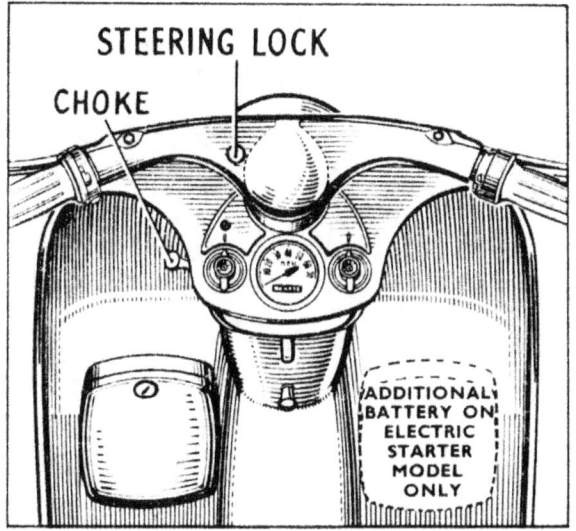

Fig. 3.

CONTROLS ON INSTRUMENT PANEL, ETC.

On the Panel.
Left — The ignition switch (on twin cylinder model).
The lighting switch (on single cylinder model).
Centre — The Speedometer.
Right — The lighting switch (on twin cylinder models only).

Below the Panel.
1. Spring loaded ring-hook for handbag, small parcels, etc.
2. The starter knob—on model equipped with electric starter.
3. Choke (see page 7)

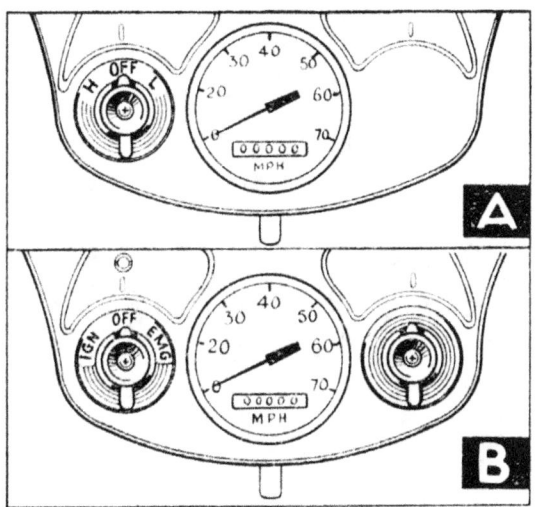

Fig. 4.

LIGHTING AND IGNITION SWITCHES

A. Single Cylinder Model.
Lighting switch on left. Positions:—
H — Headlight.
Central — Off.
L — Pilot and parking light.

B. Twin Cylinder Models.
Ignition switch on left. Positions:—
IGN — Ignition switched on.
OFF —
EMG — For starting with a discharged battery (see page 29).

Lighting switch on right. Positions (not marked on switch):—
Left — Headlight.
Central — Off.
Right — Pilot or parking light.

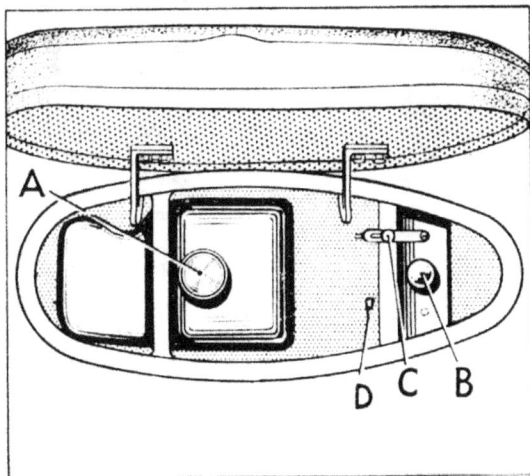

Fig. 7.

FUEL & OIL SUPPLY FOR ENGINE

The petrol tank is mounted at the rear of the frame under the hinged dual seat.
A. The petrol filler cap.
B. The oil filler cap (twin cylinder model only).
C. The petrol tap. Pull knob to turn petrol on. Push knob to turn petrol off. Pull knob and turn clockwise for reserve fuel supply.
D. Sump Dipstick (twin only).

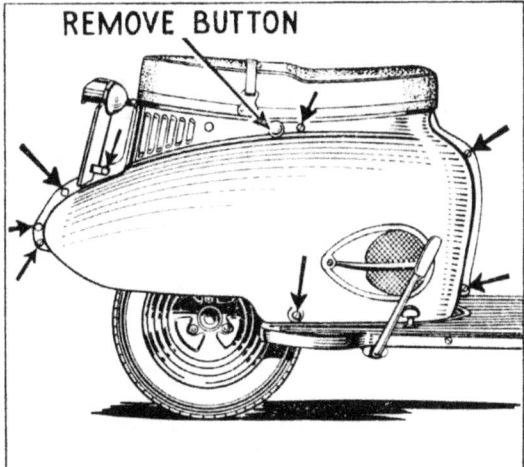

Fig. 8.

REMOVAL OF VALANCES

The valances are attached to the frame and to each other by means of the nuts and bolts marked in the diagram above.

Removal of these enables the valances to be quickly detached for engine maintenance, etc.

Fig. 9.

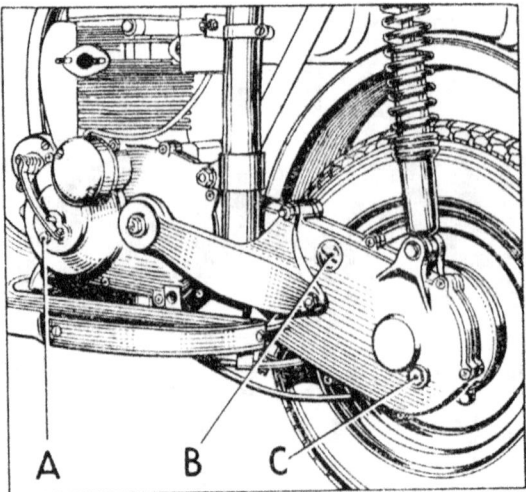

Fig. 10.

LUBRICATING THE GEARBOX

Remove the right-hand gauze cover and unscrew filler plug (A) and level plug (B).

Fill with oil until it starts to flow out through the level plug hole at B. Then replace both plugs. (Drain plug at C.)

For Oil Recommendations see page 11.

LUBRICATING THE TRANSMISSION

Remove the left-hand valance (see Fig. 8).
Primary Drive.—(Two-Stoke model only) Unscrew plug A and pour oil in until it reaches the level of the hole, and replace plug.
Rear Drive.—Unscrew filler plug B and level plug C. Fill with oil until it starts to flow out through the level plug hole at C. Replace both Plugs.

For Oil Recommendations see page 11.

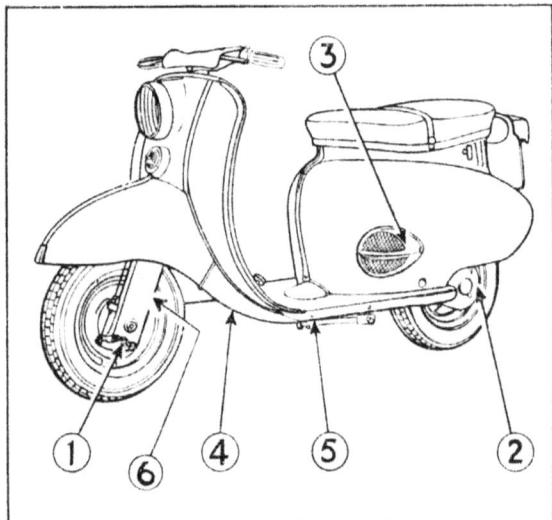

Fig. 11.

THE GREASE GUN

There are Seven grease nipples on the Scooter
1. The front brake cam spindle.
2. The rear brake cam spindle. (remove wheel)
3. The nearside swinging arm bearing.
4. The foot change pivot pin.
5. The kick starter pivot spindle. (2)
6. The fork leg. (remove wheel)

Lubricate those regularly as outlined on page 11.

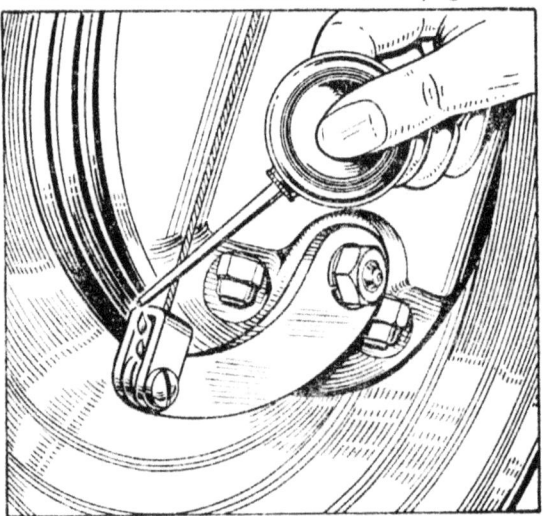

Fig. 12.

THE OILCAN

Oil exposed joints, cables etc., weekly. Use thin engine oil or ordinary cycle oil.

Fig. 13.

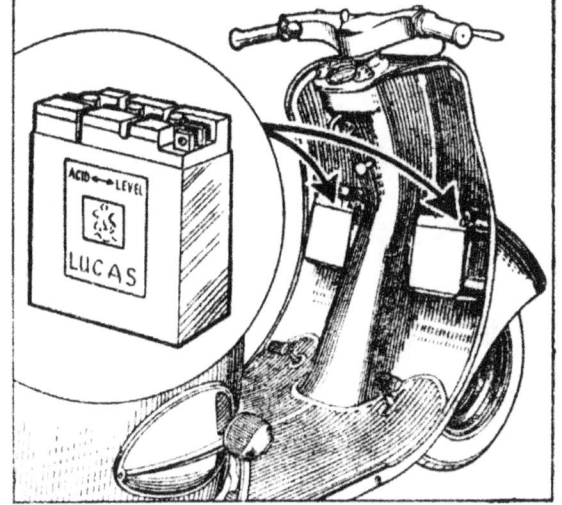

Fig. 14.

TYRE PRESSURES

Check your tyre pressures weekly.

The correct pressures are:—
Front: 17 lbs. (p.s.i.).
Rear: 24 lbs. (p.s.i.).

If a pillion passenger is carried increase the rear tyre pressure 3 or 4 p.s.i.

The inflator is mounted under the left side of the floorboard.

EXAMINE THE BATTERY

Check the battery level at least once every week and top up if necessary as described on page 28.

More frequent examination is advisable in a hot climate.

When ordering Spares or making any enquiry for your machine, the Frame and Engine numbers should be quoted. The Engine number can be found to the rear of the offside cylinder, and the Frame number is stamped on the kickstart pivot bracket.

Part Two

GENERAL INSTRUCTIONS FOR

RIDING

LUBRICATION

ADJUSTMENTS

DECARBONISATION

ELECTRICAL SYSTEM

ETC.

TAKING THE SCOOTER ON THE ROAD

Filling up with Petrol and Oil. The petrol tank is mounted on a special frame bracket and is seen when the dual seat is raised on its hinges (see Fig. 7). Its capacity is 1½ gallons. (See special instructions on filling up with petroil mixture for the single cylinder two-stroke model on page 31).

The oil sump, capacity 2½ pints, is situated under the engine and the filler cap B (Fig. 7) is on top of the rocker box cover. The dipstick indicates the oil level. For recommended fuels and oils see page 11.

The gearbox and transmission will in most cases have been filled to the correct level by the dealer before delivery, but if this is in doubt access to the filler plug for the former can be obtained by removing the right hand side valance (Fig. 8). The filler cap and the level plug will then be seen at A and B, Fig. 9. The primary drive filler plug and the rear drive filler and level plugs are seen in Fig. 10 at A, B and C respectively. Recommended oils are listed on page 11. (See also Fig. 19).

To Start the Engine. Turn on the petrol, depress tickler for a moment and pull out the choke (see Fig. 3). Place the gear in neutral by moving the gear change pedal forward once, or more if necessary, until bottom gear is engaged. Then operate the neutral finder pedal (Fig. 5) once. This will bring the gear into the neutral position between first and second gears.

Switch the ignition to the IGN position, (twin cylinder model only), and pull the electric starter knob smartly. This will cause the engine to rotate and it should fire at once. Release the starter knob immediately the engine fires.

In the case of models not provided with an electric starter the kick-starter should be operated instead. Depress the pedal gently until the rachet engages, and then push down sharply.

For starting without a battery or if the battery is discharged see instructions on page 29.

When the engine is running the choke should be pushed in as soon as possible.

Note. Do not use the choke when starting if the engine is warm.

To Engage Low Gear and Move Off. Pull the clutch lever up to the handlebar, thus dis-engaging the clutch, and engage low gear by moving the gear change pedal forwards (see Fig. 5), releasing the pedal as soon as the gear is felt to go in. Then accelerate the engine slightly by means of the twist grip, and gently release the clutch lever. The scooter will move forward smoothly and accelerate as the throttle is opened further.

To Change Up. As soon as the scooter is well under way, which on level ground should amount to no more than a yard or two, second gear should be engaged by moving the gear change pedal to the rear and releasing it again, at the same time momentarily dis-engaging the clutch by means of the lever on the left handlebar. Changing to third gear and finally to top are effected in precisely the same manner.

To Change Down. Declutch and simultaneously move the gear change pedal forward releasing both as soon as the gear is felt to go in.

This operation is carried out in the same manner when changing from top to third, third to second, and second to first.

The Art of Smooth Gear Changing. The gearbox is of a very robust construction, and the gear change mechanism is positive in action so that gear changes will be made without fail even by a novice if he follows the instructions given above, but with practice and the application of a little skill to the manipulation of the various controls a smooth and silent gear change can be achieved, which will give satisfaction to the rider and bring credit to the scooter, for there is nothing more gratifying to the experienced rider than the knowledge that he has the ability to make a smooth and silent gear change at all times, and that his scooter will respond in this matter to his expert manipulation of the controls.

For example, when changing up the rider should not only select a suitable speed at which to perform the operation, but he should also time his gear changes in such a way that engine speeds and the speeds of the moving parts in the gearbox should be allowed to coincide as far as possible. This latter requirement is met usually by momentarily closing the throttle before de-clutching for the gear change, thus removing the power drive from the gearbox and letting it slow down to the lower speed at which it will operate in the higher gear about to be engaged. As soon as the gear is engaged and the clutch is released the throttle should be opened again smartly, but without a sudden jerk. If gear changes are made in this manner, and this applies to all changes up from low gear upwards, then the operation can be performed silently and smoothly with only an alteration in the engine note to indicate that the change has been made.

When changing to a low gear it will be seen from a consideration of the conditions described above that the engine speed has to be increased relative to that of the scooter and the throttle should not therefore be closed while making the change. As soon as the clutch is released the engine will automatically speed up and if the change is made smartly and confidently, the lower gear selected will slide into engagement quietly at the correct engine speed.

To the novice the above instructions may sound somewhat complicated although they are in fact extremely simple, and riders of average potential skill and ability rapidly acquire the correct knack in a very short mileage after first acquaintance with the scooter, so that neat and precise gear changing quickly becomes second nature.

It is emphasized that it is desirable to acquire the ability to operate a gear change mechanism smoothly not only from the viewpoint of personal satisfaction, but also because silent and shock free changes naturally impose less strain on the rapidly moving parts, with the result that wear and tear are reduced to the absolute minimum, and the scooter will continue to operate in a state of mechanical perfection throughout its useful life.

To Stop the Engine. Select neutral gear close the throttle, and turn the ignition switch to the "OFF" position. On twin-cylinder models, if the ignition is left switched on and the engine is stationary, the red light serves as a reminder that the switch is incorrectly positioned.

LUBRICATION SYSTEM. (Twin Cylinder Model).

The Engine. The engine is lubricated by a circulating system in which oil is drawn from a reservoir, supplied under pressure to various working parts of the engine, and thereafter returned to the reservoir for re-circulation. The system operates in the following manner:—

The reservoir takes the form of a sump bolted to the underside of the crankcase, and a supply pipe draws oil from this sump through a filter and carries it to the oil pump. This pump, which is of the plunger type is driven by a connecting rod by an eccentric on the camshaft, and draws the oil through the supply pipe referred to above, and delivers it under pressure through drilled passages, first to the offside crankshaft bearing and then through oil-ways drilled in the crankshaft itself to the connecting rod big-end bearings. After lubricating these bearings, the oil emerges into the crankcase in a finely divided condition which is churned up into mist by the rapidly rotating parts and spreads over the entire internal structure of the engine, thus providing lubrication for the connecting rod small ends, the pistons, the cylinder bores, the nearside crankshaft bearing, which is a ballrace, and the timing gear. The oil then condenses into liquid form, and returns by gravity through a filter tray to the sump. A by-pass is also taken from the pump supply, and this is taken first to the camshaft and then through a metering hole in the offside bearing to an external pipe which feeds it to the overhead rocker spindles. It then drains back from the rocker box through drilled passages into the timing gear, and finally to the sump.

The lubrication system is thus self-contained and fully automatic in action. It is quite foolproof and calls for no attention on the part of the rider apart from the obvious precaution of checking the oil in the sump at regular intervals by inspecting the dipstick (Fig. 7) to ascertain that the correct level is maintained.

As seen in the maintenance instructions it is recommended that the sump should be drained and refilled with fresh oil every 2,000 miles. The sump should be removed for cleaning every 6,000 miles and this involves raising the scooter on a trestle or a couple of suitable boxes so that the twelve screws by means of which it is bolted to the crankcase may be taken out. When this is done the filter tray and also the supply filter should be removed and thoroughly cleaned by rinsing in paraffin.

Primary Drive. This consists of a clutch on the engine shaft coupled to the engine shaft pinion which drives a larger pinion on the gearbox mainshaft, thus giving the primary reduction.

The case forms part of the engine lubrication system on the 250 c.c. models and after the initial filling there will be no need for further attention.

With the two-stroke model the primary drive oil level should be checked periodically (see page 4 and Fig. 10).

Gearbox. The gearbox has an entirely independent oil system which is supplied through a filling orifice on top of the box (see Fig. 9). There is also a plug which determines the correct level. It is so arranged that the larger of mainshaft gears dip into it and pick up sufficient oil to churn it into mist for distribution throughout the entire box, including the gear change mechanism. The only maintenance necessary is to check the level at intervals as described under Routine Maintenance, and to drain and refill after prolonged mileages by which time the lubricating qualities of the oil may have become somewhat impaired.

Rear Drive. The rear drive, which is by chain, operates in a cast aluminium oilbath chaincase, and it is provided with an independent oil supply which is controlled at the correct level by the filler plug seen in Fig. 10. The level plug is so positioned that it ensures the correct quantity of oil being poured in.

The rear drive lubrication system requires no attention beyond a periodical check of the oil level, together with draining and refilling when necessary as described under Routine Maintenance.

Other Parts. Grease gun lubrication is provided for the brake cam spindles, the front fork, the nearside rear suspension swinging arm, and the foot gear change pivot as outlined on page 11.

Other working parts which require lubrication are packed with grease during assembly and this should suffice until such time that a major overhaul becomes necessary

*OIL AND GREASE RECOMMENDATIONS
(Twin Cylinder Model)

BRAND	OIL — Engine, Gearbox, Primary and Rear Drive		GREASE
	†Summer	Winter	
B.P. Energol	S.A.E. 30	S.A.E. 20	Energrease L2.
Castrol	XL	Castrolite	Castrolease LM
Esso Extra	20W/30	20W/30	Esso Multi-Purpose G.H.
Mobiloil	A	Arctic	Mobilgrease MP
Shell	X100-30	X100-20	Retinax A
Regent	Havoline S.A.E. 30	Havoline S.A.E. 20W	Marfak Multipurpose 2

*For single cylinder two-stroke model see page 33.
†Use S.A.E. 40 grade for tropical conditions.

SUMMARY OF ROUTINE MAINTENANCE

Weekly.
  Check the tyre pressures and examine the treads (Fig. 13).
  Oil all exposed joints and cables (Fig. 12).
  Examine the battery (Fig. 14).

Every 1,000 Miles.
  Grease the brake cam spindles (Fig. 11).
  Grease the foot gear change pivot pin.
  Grease the kick starter pivot spindle.

Every 2,000 Miles.
  Grease the nearside swinging arm bearing (Fig. 11).
  Grease fork leg (Fig. 11).
  Drain and refill oil sump and check the oil level in gearbox and rear drive. Also front drive on Two-Stroke model (Figs. 9 and 10).
  Check the rear chain tension and adjust if necessary (page 14).
  Check the contact breaker adjustment and lubricate.

Every 6,000 Miles.
  Remove and clean oil sump and filters.
  Drain and refill gearbox and rear drive, (Figs. 9 and 10).
  Drain and refill front drive (Fig. 10.) (Two-Stroke model only)

THE TRANSMISSION

Clutch Control Adjustment. As indicated under Fig. 15 there must be a positive but not excessive amount of free play at the clutch lever in order to ensure that the clutch is properly in engagement. This should amount to about 1/4 in. If it is less than

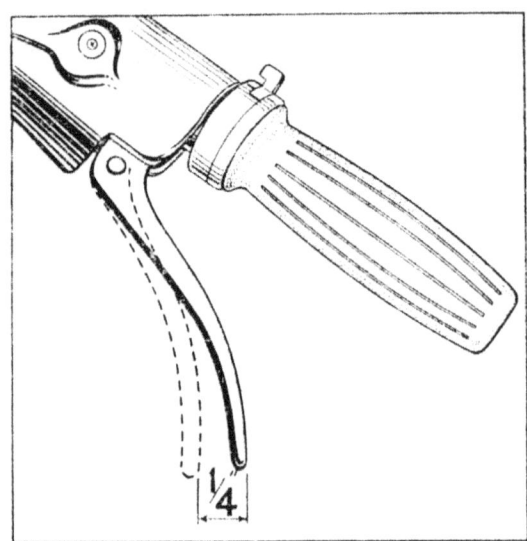

Fig. 15. Clutch Control Adjustment.

this there is a risk of inadequate clearance at the clutch operating mechanism inside the primary drive due to the normal working temperature rise with expansion of the withdrawal mechanism and consequently a tendency for the clutch to slip. If the play is excessive

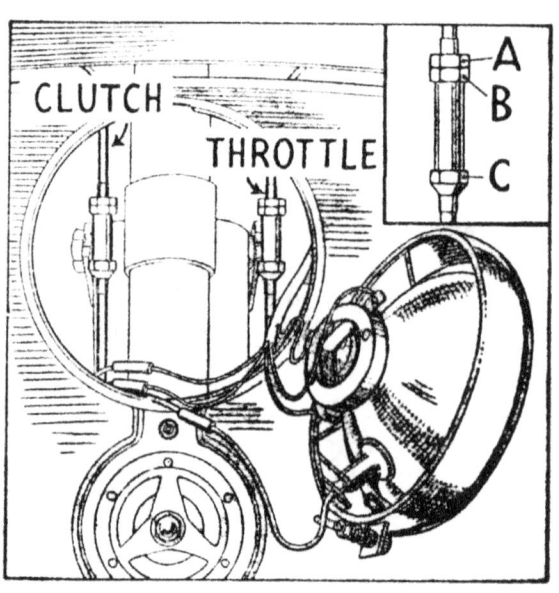

Fig. 16. Adjusting the Clutch Cable (also Throttle)

the clutch may not be free completely when the lever is pulled towards the handlebars for declutching and gear changing will be difficult. There will also be a tendency for the scooter to creep forward when held stationary with the clutch dis-engaged, as for example at traffic lights.

Adjustment of the clutch cable to provide the correct amount of play is carried out by means of the adjuster cable, see Fig. 16.

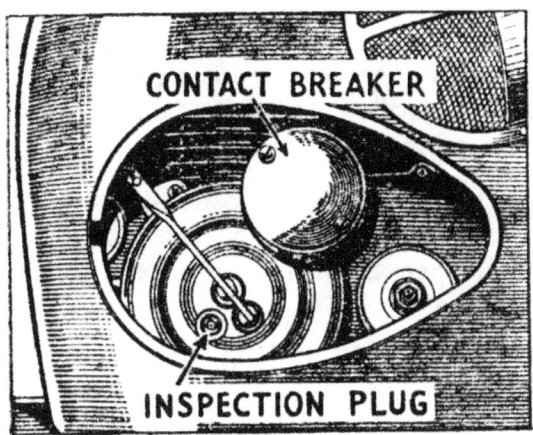

Fig. 17.
Clutch Spring Pressure.

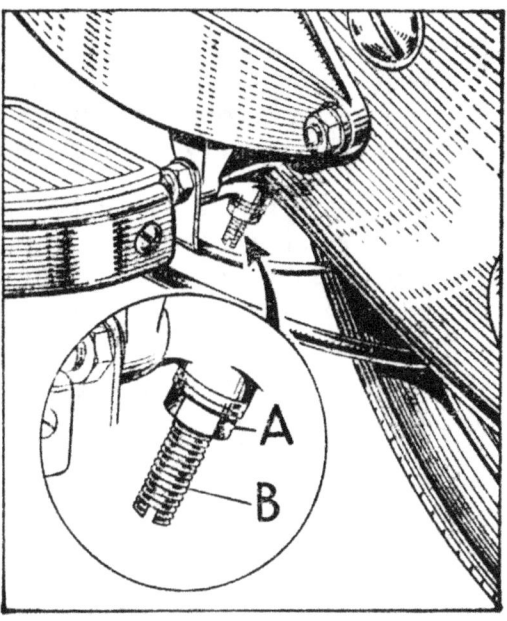

Fig. 18. Rear Chain Adjuster

Slacken off the lock nut and screw the adjuster out until the correct amount of play is felt at the handlebars as indicated in Fig. 15. Then re-tighten the lock nut.

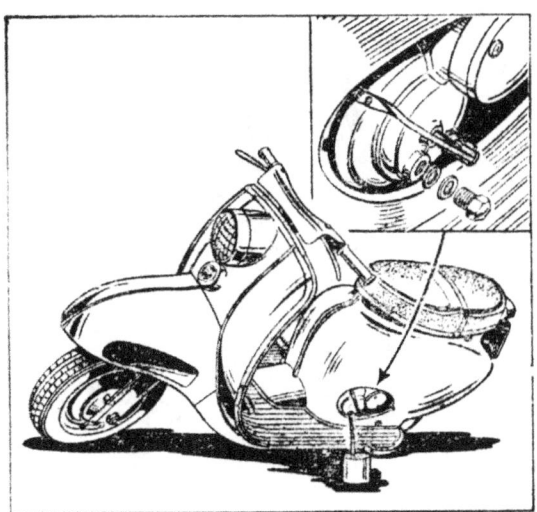

Fig 19. Draining the Primary Drive.

Clutch Spring Pressure. After very considerable mileages it may be desirable to increase the clutch spring pressure slightly. To do this remove the inspection plug Fig. 17 and turn the engine by engaging top gear and rotating the rear wheel until one of the three adjusters comes into view as shown. Screw this in about one turn clockwise, and bring the other two adjusters into view successively in order to screw them in exactly the same amount. If the three adjusters are not turned equally the clutch pressure plate may tilt with a consequently adverse effect on clutch operation. Do not forget to replace the plug firmly after adjustment.

Primary Drive. The primary drive, comprising a pair of gears, requires no adjustment and the only maintenance needed is a regular check on the oil level on the two-stroke model (see page 10). To drain the primary drive tilt the scooter as shown in Fig. 19.

Rear Drive. The rear drive is by a totally enclosed duplex chain running in an oilbath and the rear sprocket incorporates a vane type cush drive with synthetic rubber inserts, which requires no adjustment nor other form of maintenance.

An inspection plug Fig. 10 is provided for testing the chain tension, which should allow a total up and down movement of $\frac{1}{4}$ in. If incorrect the tension can be re-set by means of the tensioner, which has an external lock nut and adjuster. To adjust, release the lock nut A, Fig. 18, and screw the adjuster B up or down until the correct tension is obtained. Then tighten the lock nut and replace the inspection plug.

Maintain the oil supply at its correct level in the chaincase as described on page 10.

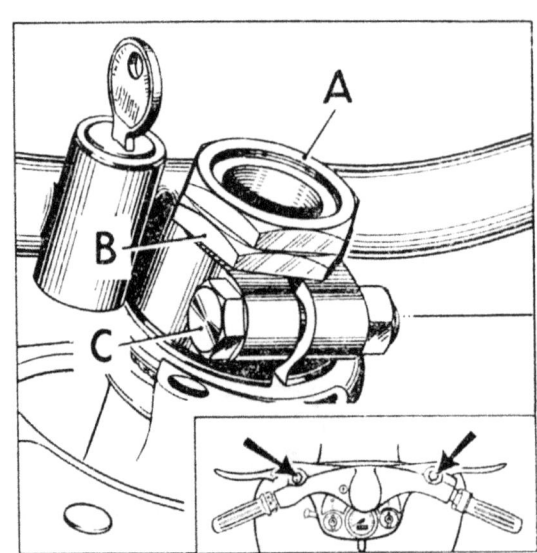

Fig. 20. Steering Head Adjuster.

The Steering Head. The steering head is of unusually generous dimensions and robust construction, so that having been correctly adjusted at the factory during manufacture, it is seldom likely to require further adjustment, except after very long periods of service.

As a precaution, however, it should be tested occasionally for play, and to ensure that the handlebars rotate freely. Place the scooter on its central stand, so that the front wheel is clear from the ground, then grasp the front fork legs and attempt to push them backwards and forwards. If any play is detected the steering head requires to be adjusted. If on the other hand there is any indication of stiffness in the motion when the handlebars are turned, this will mean that the setting is somewhat on the tight side, and it should, of course, be eased back slightly.

To adjust, remove the handlebar cover (Fig. 20) which is held by two screws (arrowed) and release the clip bolt C and the locknut A. Then screw the adjuster B up or down, as the case may be, until the adjustment is felt to be correct, (i.e., with just the least perceptible amount of shake when the fork legs are tested as described above). Then, still holding the adjuster re-tighten the lock nut and test again to see whether the tightening process has disturbed the adjustment. Finally tighten bolt C and replace the handlebar cover.

THE SUSPENSION SYSTEM

Front Suspension. This comprises two telescopic legs mounted side by side on the left of the wheel and terminating in a substantial cast aluminium housing which also accomodates the brake and wheel spindle with bearings. The rear telescopic leg houses the suspension spring while the other serves as an hydraulic damper, and is filled during assembly with a special fluid. No maintenance is required apart from greasing (see Fig. 11).

Rear Suspension. This of the swinging arm type in which the arm consists of the rear chaincase swivelling on a large spigot mounted concentrically with the gearbox mainshaft, and an auxiliary arm bolted to it and swivelling on a spigot mounted on the primary drive case, thus providing great lateral rigidity.

In operation under the action of road irregularities the wheel moves up and down carrying the swinging arm with it and this movement is controlled by a single combined coil spring and hydraulic damper unit, which is supported at its lower end by a silentbloc bearing carried on a bolt between two lugs on the rear chaincase and at its upper end by a similar silentbloc attached to the frame.

The spring requires neither lubrication nor other attention, and the hydraulic unit is sealed and completely self-contained, so that it also is entirely automatic in action, the hydraulic fluid contained within it being virtually everlasting.

If after considerable mileages it is felt that the hydraulic damping may not be functioning at full efficiency, it can be easily withdrawn for test by removal of the two bolts through the silentblocs, but this is an extremely unlikely contingency. If, however, it is taken out for this purpose it should be submitted to your dealer, as dismantling and re-assembly are beyond the capacity of the private owner, without the aid of special tools.

The swivel bearing for the chaincase portion of the swinging arm is automatically lubricated from the transmission, and a grease nipple is provided for the auxiliary arm swivel bearing (see Fig. 11).

THE WHEELS.

The wheels fitted to the scooter are of the quickly detachable and interchangeable type, resembling in principle those fitted to the majority of present-day cars.

They are fixed to their three attachment studs by means of conical seated nuts.

To Remove the Wheels. Place the machine on its stand and by means of the box spanner supplied in the toolkit undo the three nuts A, Fig. 21. Lay the scooter on its side, and the wheel can then be lifted clear.

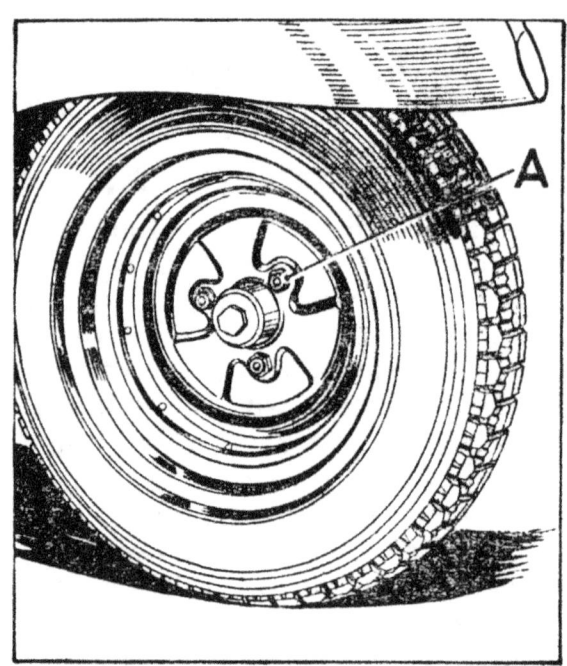

Fig. 21.
Front Wheel Removal.

To Attach the Wheels. As already pointed out the wheels are interchangeable, but it must be noted when attaching that the respective positions of the front and rear wheels are the reverse of each other (i.e., the convex side of the wheel disc faces the left, in the case of the front wheel and the right in the case of the rear wheel as shown in Fig. 22.

Wheel Bearings. The front hub is fitted with ball journal bearings, which are non-adjustable, and provided that they are correctly lubricated they will run indefinitely without any attention whatsoever. For this purpose the hub is packed with grease during assembly at the factory and this should last for very considerable mileages. It can be replenished when necessary by unscrewing the end cap Fig. 21 filling it with grease and screwing it on again tightly.
This cap has a left-hand thread.

In the case of the rear wheel this is carried on a flange forming part of the rear drive spindle to which the rear sprocket is coupled, and this spindle runs on two large ball journal bearings housed in the rear chaincase. These bearings require no adjustment and they are automatically lubricated by the oiling system operating inside the chaincase.

Brakes. Both brakes are of the cam operated internal expanding type with cable control and the correct setting is obtained in the normal manner by means of the cable adjustment seen in Figs. 13 and 23 for front and rear respectively. When a brake is correctly adjusted there should be a small amount of play in the cable, represented by a free movement of about 1/8 in. at the lever or pedal before the brake operation is felt to become effective when the handlebar lever is pulled or the pedal is depressed. If there is an excessive amount of free movement due to wear at the brake shoe linings, this should be rectified by releasing the locking nut A and screwing adjuster B out until the correct setting is obtained, thereafter re-locking nut A.

When all the adjustment has been taken up in this manner after a considerable mileage and numerous re-settings it will be an indication that the linings are excessively worn and require replacement.

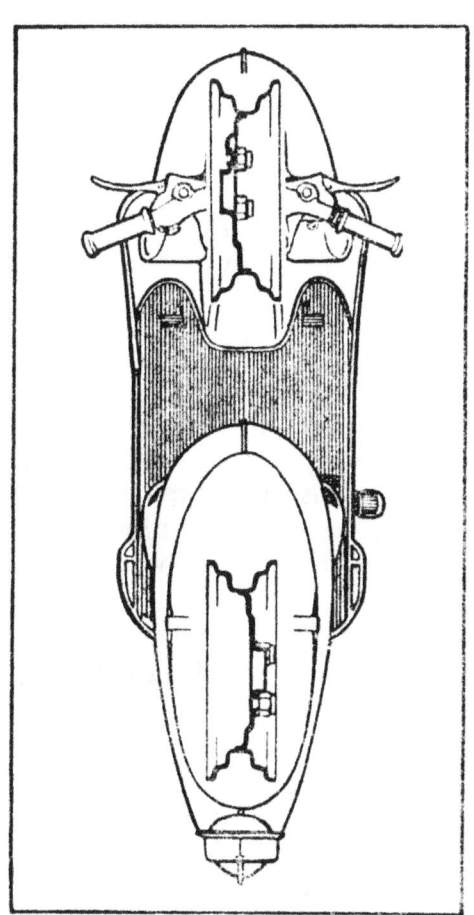

Fig. 22. Right Way Round for Wheels.

ENGINE MAINTENANCE. (Twin Cylinder Model).

Before any work can be done on the engine it is necessary to remove the body valances as shown in Fig. 8.

Valve Clearance Adjustment. This is commonly known as tappet adjustment, but the name does not properly apply in this case because the adjusting pins are mounted directly above the valves at the ends of the overhead valve rockers. Detach the sparking plug leads. Access to the rocker and valve gear is obtained when the rocker box cover is removed. It is held by two nuts and a joint washer is provided for sealing purposes (see Fig. 24). If this washer should be damaged when removing the cover, it will have to be replaced by a new one, but if it is found to adhere firmly to the face of the cylinder head or to the cover itself so that it remains in position when the cover is lifted there will be no need to disturb it.

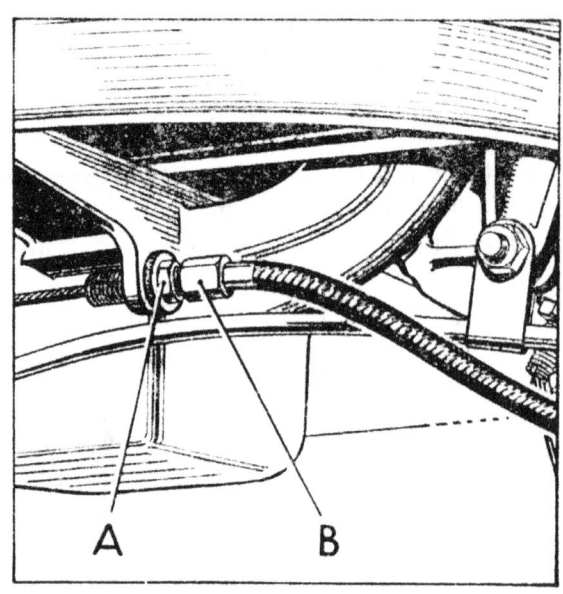

Fig. 23. Rear Brake Adjustment.

Turn the engine by means of the kick-starter or by rotating the rear wheel with top gear engaged until Valve No. 1 (Fig. 24) is fully open. Valve No. 4 will then be in the correct position for checking its clearance. Check all the valves in this way in accordance with the table below. This operation should always be carried out when the engine is cold (i.e., at atmospheric temperature) and under these conditions the correct valve clearances are .005".

HOW TO SET THE VALVES FOR CHECKING CLEARANCES

When No. 1 Valve is fully open check No. 4 Valve.

When No. 2 Valve is fully open check No. 3 Valve.

When No. 3 Valve is fully open check No. 2 Valve.

When No. 4 Valve is fully open check No. 1 Valve.

The clearances are most conveniently checked by means of a feeler gauge inserted between the end of the valve stem and the adjusting pin in the rocker, as seen in Fig. 24.

If the clearance is found to be incorrect it should be adjusted in the following manner. With the tappet spanner supplied in the toolkit, release the lock nut B, and while holding this nut with the spanner apply the other tappet spanner to the square head A on the adjusting pin. Turn this to the right or left as the case may be, until the correct clearance is obtained when tested with the feeler gauge. When the correct clearance has been found in this manner re-tighten lock nut B while holding the adjusting pin with the other spanner. After firmly re-tightening the lock nut check the clearance again to see that it has not altered during the tightening process. The operation of valve clearance adjustment is completed when the rocker box cover is replaced and its two fixing nuts finally tightened.

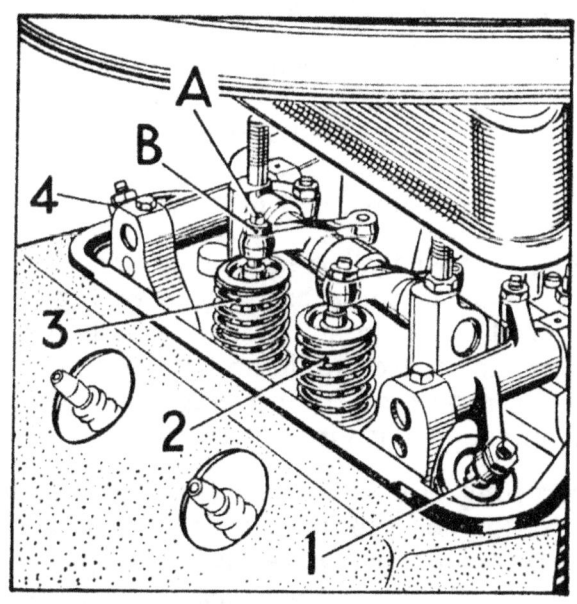

Fig. 24. Tappet Adjustment.

Decarbonisation. Decarbonisation should only be carried out when there are definite symptoms that excessive carbon build-up inside the engine is interfering with performance. The usual symptoms are an increased tendency to pink (a metallic knocking when under a heavy load) and a general falling off in performance with a tendency for the engine to run hotter than usual.

It is customary to attend to the valves during decarbonisation as this provides a reasonable interval between valve overhaul, and avoids the necessity for dismantling the engine specially for this purpose at a later date.

Detach the sparking plug leads and remove the rocker box cover as described above, detach the oil feed pipes to the rocker assembly. Dismantle the air ducting surrounding the cylinder head and disconnect the exhaust pipes at their flange joints with the head.

Uncouple the elbow carrying the carburetter; remove both as a unit, next undo the nuts on the seven studs holding the cylinder head, and lift the head off, noting that a plexeal gasket is interposed between the joint faces. This should be wiped carefully and placed on one side for refitting in due course.

Remove all the carbon deposit which has accumulated inside the combustion recesses in the cylinder head and on the valve heads, using a suitable tool for this purpose such as a slightly blunt screwdriver or narrow scraper, and take care not to damage the comparatively soft aluminium alloy material of which the head is made. This is particularly important in the case of the actual joint face, for although there is not likely to be any carbon deposit there, incautious use of the scraper or the employment of an unsuitable tool might result in its surface being scored with a consequently adverse effect on its gas retaining properties. Precisely the same remarks apply with regard to the joint face of the cylinder barrel, as this also is of aluminium alloy and liable to be badly scored if the scraper slips.

Before attempting to remove the carbon from the piston crowns the engine should be turned until the pistons are at Top Dead Centre (i.e., as far up as they will come). Carefully remove the carbon deposit from the piston crowns, bearing in mind that these also are made of aluminium alloy, and must not be scratched.

Having removed all traces of carbon from the heads, pistons, and valves, wipe all these parts clean with a slightly oily rag. This operation will show up any traces of carbon which may have been over-looked, and these should now be removed also, as small isolated particles of carbon tend to encourage the formation of fresh deposit when the engine is put into service again.

Examining the Valves. Having completed the operation of decarbonisation and subsequent cleaning, the opportunity should be taken of examining the valves before replacing the cylinder head. If the engine has been running satisfactorily, apart from the symptoms described earlier which indicate the presence of carbon deposit, it is probable that the valves will be in good condition and probably fit for further period of service before removal. If, however, there is the slightest reason to doubt the soundness of their condition then they should be removed without hesitation, and rectified in the manner described in the following section.

Removal of Valves. To remove the valves, place a wooden block which will fit inside the cylinder head on a bench and then lay the head over the block with the valve heads resting on it. Compress the valve springs until the split collets can be lifted out. When the collets are out, the valve springs and top collar can be removed. Examine the valve springs and if they have shortened appreciably they should be replaced. Valve springs are not expensive items and it is false economy to continue to use them when they are no longer at full efficiency. The correct free length of these springs when new is : outer 1-9/16", inner 1½" approx.

The inside of the valve ports must be carefully scraped free of carbon. Take care not to damage the valve seat faces with the de-carbonising tool. If any carbon falls into the valve guides, it must be carefully removed with a piece of clean rag.

If the valves and their seats are only discoloured or lightly pitted, then it will be sufficient merely to grind them in with a little grinding paste, but if there is considerable evidence of pitting, then the faces must be re-cut with proper equipment. If a valve is pitted it should be returned to the dealer for re-grinding, as attempts to grind the valve in with grinding paste will only cause excessive wear of the valve seat in the cylinder head. Probably this will still be in good condition, but if it too is pitted, the head must be removed and sent to your dealer for re-facing with a proper valve seat cutting tool. The valve seat angle is 45°.

Even with the valves and seats in good condition, they will still require to be lightly ground-in before assembly to ensure that a good gas seal is created. Smear a small quantity of fine grinding paste on to the face of the valve head and return the valve to its seat. A light spring inserted under the valve head greatly facilitates the grinding operation as it assists in raising the valve so that it can be rotated to a new position. Hold the valve stem with a special tool provided in the kit, and rotate the valve backwards and forwards whilst maintaining light pressure. Raise the valve and turn it to a new position after every few movements. Grinding should be continued until both the valve and seat show uniform metallic surfaces all round.

Before re-assembling the valves and springs all traces of grinding paste must be removed from both the valve and seat, and the valve stem and smeared with clean engine oil. Replace the valves, then compress the valve springs with the aid of a suitable tool until the collets can be inserted. A blob of grease on the valve stem will assist in keeping the collets in position as the valve spring is released. Make sure that the collets are correctly seated in the recess on the valve stem.

Removal of Pistons. Under normal conditions this operation should rarely be necessary but after very considerable mileages excessive oil consumption may develop, accompanied by continuous blue smoke in the exhaust or by piston tap or rattle. These symptoms will probably indicate that the piston rings require examination and probable replacement on account of wear, or even in extreme cases that the cylinder liners are unduly worn, and may require to be reground, which is, of course, beyond the capacity of the private owner. The fitting of new piston rings, on the other hand, is a simple matter of which many owners will prefer to do themselves.

As the cylinder barrels and crankcase are cast in one unit, it is not possible to separate them in order to provide access to the pistons, and the correct procedure therefore is to split the big-end bearings, and draw the pistons out complete with their gudgeon pins and connecting rods.

To do this remove the sump as described on page 10, and turn the engine until the pistons are at the bottom of their stroke as this will bring the big-end bolts within easy reach. Then with a suitable spanner unscrew the bolts, nuts and washer from the big-end and tap the latter up gently with a soft hammer to release the big-end caps. When this is done turn the engine again until the pistons are at the top of their stroke, and with the hand or suitable wooden rod push the connecting rods upwards until the pistons come far enough out of the cylinder to enable them to be grasped and pulled clear of the engine. Re-tighten the big end bolts with a torque spanner set to 140-180 lbs. ins.

If on account of excessive cylinder bore wear a ridge has been left at the end of the cylinder liners just beyond the tops of the pistons it may not be possible to draw the pistons outwards from their bores, and if this should prove to be the case it will be necessary to strip the engine completely in order to draw the pistons out from the crankcase end. This is not likely to occur, however, except in extreme cases where the engine has been allowed to run long after the symptoms calling for early attention have developed and been ignored. In such circumstances unless the owner is sufficiently experienced to undertake the complete dismantling of the power unit, the job should be entrusted to the dealer from whom the scooter was purchased, or to a qualified repairer.

Examination of Pistons and Rings. If it is desired for convenience of handling to remove the pistons from the connecting rod this is done by extracting one of the circlips which locate the gudgeon pin. These are made of spring steel wire and can be prised out of their grooves by means of a pair of pointed nose pliers or failing this the tang of a file or other sharp instrument. When one circlip has been removed the gudgeon pin can be pushed out by pressure at its other end, but if it does not yield freely to pressure, or light tapping with a suitable punch, it can be freed by wrapping a piece of rag, which has been soaked in hot water and wrung out, round the piston for a few moments. This will cause the aluminium piston to expand more than the steel gudgeon pin with the result that the latter will become free and can be pushed out quite easily. This is the best way to remove the gudgeon pin in case of difficulty, and the temptation to lay the piston on a block of wood and hammer the gudgeon pin violently in order to shift it should be resisted as this will cause serious distortion of the piston.

When the piston is free, mark the inside of the skirt at the back of its upper face, so that it can be replaced the correct way round.

If the rings are stuck in their grooves they will need to be carefully prised free and removed from the piston. All carbon deposit should be carefully scraped from the grooves and the inside edges of the rings. If a ring shows brown patches on its periphery, replace with a new one.

Check the piston ring gaps by inserting the piston in the barrel and sliding each ring independently up to the skirt of the piston. Check the gap with a feeler gauge. It should not be less than .006 in., or more than .010 in. Fit new rings if the gap greatly exceeds the figure stated. It is advisable to check the gap of new rings before fitting, and if the gap is less than .006 in., the ends of the rings should be carefully filed to the correct limit.

It should be noted that piston rings are very brittle, and unless handled very carefully are easily broken.

THE SPARKING PLUGS

Adequate attention to the sparking plugs is of great importance in obtaining satisfactory engine performance. The Champion L7 sparking plugs fitted at the factory have been adopted after careful tests and nothing will be gained by trying an alternative type of plug.

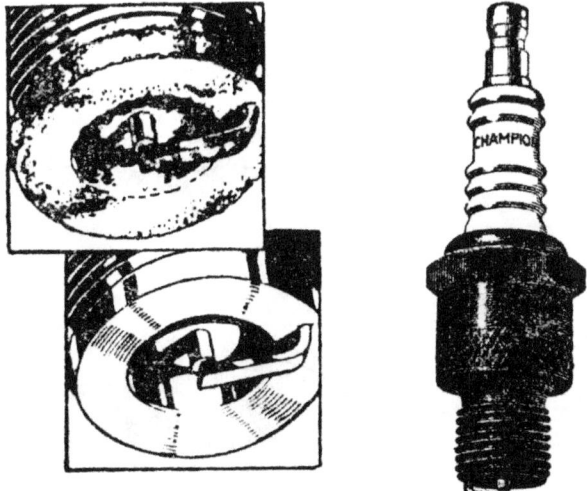

Fig. 25. The Sparking Plug.

Remove the plugs every 1,000 miles (1,500 km.) or so for inspection. Providing that the carburation is correct the sparking plug points should remain clean almost indefinitely and should appear as shown in the lower view Fig. 25. The bottom of the plug body should remain a smooth black and the central insulation should remain a natural colour. If the mixture is too rich, a sooty deposit will form on the body of the plug as in the upper view of Fig. 25, but a weak mixture will cause the end of the plug to go white. A heavily leaded fuel may cause a greyish deposit to form on the plug and excess oil will show its presence by a shiny black deposit and gum.

A light deposit due to any of these causes can easily be removed by cleaning the plugs on a proper air blast unit such as is to be found at most garages, but if it is found necessary to clean the plugs frequently the cause should be investigated. If the deposit is allowed to accumulate, particularly inside the plug body, they may spark internally. This will cause difficult starting and have an adverse effect on performance; it may even stop the engine altogether. If eventually the cleaning process fails to restore the plugs to their original efficiency, then a new set should be fitted.

It is most important that the plug gap is kept correct. Whenever a plug is removed for inspection, the gap should be tested and if necessary reset. The correct gap is .020—.025 inches (.50—.62 mm.) and it should be measured by means of feeler gauges inserted between the side wire and the central electrode. If the gap is not correct it should be adjusted by bending the side wire, but in no circumstances must any attempt be made to bend the central electrode as this will damage the insulation and make the plug ineffective.

The gap is most easily adjusted with the aid of the special tool illustrated in Fig. 26, which also has feeler gauges attached to assist in measuring the plug gap. This tool is obtainable, price 2/- from any Champion Plug Stockist, or from Champion Sparking Plug Co. Ltd., Feltham, Middlesex.

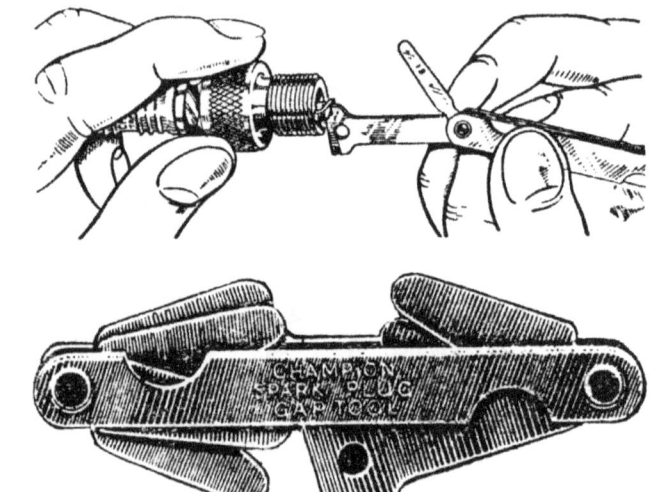

Fig. 26. Setting the Points.

Before replacing a plug make sure that the threads are clean and that the copper washer is in good condition. If it has become worn or badly flattened a new one must be fitted to ensure a gas-tight seal. Screw the plugs in as far as possible by hand, then use a tubular box spanner for final tightening, to avoid the possibility of damage to the insulators. In no circumstances should an adjustable spanner be used.

The insulation on the top of the plugs should be wiped quite clean before replacing the caps and then finally the caps themselves should be wiped to remove dirt and grease.

THE CARBURETTER

The Zenith 17 MXZ Carburetter is a compact instrument designed for trouble-free operation. The jet sizes have been chosen only after extensive testing and for normal purposes no improvement can be made by fitting alternative jets. When cleaning the jets swill them thoroughly in clean petrol and blow out with compressed air; never poke wire or needles through the jets.

Operating Instructions. When starting from cold pull out the choke which depresses the brass plunger (8). The metering hole in the plunger mates with an air passage in the carburetter body and petrol is drawn through the slow running jet (16) and mixed with air drawn through a small fixed air-bleed hole. This provides a rich mixture for starting. After about 30 seconds, push in choke to its full extent to return the brass plunger to its normal position.

In this position a smaller metering hole connects with the air passage in the body and provides the correct volume of mixture for normal slow running. The slow running speed is adjusted by the throttle stop screw (15). Turn clockwise to increase the speed and anticlockwise to reduce the speed.

The carburetter is also provided with a pilot jet control (10). This is set at the works before despatch and seldom requires attention. To enrich the slow running mixture for a reliable tick-over the control should be screwed in a fraction of a turn. Screwing in the reverse direction tends to give a faster and less reliable tick-over.

When the carburetter is used at larger throttle openings, the tapered needle portion of the slide (32) will progressively withdraw from the top of the emulsion tube (22) and consequently the depression from the inlet manifold will draw a correspondingly greater volume of petrol through the main jet (21). This mixes with air drawn through the small hole in the side of the emulsion tube and in drawn into the main carburetter choke tube and thence to the engine. When parking the machine always turn off the petrol tap.

Maintenance. The carburetter should be dismantled and cleaned at regular intervals, paying particular attention to the filter gauze in the inlet union and the various jets. The float needle and seating unit is pressed into the body and cannot be removed. When replacing the carburetter make sure that the body is pressed on to the adaptor as far as possible before the clip is tightened. Particular attention should be paid to cleanliness at this point, as an air leak will cause very poor slow running.

THE ELECTRICAL SYSTEM (Twin Cylinder Model)

Contact Breaker.

The contact breaker is mounted on the left side of the engine and is protected by a cover held by two screws. The ignition operates on the double coil system with a separate coil for each cylinder

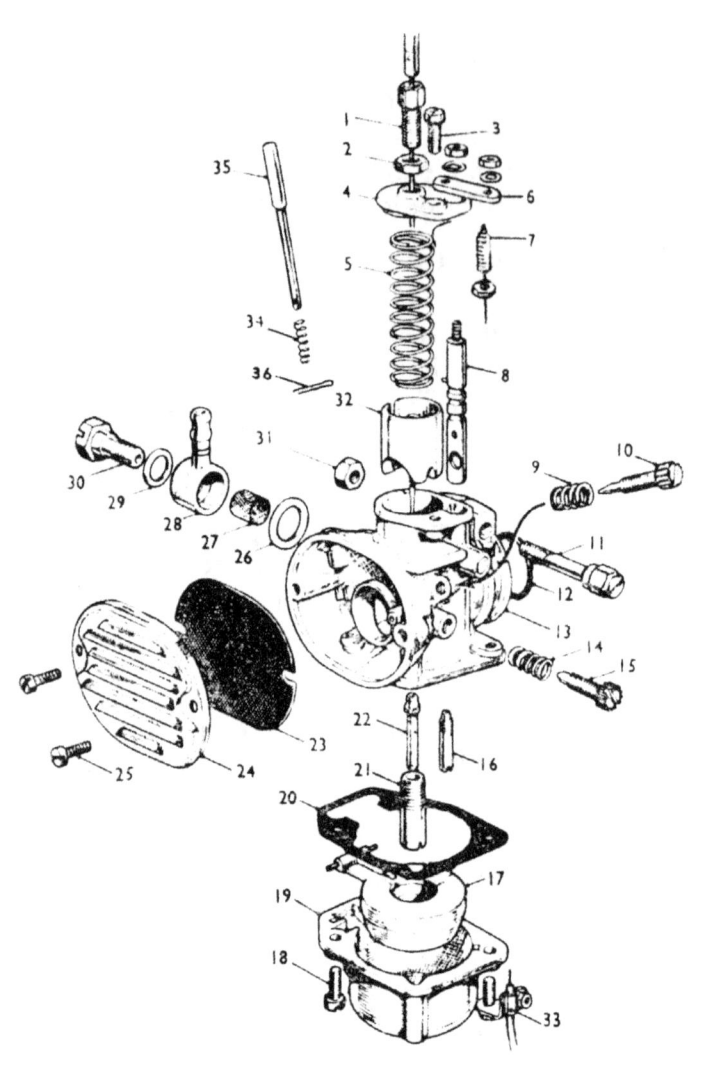

1. Cable Adjuster.
2. Locknut for Cable Adjuster.
3. Cover Plate Screw.
4. Cover Plate.
5. Spring, Main Side.
6. Choke Operating Arm.
7. Choke Cable Anchor.
8. Starter Slide.
9. Spring, Pilot Air Screw.
10. Pilot Air Screw.
11. Clamping Screw.
12. "O" Ring.
13. Carburetter Body.
14. Spring, Throttle Adjustment Screw.
15. Throttle Adjustment Screw.
16. Slow Running Jet.
17. Float.
18. Carburetter Bowl Screw (2).
19. Carburetter Bowl.
20. Gasket.
21. Main Jet.
22. Emulsion Tube.
23. Air Intake Gauze.
24. Cover for Air-Intake Gauze.
25. Cover Screw (2).
26. Filter Elbow Washer.
27. Filter Gauze.
28. Filter Elbow.
29. Filter Plug Washer.
30. Filter Plug.
31. Clamping Screw Nut.
32. Main Slide and Needle.
33. Choke Outer Cable Securing Clip.
34. Spring for Tickler.
35. Tickler Stem.
36. Split Pin

Fig. 27. The Carburetter.

and two pairs of contact breaker points actuated by the single contact breaker cam, see Fig. 28. The gap between the points when they are fully open should be .015 ins. Rotate the engine slowly until the upper rocker arm A is on the peak of the cam, then check the gap at B with the aid of feeler gauges. If the gap is incorrect, slacken screw C and move the plate carrying the fixed point until the adjustment is correct, then re-tighten the screw, and recheck for adjustment. Repeat this procedure for the other pair of points.

Approximately every 3,000 miles apply a smear of thin grease to the felt pad D lubricating the cam. Do not over lubricate or surplus grease may find its way on to the contact breaker points.

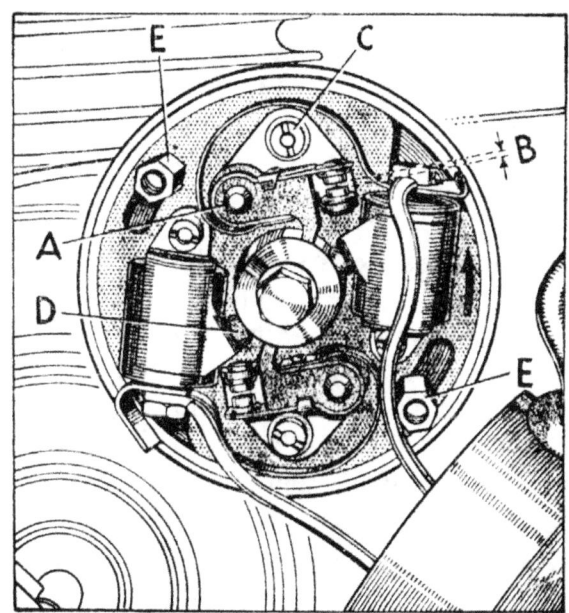

Fig. 28.
The Contact Breaker (250 c.c.).

Ignition Timing.

It is a rare occurrence for the ignition timing to alter and it is not advisable to interfere with the standard setting unless it is known to be at fault. It is, however, advisable to check over the timing after carrying out any adjustment to the contact breaker points as a slight variation of the points gap tends to alter the timing. (Opening the points advances the timing; closing them retards the timing).

Whenever the ignition timing requires checking the contact breaker gaps should also be checked and, if necessary, re-adjusted as described above.

Remove the sparking plugs and insert a length of rod through the nearside plug hole so that the piston crown can be felt and its position determined. Rotate the engine until it is at top dead centre on the compression stroke. The engine is most easily rotated by engaging top gear and turning the rear wheel. Keep the rod as vertical as possible and check that both valves in this cylinder are closed, as if either of them is open, the nearside piston is not on its compression stroke, and the engine must be rotated one revolution.

Rotate the engine backwards through about 45 degrees and then bring it forward again until the upper contact breaker points are just about to open. This is best determined by inserting a piece of fine paper (such as cigarette paper) between the points. The points are just on the point of opening when the paper is only lightly gripped and can be withdrawn with a gentle pull. The piston should then be five degrees before top dead centre. A convenient way of checking this position without the use of a degree plate is to observe the vanes on the cooling fan on the other side of the engine. These vanes are spaced roughly 11 degrees apart, so that half of the distance between two vanes is very near to five degrees.

If the ignition setting is incorrect, rotate the engine until the piston is five degrees before top dead centre, slacken the two long hexagons E, which secure the contact breaker back plate, and rotate the plate until the contact breaker points are just about to open. Then re-tighten the two hexagons. Finally recheck the adjustment and replace the sparking plugs.

Advance and Retard Mechanism.
The timing is automatically advanced and retarded by means of a governor mechanism behind the contact breaker plate. When the engine is stationary, therefore, the timing is fully retarded and this is the normal condition for checking the setting. As the engine speed increases the ignition timing is progressively advanced until it is fully advanced at normal road speeds.

To expose the advance and retard mechanism remove the two hexagons E, Fig. 28 and detach the contact breaker back plate. Inspect the mechanism and make sure that the bob-weights move freely. Oil the bearings with a few drops of light oil. Do not over lubricate or the excess may find its way on to the contact breaker points. Note that the ignition must be retimed when the contact breaker back plate is replaced.

Battery. The standard model is provided with one 6 volt battery and the electric starter model has two such batteries connected in series thus giving 12 volts. They are mounted in special housings at the back of the legshields.

Check the acid level weekly. This can be seen through the walls of the battery case and should be maintained at the level indicated by the blue line.

Initial Filling and Soaking of MLZ9E Batteries. Discard the vent hole sealing tapes.

Pour into each cell pure dilute sulphuric acid of appropriate specific gravity to the COLOURED LINE DENOTING THE MAXIMUM FILLING LEVEL and allow the battery to stand at least one hour. Thereafter keep the acid just level with the coloured line by topping-up with distilled water.

Specific gravity of electrolyte (corrected to 60°F., 15.5°C.) for filling both uncharged and dry-charged batteries:—

   (a)   In climates ordinarily below 90°F. (32.2°C.) use acid of 1.270 s.g. (corrected to 60°F.).

   (b)   In climates ordinarily above 90°F., use acid of 1.210 s.g.

Battery Topping-up. During charging water is lost by gassing and evaporation. At regular weekly intervals (see Routine Maintenance, page 11), and more frequently in warm climates, check the electrolyte level in the battery cells; if necessary add distilled water to maintain the level indicated by the blue line. Do not use tap water, as it may contain impurities detrimental to the battery, nor use naked lights when examining the condition of the cells.

Cleaning. Wipe away all dirt and moisture from the top of the battery.

Battery — Maintaining Condition. Never leave the battery in a discharged condition. If the motor cycle is to be out of use for any length of time, have the battery fully charged and every fortnight give it a short refreshing charge at about 1.5 amperes to prevent any tendency for the plates to become permanently sulphated.

A positive earth wiring system is employed. Make sure that the battery is connected correctly, i.e., with the positive or + side of the battery connected to earth.

Starting with a Discharged battery. Turn the ignition switch to the EMG position (Fig. 4) and operate the kick starter. As soon as the engine fires turn to the IGN position.

The A.C. Generator. This is in two parts, the rotor which is built into the engine flywheel and is mounted directly on the engine shaft, and the stator which is bolted to the crankcase cover. The generator is entirely self-contained and requires no maintenance whatsoever.

Rectifier. This is fitted on the left of the main frame tube in a position that ensures adequate air cooling and it is most important that nothing is near it which might obstruct the air flow. The only attention which the rectifier requires is an occasional check to ensure that the leads are securely attached as loose contacts may affect its life.

Ignition Coils. No maintenance is required except to ensure that the terminals and terminal moulding are kept clean and tight.

Electric Horn. The horn is adjusted at the works to give its best performance and will give a long period of service without any attention. If it becomes uncertain in action, giving only a choking sound, or does not vibrate, it does not follow that it has broken down. First ascertain that the trouble is not due to some outside source such as a discharged battery, or a loose connection or short circuit in the wiring.

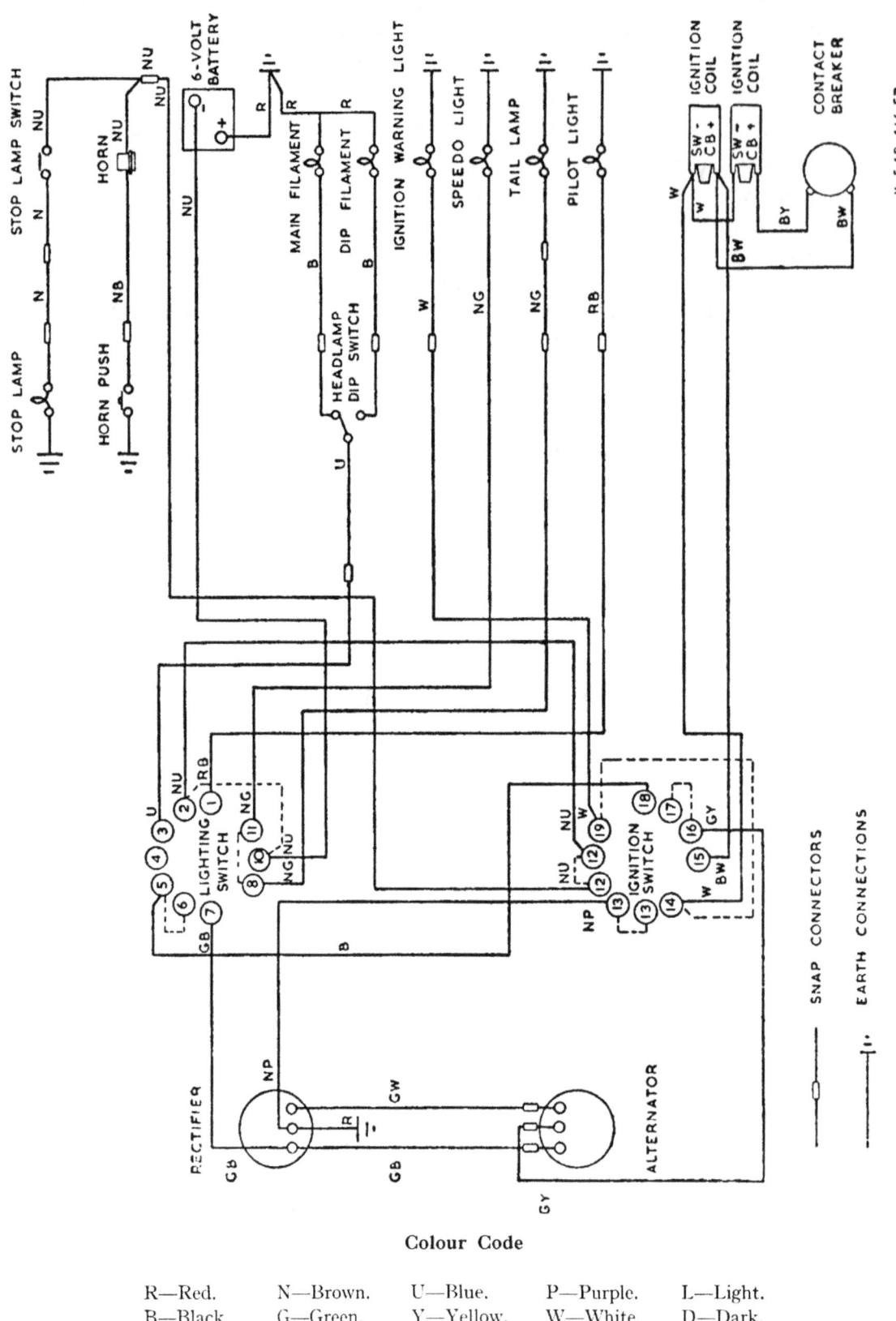

Fig. 29. Lucas Diagram. (Twin Cylinder Model)

If the horn still gives trouble it should be removed and returned to the manufacturers.

Headlamp. The headlamp is of the sealed unit type employing a prefocus bulb. To gain access to the bulbs, the headlamp rim complete with light unit must be removed by the slackening screw below the headlamp shell and pulling the rim away. The headlamp bulb is retained by a bayonet fitting cap. Push on the cap, turn it to the left and then withdraw. The bulb is located by a flange which has a notch engaging with a projection inside the holder to ensure that it is correctly positioned.

Note that the prongs of the bayonet fitting cap are not symmetrical so that it can only be replaced in the correct position.

The reflector is sealed to the glass and in the event of either becoming damaged the complete unit must be replaced.

Tail Lamp. Access to the tail lamp is obtained by removing the two screws securing the red transparent plastic cover. Note that the locating prongs of the bulb are offset so that it can only be replaced one way round.

Bulbs. The correct replacement bulbs are as follows:—

Head	6v. (12v.)	30/24 watts. (24/24)
Pilot	6v. (12v.)	3 watt. (6)
Speedometer ...	8v. (12v.)	1.8 watts. (2.2)
Stop Tail ...	6v. (12v.)	6/18 watt. (6/21)
Ignition Warning	6v. (12v.)	.6 watts. (2.2)

(The figures in brackets are for models with electric starter)

Circuit Diagram.

Diagrams of the electrical circuit appear on pages 30 and 32.

The rubber insulation of the wires is individually coloured and these colours are indicated on the diagram.

SPECIAL INSTRUCTIONS FOR THE SINGLE CYLINDER TWO-STROKE MODEL

This model is practically identical with the twin cylinder model apart from the engine, and maintenance instructions differ only with regard to this item.

FUEL AND OIL SUPPLY.

The engine is lubricated by the "Petroil" system which means that the lubricating oil is dissolved in the petrol to form petroil mixture. This mixture is available at most garages either from special petrol dispensers or pumps, or by the injection into the tank of the requisite quantity of self-mixing oil after the desired quantity of petrol has been poured in, and in both these cases the correct proportions of oil and petrol are automatically provided.

Alternatively, the rider may prefer to make his own petroil

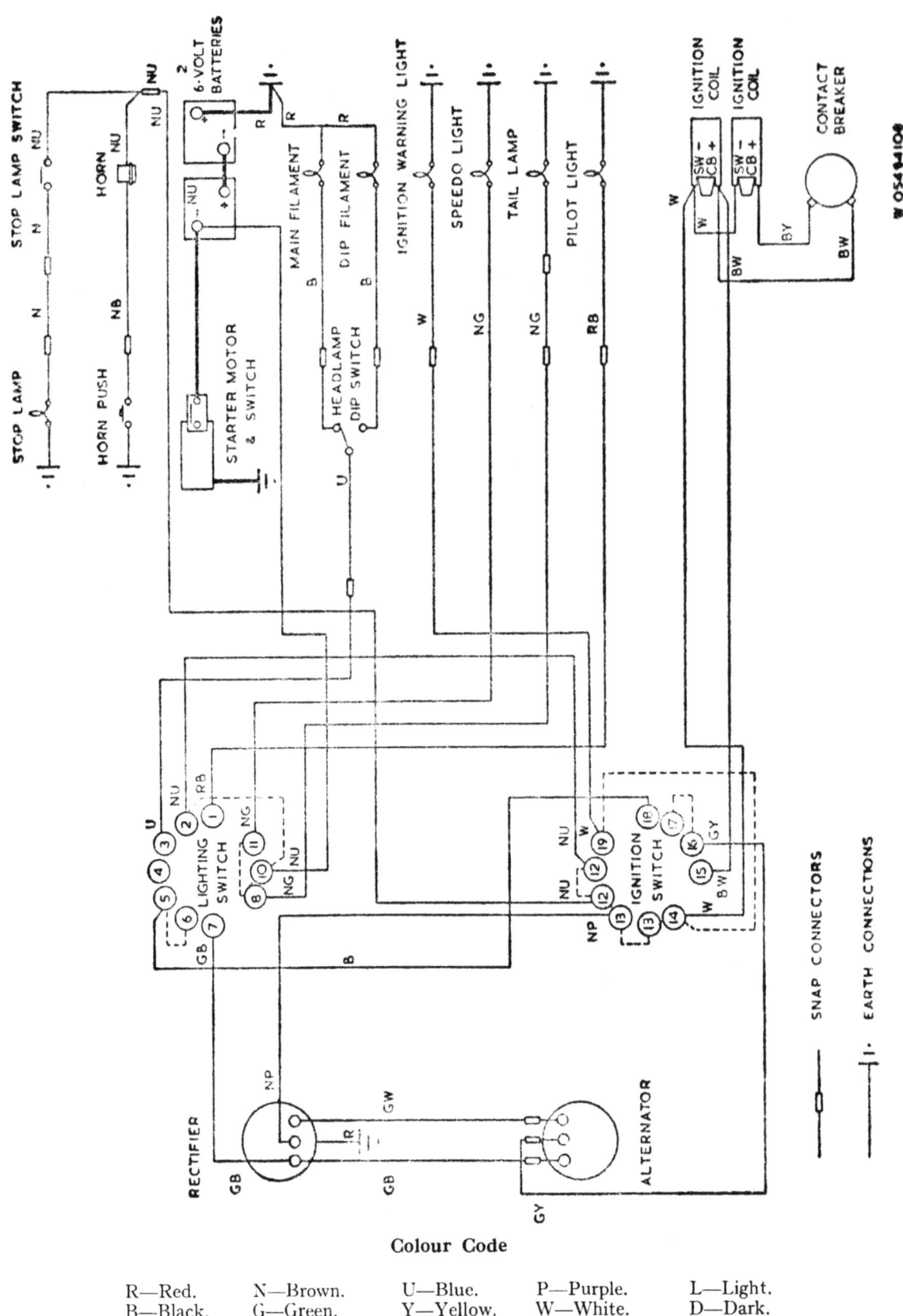

Fig. 30. Lucas Diagram (Twin Cylinder Model with Electric starter)

mixture, and for this purpose a measure is incorporated in the tank filler cap. For correct running of the engine and also for adequate lubrication, it is essential that the oil should be completely dissolved in the petrol, and it is, therefore, preferable to mix the two in a separate container before pouring into the tank. If this is not possible, however, as for instance, when obtaining petrol from a wayside pump, the oil should be put into the petrol after filling up with the latter and the machine should be shaken thoroughly to ensure correct mixing of the two liquids. If this is not done, there is the risk of liquid oil undiluted with petrol reaching the carburetter and clogging the fuel supply system.

The correct mixture strength for the standard engine oils is 1 in 20, but for self-mixing oils this should be increased to 1 in 16. For oil recommendations see table below.

RECOMMENDED OIL FOR THE SINGLE CYLINDER TWO-STROKE ENGINE
(Summer and Winter)

BRAND	ENGINE OIL
Wakefield	Castrol Two-Stroke Oil (1 in 16) or Castrol XXL
Shell	2T Mixture or 2T Two-Stroke Oil
Esso	Esso Two-Stroke Motor Oil (1 in 16) or Essolube 40
Mobil	Mobil Mix TT (1 in 16) or Mobiloil BB
B.P.	BP Zoom or Energol Two-Stroke Oil
Regent	Motor Oil 2T

Mix one of the above oils with petrol in the ratio of 1 in 20 unless otherwise shown.

DECARBONISATION.

The symptoms indicating that decarbonisation is necessary are similar to those described on page 19 with the addition of excessive four and eight stroking. The operation consists of removing the carbon deposit from the cylinder head and piston crown as described previously, together with the cleaning of any deposit which may have formed in the cylinder exhaust port where the exhaust pipe is attached.

First remove the side valances (see Fig. 8) and then take off the cylinder head and barrel ducting by undoing their fixing screws. Disconnect the fuel pipe from the carburetter, and remove the latter.

Then undo the four fixing nuts on the cylinder head and lift the head clear. Bring the piston to the top and remove the carbon from piston and cylinder head.

To remove the cylinder barrel slacken off the exhaust pipe clip and draw the barrel up and clear of the four long studs. Any carbon in the exhaust port can then be removed.

PISTON AND RINGS.

Examine these as described on page 22, noting that the rings are located in their grooves by pegs at the ring ends (i.e., in the gaps) and that these must be correctly positioned when replacing the cylinder barrel. Note also that the piston must be replaced in its original position with the gaps towards the rear. The correct piston ring gaps are .009" to .013".

THE CARBURETTER.

This is an Amal Monobloc, type 363/11, and the strangler is of the push-pull variety, the operating knob protruding through the left-hand weather shield. To close the strangler when starting from cold, pull the knob out. Push the knob in to open the strangler again as soon as possible after the engine fires.

THE ELECTRICAL SYSTEM.

The equipment consists of a permanent magnet alternator which provides direct lighting for the headlamp and also a trickle charge for the battery through a rectifier. The headlamp therefore does not operate when the engine is stationary, although current for the other items (pilot light, horn, etc.) is supplied by the battery.

Battery. See instructions for twin-cylinder model.

Alternator. The flywheel comprises six high grade cast magnets with laminated pole pieces. It is *self-keeping* and may be separated from the stator without any loss of magnetism.

The set requires very little maintenance, and if the following notes are observed the life of the machine should prove trouble-free. Check and if necessary readjust the contacts once every 5,000 miles (8,000 km.) as described on page 35.

Occasionally clean the contacts by inserting a dry smooth piece of paper between them and withdrawing while the contacts are in the closed position. Do not allow the engine to run with grease or petrol on the contacts or they will start to burn and blacken. If they do, lightly polish with a piece of smooth emery cloth.

Smear the cam lubricating pad with a little high melting point grease every 5,000 miles (8,000 km.). Do not run with a faulty or damaged high-tension lead, and occasionally clean away mud and dirt from around the high-tension insulator.

If the Unit requires any attention beyond the replacement of contact points and condenser, it is recommended that the complete machine should be sent to an authorised Wico service station.

SPARKING PLUG.

Champion L5 (Maintenance as with twin cylinder model).

CONTACT BREAKER.

The ignition timing is of the "fixed" variety and it is only necessary to check the contact breaker points gap from time to time, say every time the engine is decarbonised.

This can be done, however, without removing the side valances, merely by taking off the grilled inspection cover on the right-hand valance by removing the single fixing screw. Take off the flywheel cover plate, held by four screws, and turn the flywheel until the contactbreaker is exposed as seen in Fig. 31. To adjust the gap slacken screw A and turn adjuster screw B with a screwdriver until the correct gap of .018" is obtained. Then retighten screw A.

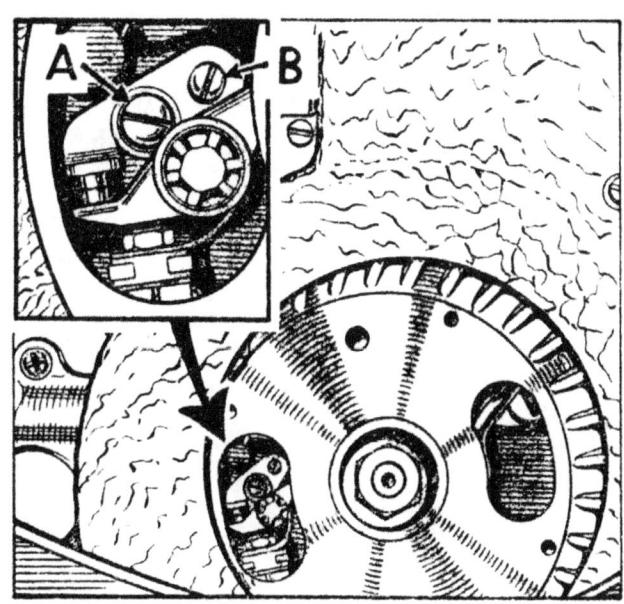

Fig. 31. The Contact Breaker (175 c.c.).

Electric Horn. The horn is adjusted at the works to give its best performance and will give a long period of service without any attention. If it becomes uncertain in action, giving only a choking sound, or does not vibrate, it does not follow that it has broken down. First ascertain that the trouble is not due to some outside source such as, a discharged battery, or a loose connection or short circuit in the wiring.

If the horn still gives trouble it should be removed and returned to the manufacturers.

Headlamp. The lamp front, together with the reflector and bulb assembly, is secured to the main lamp casing by means of a slotted screw under the lamp. To replace a bulb therefore, it is only necessary to loosen the screw until the rim can be removed.

Stop Light Switch. This is operated by the brake rod through a spring. It is desirable to see that any mud or grease is periodically cleared away from the switch, and the operating mechanism should be oiled occasionally with thin oil.

GENERAL NOTES.

The wiring is connected by means of snap connectors at various convenient places on the machine and it is desirable occasionally to check it over and make certain that these connectors are tight.

BULB TYPES.

Headlamp (main bulb)	6 volt, 24/24 watt.
Headlamp (pilot bulb)	6 volt, 1.8 watt. Screw fitting.
Speedometer	8 volt, 1.8 watt.

Rear and Stop lamp incorporating three bulbs

Rear lamp bulb	6 volt, 3 watt.
Two Stop light bulbs	6 volt, 6 watts. (2 off) Screw fitting.
Ignition Warning	6 volts, .6 watts.

WIRING WIPAC DIAGRAM

B.S.A. SUNBEAM AND TRIUMPH TIGRESS
175 c.c. SCOOTER, (A.C. LIGHTS, D.C. TRICKLE CHARGE)
MODELS PRODUCED FROM OCT. 1958 TO SEPT. 1963

THE WIPAC GROUP · BUCKINGHAM · BUCKS

UNIT FOR SPARES	PART No.
Headlamp Unit	S0867
Harness (Main)	S0869
Switch Unit (Lights)	S0868
Dipper Switch	S1104
Leads Set (Dip Switch)	S1105
Rectifier	S1044
Stop Switch	S2370
Leads Set (Stop Switch)	S0870
Stop and Rear Lamp	S0088
Ignition Generator	IG1555

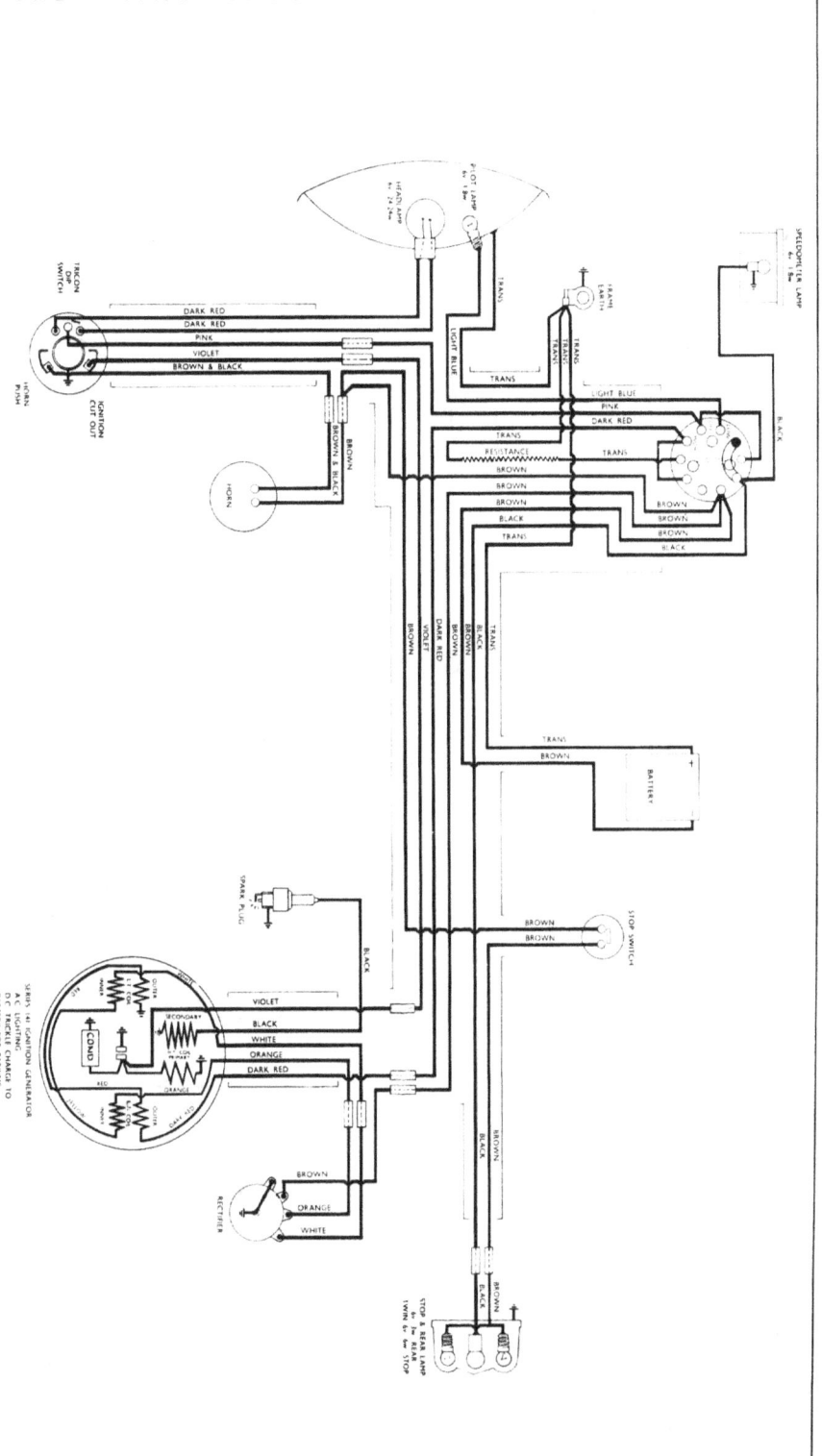

REF. WD/27/742/2

WIRING WIPAC DIAGRAM

B.S.A. SUNBEAM AND TRIUMPH TIGRESS
175 c.c. SCOOTER, (D.C. COIL IGNITION)
MODELS PRODUCED FROM OCTOBER 1963

THE WIPAC GROUP · BUCKINGHAM · BUCKS

UNIT FOR SPARES	PART No.
Headlamp Unit	S0867
Harness (Main)	S3544
Switch Unit (Lights)	S0868
Switch Unit (Ignition)	S3545
Dipper Switch	S1216
Leads Set (Dip Switch)	S1217
Rectifier	S1044
Stop Switch	S2370
Leads Set (Stop Switch)	S2862
Stop and Rear Lamp	S0088
Ignition Generator	I.G.1676
Ignition Coil	S0769

Ref. WD/66/925

Scooter Data

B.S.A. SCOOTERS B1 AND B2

CONTENTS

Item	Page
ENGINE SPECIFICATION	2
ENGINE DATA	3, 4
CARBURATION	5
TRANSMISSION	6
TYRES, PRESSURES, WHEELS, BRAKES	7
SUSPENSION	8
LUBRICATION, CAPACITIES	9
ELECTRICAL EQUIPMENT	10
BEARINGS (Main and Big-end)	12
DIMENSIONS, WEIGHTS	11

ENGINE SPECIFICATION

	B1	B2
Number of Cylinders	1	2
Valve arrangement	Two-stroke	O.H.V.
Cylinder arrangement	Vertical	Vertical
Cylinder head	Al. alloy	Al. alloy
Cylinder barrel	C. iron	Al. alloy
Cylinder liner	—	Pearlitic C. iron
Capacity (c.c.)	173	249
Bore (mm./inches)	61.5 (2.42)	56 (2.20)
Stroke (mm./inches)	58 (2.28)	50.6 (2.00)
Lubrication system	Petroil	Wet sump
Oil pump	—	Plunger type

ENGINE DATA

	B1	B2
*Compression ratio	7.6	6.5
Sparking plug	L5	L7/JA/548
Sparking plug gap (inches/mm.)	.025 (.635)	.025 (.635)
Valve timing: Inlet open B.T.D.C. (degrees)	—	10
Inlet closed A.B.D.C.	—	50
Exhaust open B.B.D.C.	—	50
Exhaust closed A.T.D.C.	—	10
Ignition timing	CR 6.5 1/16" B.T.D.C. (CR 7.6 5/32" B.T.D.C.)	5° B.T.D.C. fully retarded
Crankshaft (degrees)	17 for 1/16" B.T.D.C. (27 for 5/32 B.T.D.C.)	5° fully retarded
Contact breaker points (inches)	.018	.015
Ignition control	Fixed	Automatic
Breather timing: Opens B.B.D.C. (degrees)	—	83
Closes A.B.D.C.	—	21
Total period	—	104
Tappet clearances (cold): Inlet (inches)	—	.005
Exhaust	—	.005
Valve lift (inches)	—	.280

*Compression ratio up to Engine No. S6001 6.5 on the B1.

ENGINE DATA—(continued)

	B1	B2
Piston rings: Plain (2 off) (inches)	.0938 × .081	.0625 × .092
Oil control (inches)	—	.093 × .092
Piston ring gap: Plain (inches)	.010	.011
Oil control (inches)	—	.011
Valve springs (free length): + or − 1.64 Inner (inches)	—	1½
Outer (inches)	—	1-9/16
Valve sizes and material (inches)	—	Inlet head 1 dia. stem 9/32. Material H18 Exhaust head 1 dia. stem 9/32. Material G2 Stellite tipped
Gudgeon pin diameter (inches)	9/16	9/16
Exhaust pipe diameter (inches)	1⅝	1

CARBURATION

	B1	B2
Air cleaner	B.S.A.	Gauze
Carburetter type	Amal No. 363/11	Zenith 17MXZ
Choke size (inches)	13/16	23/32
Main jet	130	82
Pilot jet	15	45
Throttle valve number	3	—
Needle position	3	—
Needle jet	106	—
Emulsion tube	—	017135
Starter slide	—	200 (starter outlet) (slow running outlet undrilled)

TRANSMISSION

	B1	B2
Standard gear ratios	4.93, 6.29, 10.08, 14.75	4, 5.2, 8, 12.1
Primary drive	Gear 2.27:1	Gear 2.0:1
Rear drive	Duplex Chain 94 links, .375 pitch	Duplex chain 94 links, .375 pitch
Teeth on primary drive gear	45T	49T
Teeth on primary driven gear	102T	98T
Teeth on gearbox sprocket	18T	19T
Teeth on chainwheel	39T	38T
Clutch friction plates	3	3
Clutch spring pressure (lbs.)	105	105

TYRES, PRESSURES, WHEELS, BRAKES

	B1	B2
Tyres	3.50 x 10 Dunlop scooter	3.50 x 10 Dunlop scooter
*Inflation pressure: Front (lbs.)	17	17
Rear (lbs.)	24	24
Wheel (inches)	10	10
Brake diameter (inches)	5	5
Brake shoe width (inches)	1	1

*(30 p.s.i. on rear tyre only when pillion passenger is carried).

SUSPENSION

	B1	B2
Front fork type	Tel. hyd.	Tel. hyd.
Front fork suspension spring	76–5020	76–5020
Front fork spring rating (lbs./in.) ...	57	57
Front fork movement (inches) ...	$4\frac{3}{8}$	$4\frac{3}{8}$
Rear suspension	Swinging arm	Swinging arm
Rear suspension damping	Hydraulic	Hydraulic
Rear suspension damping movement (in.)	2-19/32	2-19/32
Rear fork damper unit	76–6035	76–6035

CAPACITIES, VISCOSITY GRADES

	B1	B2
Petrol tank capacity (gal./litre)	$1\frac{1}{2}$ (6.8)	$1\frac{1}{2}$ (6.8)
Oil capacity: Engine (pints/c.c.) ...	Petroil	$2\frac{1}{2}$ (1420)
Primary drive (fl. oz/c.c.)	9 (250)	9 (250)
Rear chain (c.c.)	120	120
Gearbox (c.c.)	125	125
Engine oil	Two-stroke or S.A.E. 40	Summer S.A.E. 30 / Winter S.A.E. 20
Gearbox oil	Summer S.A.E. 30 / Winter S.A.E. 20	Summer S.A.E. 30 / Winter S.A.E. 20
Rear drive	Summer S.A.E. 30 / Winter S.A.E. 20	Summer S.A.E. 30 / Winter S.A.E. 20
Primary drive	S.A.E. 20	Summer S.A.E. 30 / Winter S.A.E. 20

ELECTRICAL EQUIPMENT

	B1	B2
Magneto	Wico-Pacy flywheel type	—
Generator	—	Lucas 6-volt AC
Coil (6-volt set)	—	MA 62 (2 off)
Coil (12-volt)	—	MA 6 (2 off)
Rectifier: 6-volt	Wico No. 08460	Lucas FSX 1849
12-volt	—	Lucas FSX 1850A
Battery	Lucas No. MLZ9E	*Lucas MLZ9E
Battery voltage and capacity	6v 13ah	6v 13ah
Horn	Lucas 5H	Lucas 5H
Headlamp diameter (inches)	5½	5½
Headlamp bulb	6v 24/24w	6v 30/24w (12v 24/24w)
Pilot bulb	6v 1.8w screw fitting	6v 3w (12v 6w)
Rear lamp	6v 3w	
Stop light bulb(s)	6v 6w screw fitting (2 off)	6v 6/18w (12v 6/21w)
Speedometer bulb	6v 6w	6v 6w (12v 2/2w)
Ignition warning bulb	6v 6w	6v 6w (12v 2/2w)

*(Two off on model B2S making 12 volts).

DIMENSIONS, WEIGHTS

	B1	B2
Overall height (inches)	37½	37½
Overall length (inches)	72	72
Saddle height (inches)	28	28
Handlebar width (inches)	24	24
Wheel base (inches)	48	48
Ground clearance (inches)	5	5
Steering lock angle (degrees)	45	45
Turning circle (feet)	8	8
Steering head angle (degrees)	65	65
Trail (inches)	3¾	3¾
Total weight unladen (lbs)	236	244
Weight on front wheel (lbs.)	88	102
Weight on rear wheel (lbs.)	148	142

BEARINGS

	B1	B2
Main bearing drive side	Ball 17 x 40 x 12 mm. Ball $\frac{3}{4}$ x $1\frac{7}{8}$ x 9/16 in. deep groove	Ball 25 x 62 x 17 mm. D/S deep groove
Main bearing timing side	Ball 17 x 40 x 12 mm. Ball $\frac{3}{4}$ x $1\frac{7}{8}$ 9/16 in. deep groove	Plain $1\frac{1}{8}$ dia. x $\frac{7}{8}$ in. wide
Big-end bearing	18 rollers 4 x 8 mm. on 1-5/32 in. crankpin	Plain $1\frac{1}{8}$ in. dia. (shaft)
Wheel bearings	Deep groove ball journals	Deep groove ball journals
Front	15 x 35 x 11 mm. 17 x 40 x 12 mm.	15 x 35 x 11 mm. 17 x 40 x 12 mm.
Rear	17 x 40 x 12 mm. 20 x 52 x 15 mm.	17 x 40 x 12 mm. 20 x 52 x 15 mm.

B.S.A. MOTOR CYCLES LTD., SCOOTER DIVISION WAVERLEY WORKS, BIRMINGHAM 10.

B.S.A. Motor Cycles Ltd. reserve the right to alter the designs or any constructional details of their manufactures at any time without giving notice

NOTES

The Triumph Tigress

SCOOTER SPARES

Catalogue No. 00-5083

NOTES

The TRIUMPH Tigress SCOOTERS

SPARE PARTS CATALOGUE

SERVICE DEPARTMENT

TRIUMPH ENGINEERING CO. LTD., SCOOTER DIVISION
WAVERLEY WORKS, BIRMINGHAM, 10

Telephone: BIRMINGHAM VICtoria 3711 *Telegrams*: TIGRESS, BIRMINGHAM, 10

SUFFIX NUMBERS TO BE USED TO IDENTIFY VARYING FINISHES.
CHIFFRES DE SUFFIXE A EMPLOYER POUR IDENTIFIER LES PRESENTATIONS VARIÉES
NACHZAHLEN ZU BENUTZEN UM DIE VERSCHIEDENEN AUSFÜHRUNGEN ZU BEZEICHNEN.
CIFRAS ADICIONALES QUE SE EMPLEA PARA IDENTIFICAR LOS ACABADOS VARIOS.

/140 Polychromatic Blue, Bleu Polycromatique, Blau Polycromatisches, Azul Polycromatico.

When ordering components with varying finishes, please state finish required by adding the APPROPRIATE NUMBER TO PART NUMBER.

En commandant des pièces avec présentations différentes, veuillez indiquer la présentation requise en ajoutant les chiffres appropriés au numéro de CATALOGUE DE LA PIECE.

Bei Bestellungen von Teilen mit verschiedenen Ausführungen, bitte die Erwünschte Ausfuhrung mit Angabe der entsprechenden Nachzahl nach dem TEILNUMMER BEZEICHNEN.

Al pedir piezas con acabados differentes, sírvase indicar el acabado requirido mediante la cifra relativa escrita después del NUMERO DE CATALOGO DE LA PIEZA.

EXAMPLE. Side Panel L/H, Polychromatic Blue, 76-9278/140.

EXEMPLE. Panneau lateral (gauche), Bleu polychromatique, 76-9278/140.

BEISPIEL. Seitenblech (Links), Blau Polycromatisches, 76-9278/140.

EJEMPLO. Panel de lado (izq.), Azul polycromatico, 76-9278/140.

PART / DESCRIPTION		French	German	Spanish	PAGE
Cylinder Head Group.	250 c.c.	Ensemble culasse	Zylinderkopfsatz	Conjunto de la culata	4
Crankcase Group.	250 c.c.	Ensemble carter	Kurbelgehäusesatz	Conjunto del cárter	8
Cylinder and Crankshaft Group.	175 c.c.	Groupe culasse et de vilebrequin. 175 c.c.	Zylinderkopf und Kurbelwellesatz. 175 c.c.	Grupo de culata y cigüeñal. 175 c.c.	12
Crankcase and Primary Drive Group.	175 c.c.	Ensemble carter et transmission primaire. 175 c.c.	Kurbelgehäusesatz und Primärantriebsatz. 175 c.c.	Conjunto del cárter y de la transmisión primario. 175 c.c.	14
Gear Cluster / Gearchange / Starting Mechanism	175 c.c. 250 c.c.	Jeu d'engrenages / Changement de vitesse / Mécanisme de demarrage	Zahnradsatz / Getriebeschaltung / Anlasswerk	Juego de engranages / Cambio de velocidad / Mecanismo de arranque	16
Primary Drive.	175 c.c., 250 c.c.	Entraînement primaire	Primar Antrieb	Transmisión primario	18
Oil Pump / Crankcase Breather	175 c.c. 250 c.c.	Pompe à huile / Renifleur de carter	Ölpumpe / Kurbelgehäuse-Schnüffel	Bomba de aceite / Respiradero del carter	20
Rear Wheel / Rear Drive	175 c.c., 250 c.c.	Roue ar / Transmission arrière	Hinterrad / Hinterradantrieb	Rueda trasera / Transmisión trasera	22
Frame / Shock Absorber	175 c.c. 250 c.c.	Cadre / Amortisseur	Rahmen / Stossdämpfer	Cuadro / Amortiguador	24
Petrol Tank / Handlebar and Controls / Dual Seat	175 c.c. 250 c.c.	Réservoir d'essence / Guidon et commandes / Selle double	Benzintank / Lenker und Steurung / Doppelsitz	Deposito de combustible / Manillar y mandos / Asiento doble	26
Foot Controls / Engine Plates / Silencer	175 c.c., 250 c.c.	Commandes à pied / Plaque d'appui pour moteur / Silencieux	Fussbetätigung / Motorabstuzblech / Schalldämpfer	Mandos de pie / Placa de apoyo del motor / Silenciador	28
Front Fork / Front Wheel	175c.c., 250 c.c.	Fourche av / Roue av	Vordergabel / Vorderrad	Horquilla delantera / Rueda delantera	30
Legshields / Front Guard / Battery Box	175 c.c., 250 c.c.	Protege-jambe / Garde-boue de roue av / Boîte à batterie	Beinschild / Vorderradschutzblech / Batteriekasten	Guardapiernas / Guardabarro del / Caja de bateria	32
Side Panels / Footboards / Number Plate	175 c.c., 250 c.c.	Panneau lateral / Repose-pieds / Plaque de police	Seitenblech / Fussraster / Nummernschild	Panel de lado / Descansa-pies / Chapa de patente	34
Electrical Equipment / Sundries	250 c.c.	Equipement electrique / Pièce variees	Elektr, Ausrung / Sonstige Teile	Equipo electrico / Piezas varias	36
Electrical Equipment / Sundries	175 c.c.	Equipement electrique / Pièce variees	Elektr, Ausrung / Sonstige Teile	Equipo electrico / Piezas varias	40
Tools.	175 c.c., 250 c.c.	Outils	Werkzeuger	Herramientos	42
Carburetters.	250 c.c.	Carburateurs	Vergaser	Carburadores	44
Carburetters.	175 c.c.	Carburateurs	Vergaser	Carburadores	46

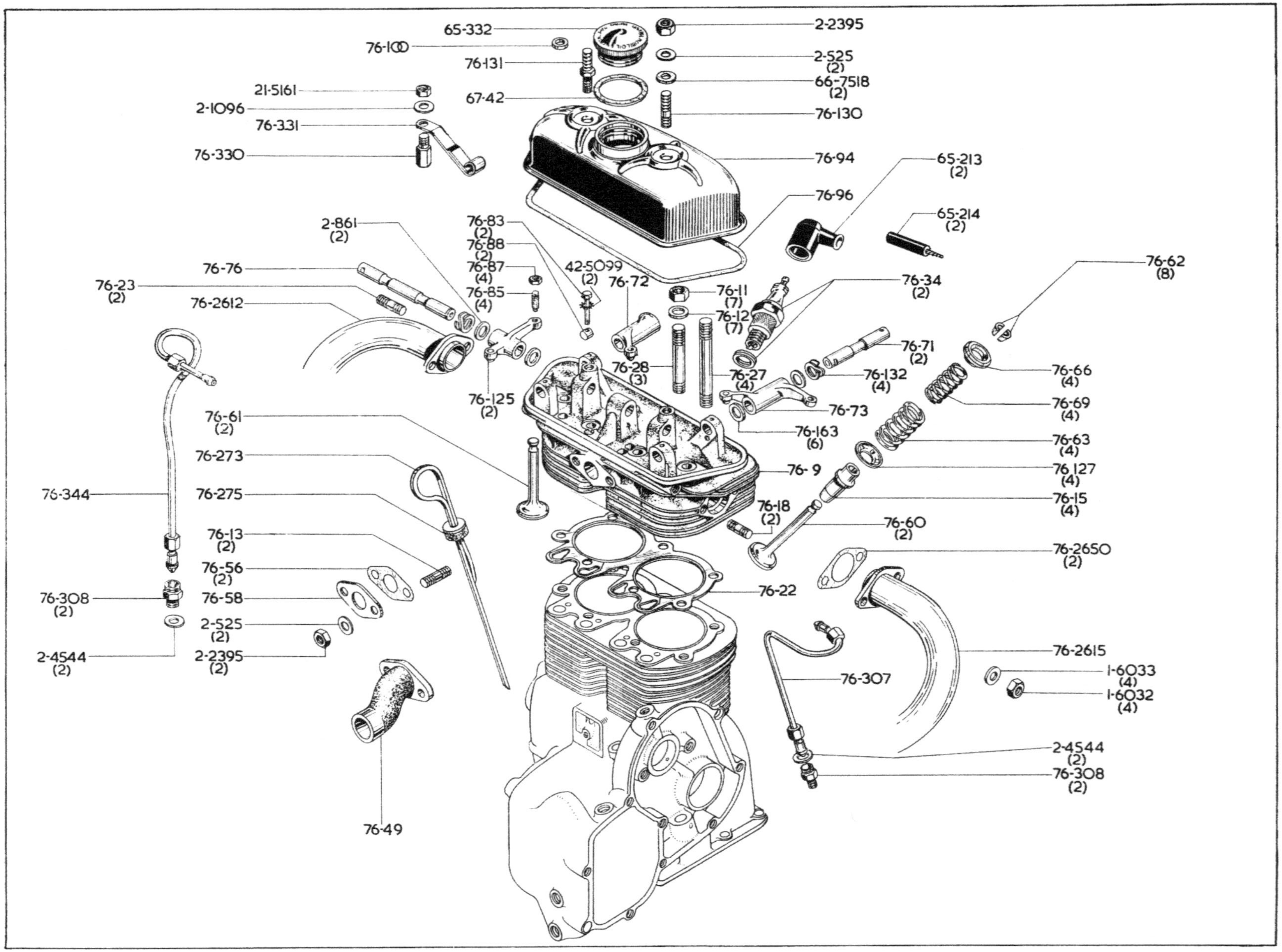
65-332
76-100
76-131
21-5161
2-1096
67-42
76-331
76-330
2-2395
2-525 (2)
66-7518 (2)
76-130
76-94
76-96
65-213 (2)
65-214 (2)
2-861 (2)
76-83 (2)
76-88 (2)
76-87 (4)
76-85 (4)
42-5099 (2)
76-72
76-11 (7)
76-12 (7)
76-34 (2)
76-62 (8)
76-76
76-23 (2)
76-2612
76-71 (2)
76-28 (3)
76-27 (4)
76-132 (4)
76-66 (4)
76-125 (2)
76-73
76-69 (4)
76-163 (6)
76-61 (2)
76-63 (4)
76-273
76-9
76-127 (4)
76-344
76-275
76-15 (4)
76-18 (2)
76-60 (2)
76-13 (2)
76-2650 (2)
76-56 (2)
76-308 (2)
76-58
76-22
2-525 (2)
2-4544 (2)
2-2395 (2)
76-2615
76-307
1-6033 (4)
1-6032 (4)
2-4544 (2)
76-308 (2)
76-49

CYLINDER HEAD GROUP 250 c.c.

Part No. No. de pièce Bestell-nr No. de parte	Description	Designation	Beschreibung	Descripción	Per Set Par jeu Pr. Satz Juego de
1-6032	Nut	Ecrou	Mutter	Tuerca	4
1-6033	Washer	Rondelle	Scheibe	Arandela	4
2-525	Washer	Rondelle	Scheibe	Arandela	4
2-861	Thrust Washer	Rondelle de butée	Druckscheibe	Anillo de empuje	2
2-1096	Spring Washer	Arrêtoir	Sicherung	Freno	
2-2395	Nut	Ecrou	Mutter	Tuerca	3
2-4544	Sealing Washer	Joint d'étanchéité	Dichtung	Arandela de reten	2
21-5161	Nut	Ecrou	Mutter	Tuerca	
42-5099	Lockwasher	Rondelle frein	Sicherungsscheibe	Freno	2
65-213	Cover	Couvercle	Schutzkappe	Tapa	2
65-214	Suppressor	Dispositif antiparasite	Wellensauge	Supresor	2
66-7518	Sealing Washer	Joint d'étanchéité	Dichtung	Arandela de reten	2
67-42	Sealing Washer	Joint d'étanchéité	Dichtung	Arandela de reten	2
76-9	Cylinder Head	Culasse	Zylinderkopf	Culata	
76-11	Nut	Ecrou	Mutter	Tuerca	7
76-12	Washer	Rondelle	Scheibe	Arandela	7
76-13	Stud	Goujon	Stehbolzen	Esparago	2
76-15	Valve Guide	Guide de soupape	Ventilführung	Guia de valvula	4
76-18	Stud	Goujon	Stehbolzen	Esparago	2
76-22	Gasket	Joint	Dichtung	Empaquetadura	
76-23	Stud	Goujon	Stehbolzen	Esparago	2
76-27	Stud	Goujon	Stehbolzen	Esparago	4
76-28	Stud	Goujon	Stehbolzen	Esparago	3
76-34	Spark Plug	Bougie d'allumage	Zündkerze	Bujía	2
76-49	Manifold	Collecteur	Verbingdungsstümck	Cabezal de union	
76-56	Gasket	Joint	Dichtung	Empaquetadura	2
76-58	Insulating Washer	Rondelle isolante	Isolierscheibe	Arandela isoladora	
76-60	Exhaust Valve	Soupape d'échappement	Ausslassventil	Valvula de escape	2
76-61	Inlet Valve	Soupape d'admission	Einlassventil	Valvula de admisión	2
76-62	Collet	Collet	Wulst	Refuerzo del cilindro	8
76-63	Spring (outer)	Ressort (extérieur)	Feder (Aussen)	Resorte (exterior)	4
76-66	Collar	Bague d'arrêt	Stelring	Anillo móvil aprisionado	4
76-69	Spring (inner)	Ressort (intérieur)	Feder (Innere)	Resorte (interior)	4
76-71	Rocker Shaft	Axe des culbuteurs	Kipphebelwelle	Eje del brazo oscillante	2

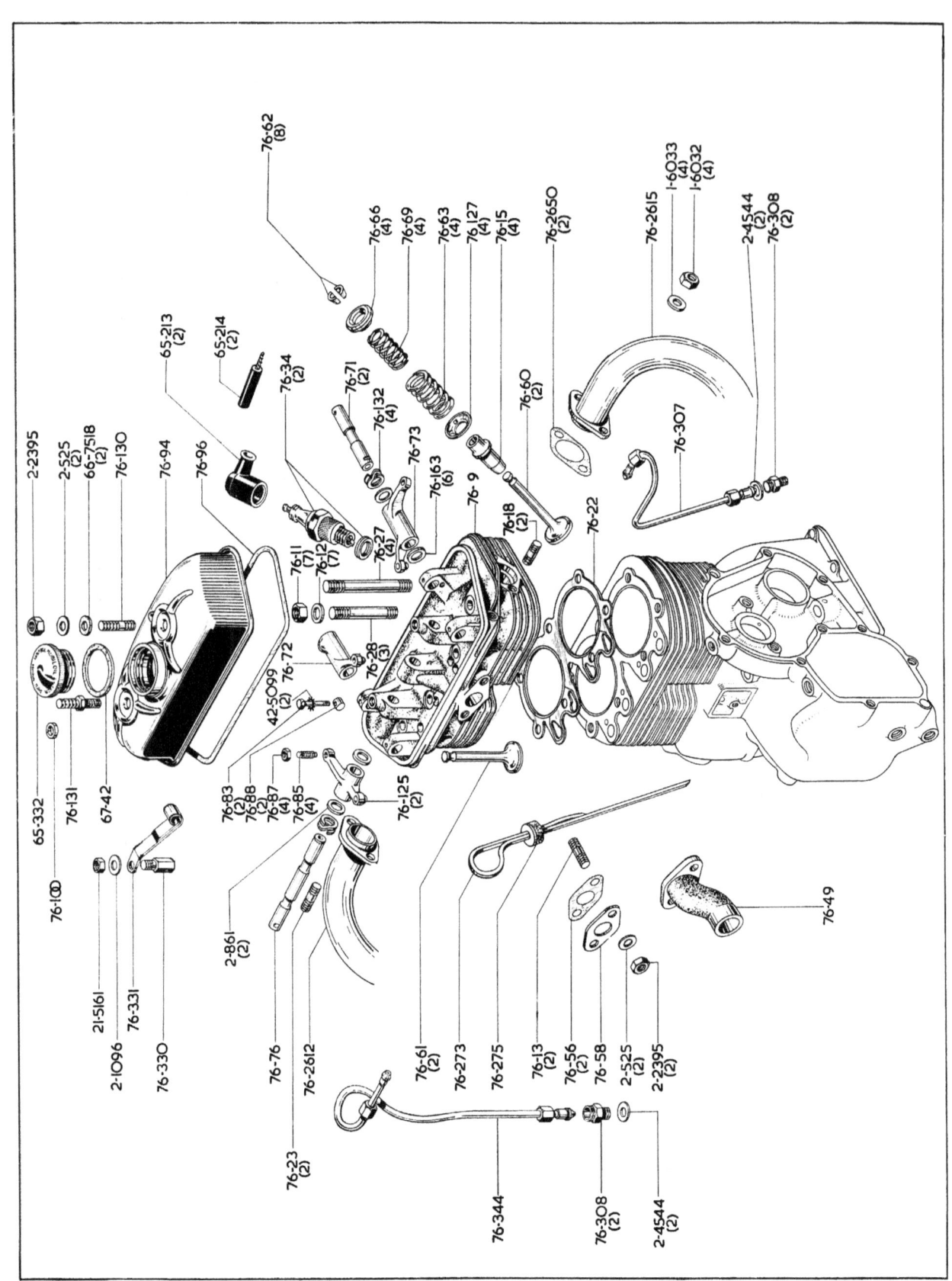

CYLINDER HEAD GROUP 250 c.c.

Part No. No. de pièce Bestell-nr No. de parte	Description	Designation	Beschreibung	Descripción	Per Set Par jeu Pr. Satz Juego de
7672	Exhaust Rocker (L/H)	Culbuteur-échappement (gauche)	Auslasskipphebel (Links)	Brazo osc. escape (izq.)	
76-73	Exhaust Rocker (R/H)	Culbuteur-échappement (droite)	Auslasskipphebel (Rechts)	Brazo osc. escape (der.)	
76-76	Rocker Shaft	Axe des culbuteurs	Kipphebelwelle	Eje del brazo oscillante	
76-83	Screw	Vis	Schraube	Tornillo	2
76-85	Adjuster	Système de réglage	Einstellschraube	Tornillo de ajuste	4
76-87	Nut	Ecrou	Mutter	Tuerca	4
76-88	Swivel Pin (screwed)	Tourillon fileté	Passchraube	Esparago can rosca	2
76-94	Cover	Couvercle	Schutzkappe	Tapa	
76-96	Gasket	Joint	Dichtung	Empaquetadura	
76-100	Spacer Ring	Tube entretoise	Distanzring	Anillo espaciador	
76-125	Inlet Rocker	Culbuteur-admission	Einlasskipphebel	Brazo osc. admisión	2
76-127	Cup	Cuvette	Schale	Copa	4
76-130/131	Stud	Goujon	Stehbolzen	Esparago	
76-132	Spring Washer	Arrêtoir	Sicherung	Freno	4
76-163	Washer	Rondelle	Scheibe	Arandela	6
76-273	Dipstick	Tige de jauge d'huile	Ölmessstab	Varilla probadora	
76-275	Sealing Washer	Joint d'étanchéité	Dichtung	Arandela de reten	
76-307	Oil Pipe	Conduit au canalisation d'huile	Ölleitung	Conexión de engrase	
76-308	Oil Pipe Union	Raccord d'alimentation d'huile	Ölzufuhrverbindung	Union de la tuberia de alimentacion de aceite.	2
76-330	Nut	Ecrou	Mutter	Tuerca	
76-331	Clip	Bride	Klammer	Grapa	
76-332	Cap	Chapeau	Abdeckkappe	Tapon	
76-344	Oil pipe	Conduit au canalisation d'huile	Ölleitung	Conexion de engrase	
76-2612	Exhaust Pipe (L/H)	Tuyau d'échappement (gauche)	Auspuffrohr (Links)	Tubo de escape (izq.)	
76-2615	Exhaust Pipe (R/H)	Tuyau d'échappement (droite)	Auspuffrohr (Rechts)	Tubo de escape (der.)	
76-2650	Sealing Washer	Joint d'étanchéité	Dichtung	Arandela de reten	2

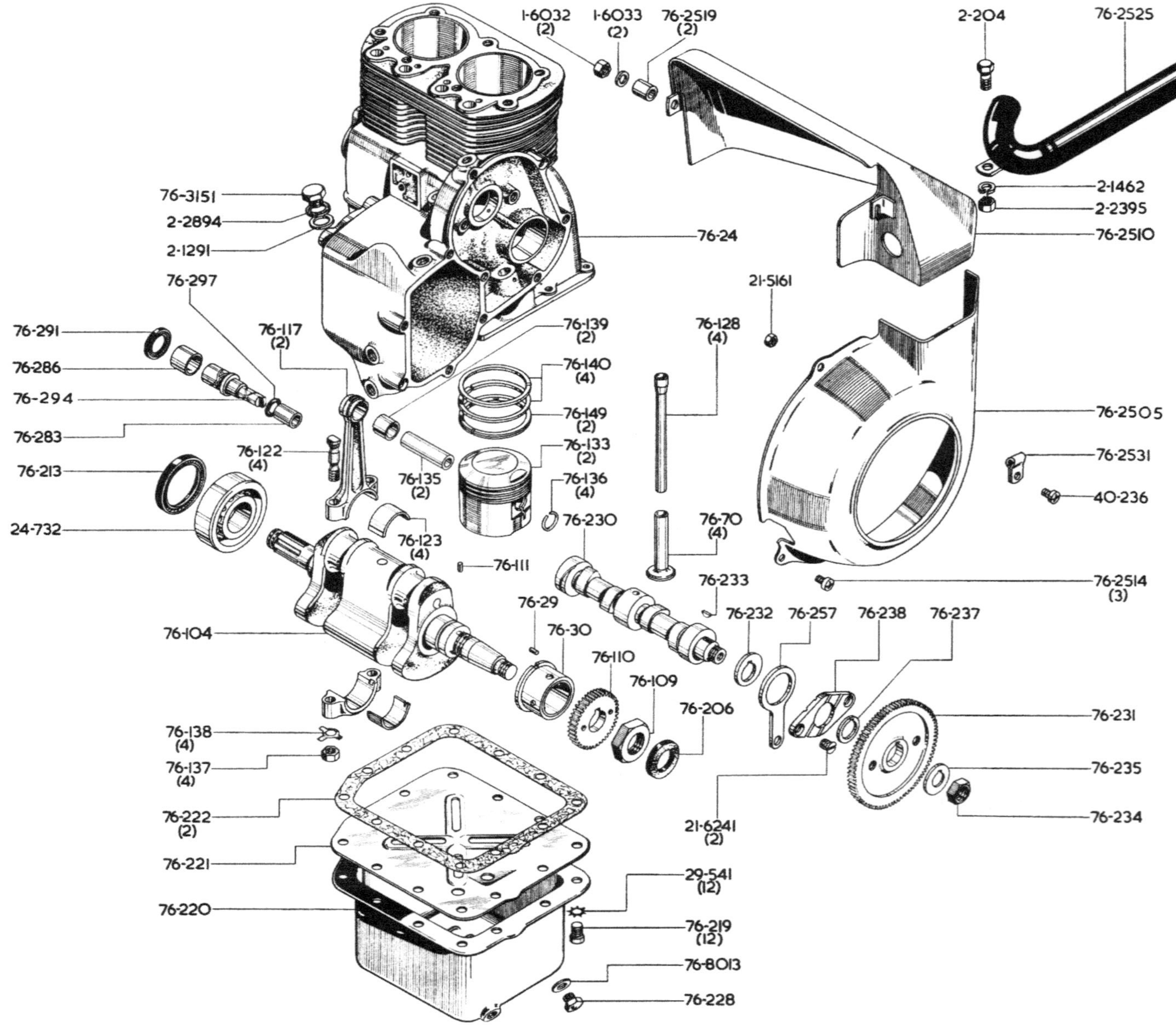

1-6032
(2)
1-6033
(2)
76-2519
(2)
2-204
76-2525
76-3151
2-2894
2-1291
76-24
2-1462
2-2395
76-2510
76-297
21-5161
76-291
76-286
76-294
76-283
76-117
(2)
76-139
(2)
76-128
(4)
76-140
(4)
76-149
(2)
76-2505
76-122
(4)
76-133
(2)
76-2531
76-213
76-135
(2)
76-136
(4)
40-236
24-732
76-123
(4)
76-230
76-70
(4)
76-111
76-2514
(3)
76-233
76-29
76-232
76-257
76-238
76-237
76-104
76-30
76-110
76-109
76-206
76-231
76-138
(4)
76-137
(4)
76-235
76-222
(2)
76-234
21-6241
(2)
76-221
29-541
(12)
76-220
76-219
(12)
76-8013
76-228

CRANKCASE GROUP 250 c.c.

Part No. / No. de pièce / Bestell-nr / No. de parte	Description	Designation	Beschreibung	Descripción	Per Set / Par jeu / Pr. Satz / Juego de
00-3120	Decoke Set	Jeu de joint pour dé cabaminage	Dichtung Satz für Entrussen	Juego de empaquetaduras para	
00-3121	Gasket Set Complete	Je de joints complet	Satz Dichtungen Kompl	Juego de empaquetaduras comp	
1-6032	Nut	Ecrou	Mutter	Tuerca	2
1-6033	Washer	Rondelle	Scheibe	Arandela	2
2-204	Bolt	Boulon	Schraube	Tornillo	
2-1291	Washer	Rondelle	Scheibe	Arandela	
2-1462	Washer	Rondelle	Scheibe	Arandela	
2-2395	Nut	Ecrou	Mutter	Tuerca	
2-2894	Sealing Washer	Joint d'étanchéité	Dichtung	Arandela de reten	
21-5161	Nut	Ecrou	Mutter	Tuerca	2
21-6241	Screw	Vis	Schraube	Tornillo	
24-732	Bearing	Roulement	Lager	Rolamiento	
29-541	Lockwasher	Rondelle frein	Sicherungsscheibe	Freno	12
40-236	Screw	Vis	Schraube	Tornillo	
76-24	Crankcase and Cylinder Block	Carter et bloc cylindre	Kurbelgehäuse und Zylinder	Carter motor y cilindro	
76-29	Dowel	Goujon	Passtift	Pasador	
76-30	Main Bearing	Palier principal	Hauptlager	Chumacera principal	
76-70	Tappet	Poussoir	Stössel	Botador de valvula	
76-104	Crankshaft	Vilebrequin	Kurbelwelle	Ciqueñal	4
76-109	Nut	Ecrou	Mutter	Tuerca	
76-110	Pinion	Pignon	Zahnrad	Piñón	
76-111	Peg	Ergot	Stift	Esparago	
76-117	Connecting Rod	Bielle	Pleuelstange	Varilla de acoplamiento	2
76-122	Bolt	Boulon	Schraube	Tornillo	4
76-123	Bearing Shell	Coquille de palier	Lager	Chumacera	4
76-128	Push Rod	Tige de culbuteur	Stösselstange	Varilla	4
76-133	Piston Complete	Piston complete	Kolben Kompl.	Embolo comp.	2
76-135	Gudgeon Pin	Axe de piston	Kolbenbolzen	Bulón de embolo	2
76-136	Circlip	Arrêtoir	Sprengring	Freno	4
76-137	Nut	Ecrou	Mutter	Tuerca	4
76-138	Lockwasher	Rondelle frein	Sicherungsscheibe	Freno	4
76-139	Bush	Douille	Büchse	Casquillo	2
76-140	Piston Ring	Segment	Kolbenring	Segmento	4
76-141	Piston Ring (+.010″)	Segment (+.254 mm.)	Kolbenring (+.254 mm.)	Segmento (+.254 mm.)	4
76-142	Piston Ring (+.020″)	Segment (+.508 mm.)	Kolbenring (+.508 mm.)	Segmento (+.508 mm.)	4
76-146	Bearing Shell (−.010″)	Coquille de palier (−.254 mm.)	Lager (−.254 mm.)	Chumacera (−.254 mm.)	4
76-147	Bearing Shell (−.020″)	Coquille de palier (−.508 mm.)	Lager (−.508 mm.)	Chumacera (−.508 mm.)	4
76-149	Piston Ring	Segment	Kolbenring	Segmento	2
76-150	Piston Ring (+.010″)	Segment (+.254 mm.)	Kolbenring (+.254 mm.)	Segmento (+.254 mm.)	2
76-151	Piston Ring (+.020″)	Segment (+.508 mm.)	Kolbenring (+.508 mm.)	Segmento (+.508 mm.)	2
76-155	Piston Complete (+.010″)	Piston complet (+.254 mm.)	Kolben Kompl. (+.254 mm.)	Embolo comp. (+.254 mm.)	2

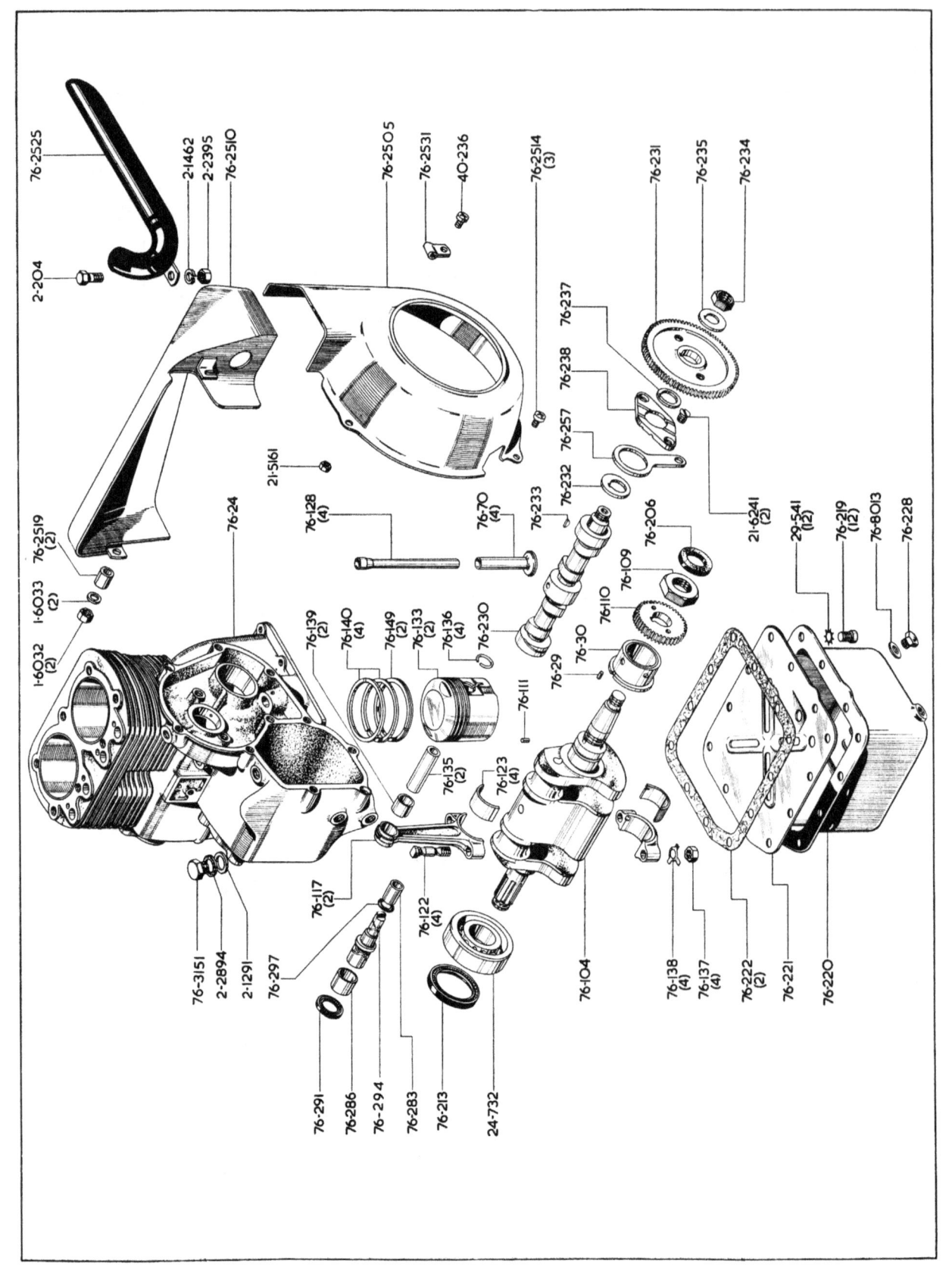

CRANKCASE GROUP 250 c.c.

Part No. No. de pièce Bestell-nr No. de parte	Description	Designation	Beschreibung	Descripción	Per Set Par jeu Pr. Satz Juego de
76-157	Piston Complete (+.020″)	Piston complet (+.508 mm.)	Kolben Kompl. (+.508 mm.)	Embolo comp. (+.508 mm.)	
76-164	Main Bearing (—.010″)	Palier principal (—.254 mm.)	Hauptlager (—.254 mm.)	Chumacera principal (—.254 mm.)	2
76-206	Oil Seal	Joint d'huile	Simmerring	Reten de aceite	
76-213	Oil Seal	Joint d'huile	Simmerring	Reten de aceite	
76-219	Screw	Vis	Schraube	Tornillo	12
76-220	Sump	Fond de carter	Sumpf	Colector de aceite	
76-221	Baffle Plate	Chicane	Stauscheibe	Placa reflectadora	
76-222	Gasket	Joint	Dichtung	Empaquetadura	2
76-228	Drain Plug	Bouchon de vidange d'huile	Ablassschraube	Tapón	
76-230	Camshaft	Arbre de cames	Nockenwelle	Arbol de levas	
76-231	Camshaft Gear	Pignon de l'arbre de cames	Nockenwellenritzel	Piñón del arbol de levas	
76-232	Camshaft Eccentric	Excentrique de l'arbre de cames	Nockenwelle, Exzentrisch	Excentrica del arból de levas	
76-233	Woodruff Key	Clavette disque	Rundkeil	Chaveta Woodruff	
76-234	Nut	Ecrou	Mutter	Tuerca	2
76-235	Lockwasher	Rondelle frein	Sicherungsscheibe	Freno	
76-237	Distance Piece	Entretoise	Distanzrohr	Distanciador	
76-238	Retainer	Arrêtoir	Sicherung	Freno	
76-257	Connector	Connexion	Verbinder	Conector	
76-283	Bush	Douille	Büchse	Casquillo	
76-286	Bush	Douille	Büchse	Casquillo	
76-291	Oil Seal	Joint d'huile	Simmerring	Reten de aceite	
76-294	Drive Shaft	Arbre d'entraînement	Antriebswelle	Arbol de transmisión	
76-297	"O" Ring	Bague "O"	"O" Ring	Anillo "O"	
76-2505	Fan Cowl	Capotage du ventilateur	Ventilatorgehause	Capuchondel ventilador	
76-2510	Air Duct (cowl)	Conduit d'air	Luftleitung	Conducto de aire	
76-2514	Screw	Vis	Schraube	Tornillo	4
76-2519	Distance Piece	Entretoise	Distanzrohr	Distanciador	2
76-2525	Air Duct	Conduit d'air	Luftleitung	Conducto de aire	
76-2531	Clip	Bride	Klammer	Grapa	
76-3151	Filler Cap	Bouchon de remplissage	Verschlusskappe	Tapa	
76-8013	Sealing Washer	Joint d'étanchéité	Dichtung	Arandela de reten	

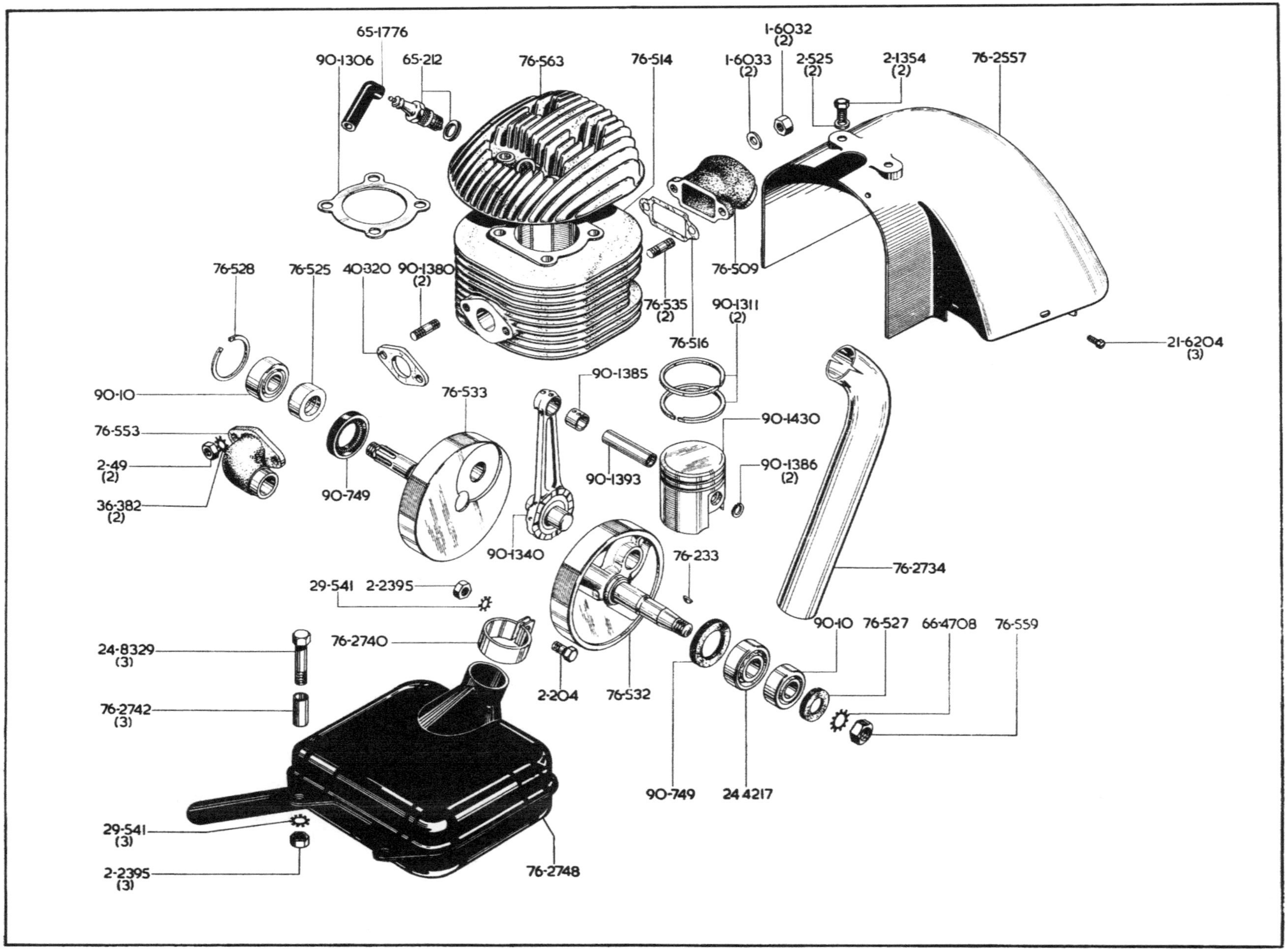
65-1776
90-1306
65-212
76-563
76-514
1-6032
(2)
1-6033
(2)
2-525
(2)
2-1354
(2)
76-2557
76-509
76-528
76-525
40320
90-1380
(2)
76-535
(2)
90-1311
(2)
76-516
21-6204
(3)
90-1385
90-10
76-533
90-1430
76-553
2-49
(2)
90-1393
90-1386
(2)
36-382
(2)
90-749
90-1340
76-233
76-2734
29-541
2-2395
90-10
76-527
66-4708
76-559
24-8329
(3)
76-2740
2-204
76-532
76-2742
(3)
90-749
24 4217
29-541
(3)
2-2395
(3)
76-2748

CYLINDER & CRANKSHAFT GROUP 175 c.c.

Part No. No. de pièce Bestell-nr No. de parte	Description	Designation	Beschreibung	Descripción	Per Set Par jeu Pr. Satz Juego de
1-6032	Nut	Ecrou	Mutter	Tuerca	2
1-6033	Washer	Rondelle	Scheibe	Arandela	2
2-49	Nut	Ecrou	Mutter	Tuerca	2
2-204	Bolt	Boulon	Schraube	Tornillo	2
2-525	Washer	Rondelle	Scheibe	Arandela	2
2-1354	Bolt	Boulon	Schratibe	Tornillo	2
2-2395	Nut	Ecrou	Mutter	Tuerca	4
21-6204	Screw	Vis	Schraube	Tornillo	3
24-4217	Bearing	Roulement	Lager	Rolamiento	2
24-8329	Bolt	Boulon	Schraube	Tornillo	3
29-541	Washer	Rondelle	Scheibe	Arandela	4
36-382	Lockwasher	Rondelle frein	Sicherungsscheibe	Freno	2
40-320	Gasket	Joint	Dichtung	Empaquetadura	
65-212	Spark Plug	Bougie d'allumage	Zündkerze	Bujía	
65-1776	Suppressor	Depositif antiparasite	Wellensauge	Supresor	
66-4708	Lockwasher	Rondelle frein	Sicherungsscheibe	Freno	4
76-233	Woodruff Key	Clavette disque	Rundkeil	Chavet Woodruff	
76-509	Manifold	Collecteur	Verbingdungstünck	Cabezal de union	
76-514	Cylinder	Cylindre	Zylinder	Cilindro	
76-516	Gasket	Joint	Dichtung	Empaquetadura	
76-525	Sleeve	Douille	Büchse	Cas juillo	
76-527	Oil Seal	Joint d'huile	Simmerring	Reten de aceite	
76-528	Circlip	Arrêtoir	Sprengring	Freno	
76-532	Flywheel (R/H)	Volant (droite)	Schwungmasse (Rechts)	Volante (der.)	
76-533	Flywheel (L/H)	Volant (gauche)	Schwungmasse (Links)	Volante (izq.)	
76-535	Stud	Goujon	Stehbolzen	Esparago	2
76-553	Manifold	Collecteur	Verbingdungsstünck	Cabezal de union	
76-559	Nut	Ecrou	Mutter	Tuerca	
76-563	Cylinder Head	Culasse	Zylinderkopf	Culata	
76-2557	Air Duct	Conduit d'air	Luftleitung	Conducto de aire	
76-2734	Exhaust Pipe	Tuyau d'échappement	Auspuffrohr	Tubo de escape	
76-2740	Clip	Bride	Klammer	Grapa	3
76-2742	Distance Piece	Entretoise	Distanzrohr	Distanciador	
76-2748	Silencer Complete	Silencieux complet	Schalldämpfer Kompl.	Silenciador comp.	
90-10	Bearing	Roulement	Lager	Rolamiento	2
90-749	Oil Seal	Joint d'huile	Simmerring	Reten de aceite	2
90-1306	Gasket	Joint	Dichtung	Empaquetadura	
90-1311	Piston Ring	Segment	Kolbenring	Segmento	2
90-1312	Piston Ring + ½ mm.	Segment + ½ mm.	Kolbenring + ½ mm.	Segmento + ½ mm.	
90-1313	Piston Ring + 1 mm.	Segment + 1 mm.	Kolbenring + 1 mm.	Segmento + 1 mm.	
90-1340	Connecting Rod Complete	Bielle complet	Pleuelstange Kompl.	Biela comp.	
90-1380	Stud	Goujon	Stehbolzen	Esparago	2
90-1385	Bush	Douille	Büchse	Casquillo	
90-1386	Circlip	Arrêtoir	Sprengring	Freno	2
90-1393	Gudgeon Pin	Axe de piston	Kolbenbolzen	Bulón de embolo	
90-1430	Piston Complete	Piston complet	Kolben Kompl.	Embolo comp.	
90-1433	Piston Complete + ½ mm.	Piston complet + ½ mm.	Kolben Kompl + ½ mm.	Embolo comp. + ½ mm.	
90-1436	Piston Complete + 1 mm.	Piston complet + 1 mm.	Kolben Kompl. + 1 mm.	Embolo comp. + 1 mm.	

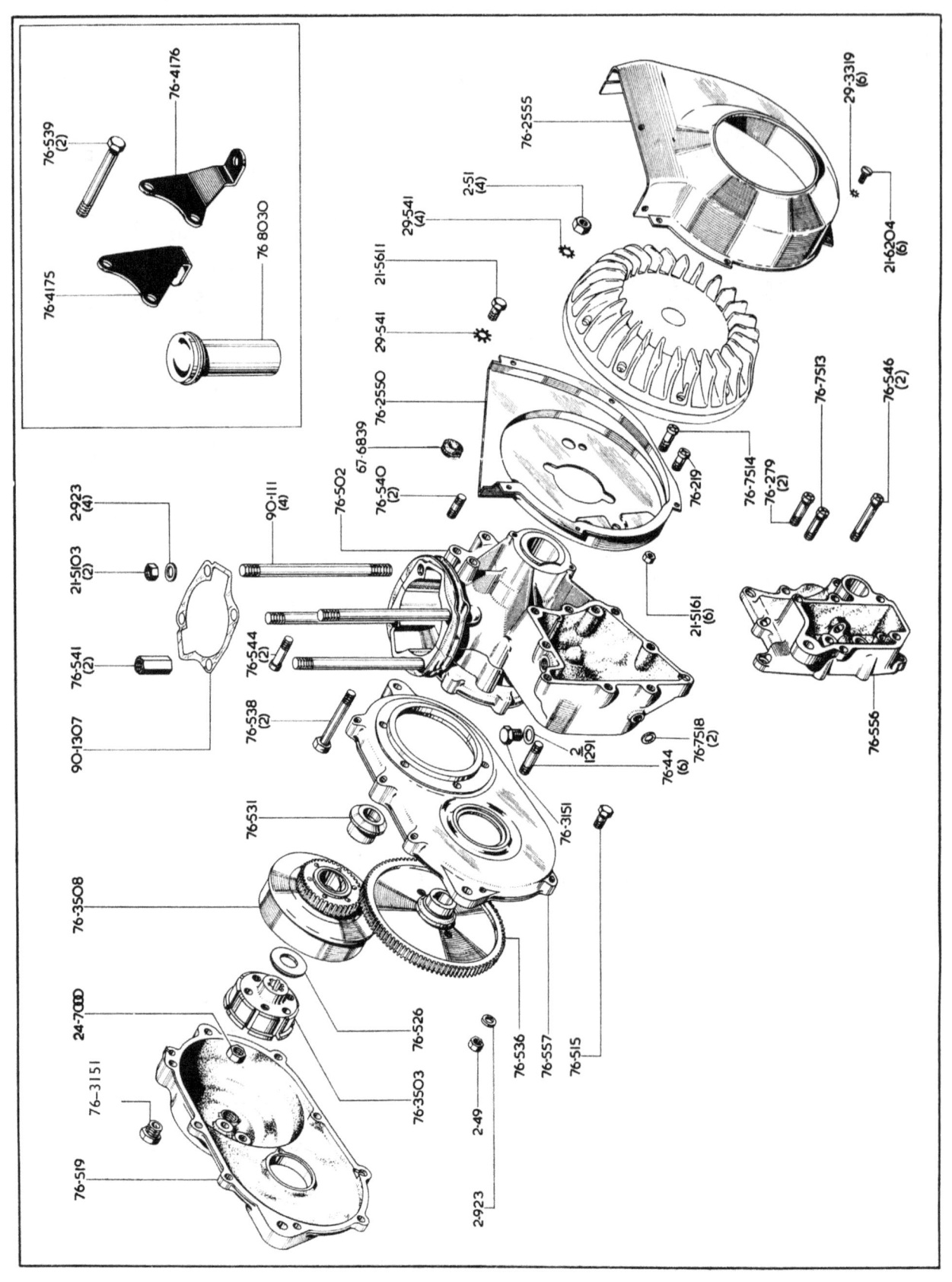

CRANKCASE & PRIMARY DRIVE GROUP 175 c.c.

Part No. No. de pièce Bestell-nr No. de parte	Description	Designation	Beschreibung	Descripción	Per Set Par jeu Pr. Satz Juego de
2-49	Nut	Ecrou	Mutter	Tuerca	
2-51	Nut	Ecrou	Mutter	Tuerca	
2-923	Washer	Rondelle	Scheibe	Arandela	5
2-1291	Washer	Rondelle	Scheibe	Arandela	
21-5103	Nut	Ecrou	Mutter	Tuerca	2
21-5161	Nut	Ecrou	Mutter	Tuerca	6
21-5611	Bolt	Boulon	Schraube	Tornillo	
21-6204	Screw	Vis	Schraube	Tornillo	6
24-36	Sealing Washer	Joint d'étanchéité	Dichtung	Arandela de reten	2
24-7000	Nut	Ecrou	Mutter	Tuerca	
29-541	Washer	Rondelle	Scheibe	Arandela	5
29-3319	Lockwasher	Rondelle frein	Sicherungsscheibe	Freno	6
76-44	Stud	Goujon	Stehbolzen	Esparago	6
76-219	Screw	Vis	Schraube	Tornillo	2
76-279	Screw	Vis	Schraube	Tornillo	2
76-502	Crankcase Complete	Carter de vilebrequin complet	Kurbelzapfen Kompl.	Caja de cigüeñal comp.	
76-515	Bolt	Boulon	Schraube	Tornillo	
76-519	Primary Cover (outer)	Couvercle primaire (extérieur)	Primarkappe (Aussen)	Tapa primario (exterior)	
76-526	Thrust Washer	Rondelle de butée	Druckscheibe	Anillo de empuje	
76-531	Sleeve	Douille	Büchse	Casquillo	
76-536	Driven Gear	Engrenage entrainé	Getriebenes Zahnrad	Engranaje impulsado	
76-538	Bolt	Boulon	Schraube	Tornillo	2
76-539	Bolt	Boulon	Schraube	Tornillo	2
76-540	Stud	Goujon	Stehbolzen	Esparago	2
76-541	Nut	Ecrou	Mutter	Tuerca	2
76-544	Screw	Vis	Schraube	Tornillo	2
76-546	Screw	Vis	Schraube	Tornillo	2
76-557	Inner Cover	Couvercle intérieur	Innere Schutzkappe	Tapa int.	
76-2550	Primary Cover (inner)	Couvercle primaire (intérieur)	Primarkappe (Innere)	Tapa primario (interior)	
76-2555	Fan Cowl (inner)	Capotage de ventilateur (intérieur)	Ventilatorgehause (Innere)	Capuchon del ventilador (interior)	
76-3151	Fan Cowl (outer)	Capotage de ventilateur (extérieur)	Ventilatorgehause (Aussen)	Capuchon del ventilador (exterior)	
76-3503	Filler Cap	Bouchon de remplissage	Verschlusskappe	Tapa	2
76-3508	Clutch Centre	Moyeux d'embrayage	Kupplungsnabe	Cubo de embrague	
76-4175	Clutch Cover	Couvercle d'embrayage	Deckel	Tapa	
76-4176	Engine Plate (L/H)	Plaque d'appui pour moteur (gauche).	Motorabstützblech (Links)	Placa de apoyo del motor (izq.)	
	Engine Plate (R/H)	Plaque d'appui pour moteur (droite).	Motorabstützblech (Rechts)	Placa de apoyo del motor (der.)	
76-6839	Grommet	Rondelle capuchon	Tülle	Manguera	
76-7513	Screw	Vis	Schraube	Tornillo	
76-7514	Screw	Vis	Schraube	Tornillo	
76-8030	Filler Cap	Bouchon de remplissage	Verschlusskappe	Tapa	
90-111	Stud	Goujon	Stehbolzen	Esparago	4
90-1307	Gasket	Joint	Dichtung	Empaquetadura	

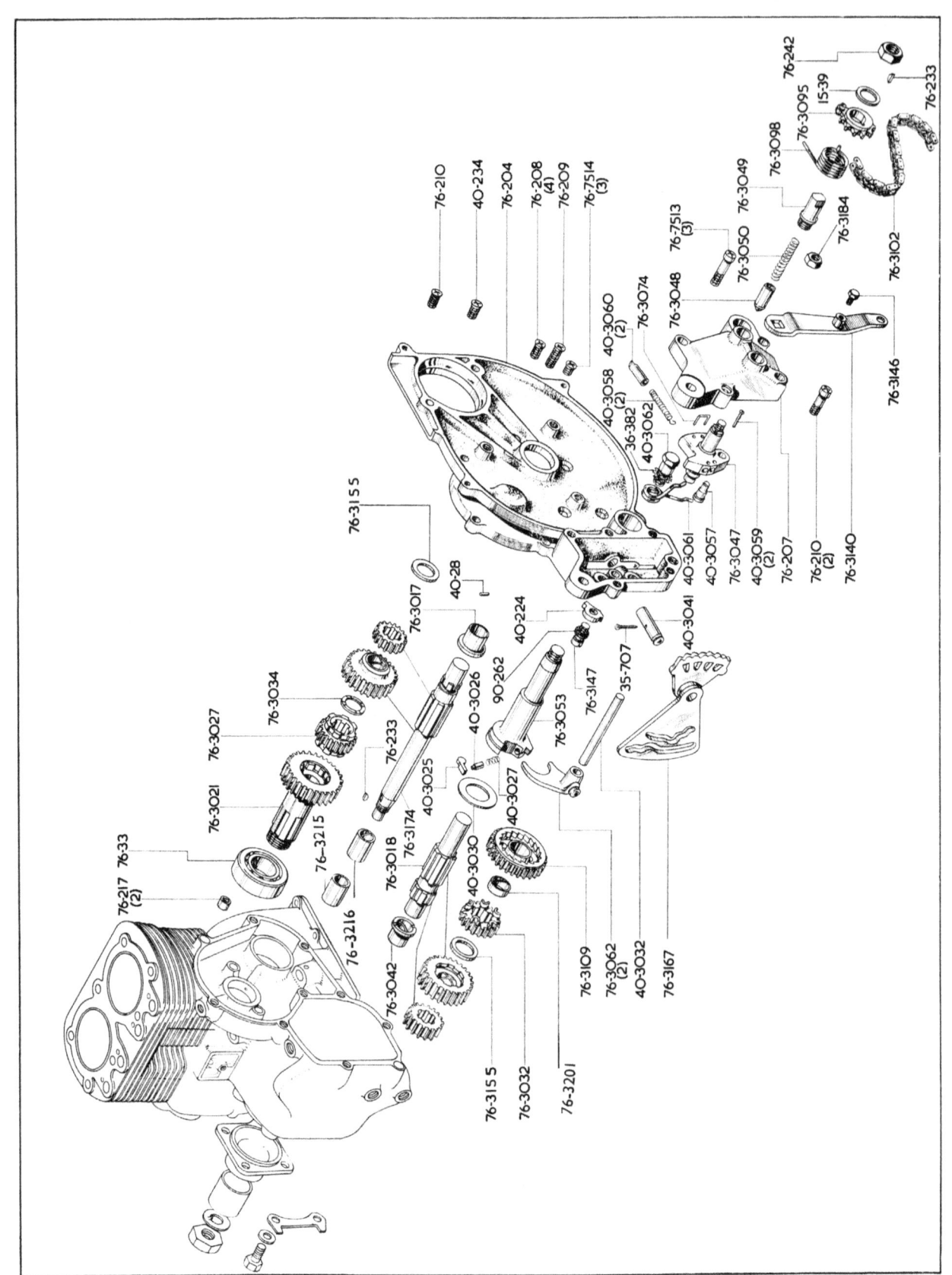

GEAR CLUSTER & GEARCHANGE & STARTING MECHANISM 175 c.c., 250 c.c. († 250 c.c.)

Part No. / No. de pièce / Bestell-nr / No. de parte	Description	Designation	Beschreibung	Descripción	Per Set / Par jeu / Pr. Satz / Juego de
15-39	Washer	Rondelle	Scheibe	Arandela	
35-707	Split Pin	Goupille fendue	Splint	Chaveta hendida	
36-382	Lockwasher	Rondelle frein	Sicherungsscheibe	Freno	
40-28	Peg	Ergot	Stift	Esparago	1
40-224	Kickstart Stop	Butée de kick	Kickstarter-Anschlag	Dispositivo de tope	
40-234	Screw	Vis	Schraube	Tornillo	
40-3025	Pawl	Cliquet	Klaue	Trinquete	
40-3026	Plunger	Plongeur	Plunger	Buzo	
40-3027	Spring	Ressort	Feder	Resorte	
40-3030	Retainer	Arrêtoir	Sicherung	Freno	
40-3032/41	Spindle	Arbre	Welle	Arbol	
40-3057	Screw	Vis	Schraube	Tornillo	
40-3058	Spring	Ressort	Feder	Resorte	2
40-3059	Rivet	Rivet	Niete	Remache	2
40-3060	Plunger	Plongeur	Plunger	Buzo	2
40-3061	Spring	Ressort	Feder	Resorte	
40-3062	Bolt	Boulon	Schraube	Tornillo	
76-33	Bearing	Roulement	Lager	Rolamiento	
76-204	†Inner Cover	Couvercle intérieur	Innere Schutzkappe	Tapa interior	
76-207	Outer Cover	Couvercle extérieur	Aussen Schutzkappe	Tapa exterior	
76-208/9/10	Screw	Vis	Schraube	Tornillo	4/-/2
76-217	Dowel	Goujon	Passtift	Pasador	2
76-233	Woodruff Key	Clavette disque	Rundkeil	Chaveta Woodruff	
76-234	Screw	Vis	Schraube	Tornillo	
76-242	Nut	Ecrou	Mutter	Tuerca	
76-3017	Bush	Douille	Büchse	Casquillo	
76-3018	Layshaft Assembled	Arbre de renvoi montée	Vorgelegewelle-Kompl	Eje secundario montado	
76-3021	Pinion Complete	Pignon complet	Zahnrad Kompl.	Piñon comp.	
76-3027	Pinion 20T	Pignon D — 20	Zahnrad Z — 20	Piñón D — 20	
76-3032	Pinion 20T	Pignon D — 20	Zahnrad Z — 20	Piñón D — 20	
76-3034	Thrust Washer	Rondelle de butée	Druckscheibe	Anillo de empuje	
76-3042	Bush	Douille	Büchse	Casquillo	
76-3047	Quadrant	Secteur	Quadrant	Sector	
76-3048	Plunger	Plongeur	Plunger	Buzo	
76-3049	Plunger Housing	Logement du plongeur	Plungergehäuse	Caja del buzo	
76-3050	Spring	Ressort	Feder	Resorte	
76-3053	Kickstarter Spindle	Arbre du kick	Kickstarterwelle	Arbol del arrancador	
76-3062	Selector Fork	Fourchette de sélecteur	Schaltgabel	Horquilla de mando de caja de velocidades.	2
76-3074	Retainer	Arrêtoir	Sicherung	Freno	
76-3095	Kickstart Sprocket	Pignon du kick	Kickstarterritzel	Piñón del arrancador	
76-3098	Spring	Ressort	Feder	Resorte	
76-3102	Chain	Chaîne	Kette	Cadena	
76-3109	Pinion 29T	Pignon D — 29	Zahnrad Z — 29	Piñón D — 29	
76-3140	Lever	Levier	Hebel	Palanca	
76-3146	Bolt	Boulon	Schraube	Tornillo	
76-3147	Screw	Vis	Schraube	Tornillo	
76-3155	Spacer Ring	Bague entretoise	Distanzring	Anillo espaciador	2
76-3167	Cam Plate	Plaque de came	Nockenplatte	Placa de leva	
76-3174	Mainshaft Assembled	Arbre primaire	Hauptwelle-Kompl	Eje primario montada	
76-3184	Nut	Ecrou	Mutter	Tuerca	
76-3201	Bush	Douille	Büchse	Casquillo	
76-3215/16	Bush	Douille	Büchse	Casquillo	
76-7513/14	Screw	Vis	Schraube	Tornillo	
90-262	Washer	Rondelle	Scheibe	Arandela	3

18

PRIMARY DRIVE 175 c.c., 250 c.c. (†250 c.c.)

Part No. No. de pièce Bestell-nr No. de parte	Description	Désignation	Beschreibung	Descripción	Per Set Par jeu Pr. Satz Juego de
2-49	Nut	Ecrou	Mutter	Tuerca	
2-1291	Sealing Washer	Joint d'étanchéité	Dichtung	Arandela de reten	
2-2395	Nut	Ecrou	Mutter	Tuerca	6
21-5202	Nut	Ecrou	Mutter	Tuerca	4
21-5359	Bolt	Boulon	Schraube	Tornillo	
36-382	Lockwasher	Rondelle frein	Sicherungsscheibe	Freno	
40-3069	Pivot Pin	Axe	Bolzen	Eje	
64-3227	"O" Ring	Bague "O"	"O" Ring	Anillo "O"	
67-3163	†Nut	Ecrou	Mutter	Tuerca	2
76-29	Peg	Ergot	Stift	Esparago	
76-39	Stud	Goujon	Stehbolzen	Esparago	2
76-43	Stud	Goujon	Stehbolzen	Esparago	
76-44	Stud	Goujon	Stehbolzen	Esparago	4
76-115	†Retaining Plate	Plaque arrêtoir	Haltescheibe	Placa retendora	
76-211	†Inner Cover	Couvercle intérieur	Innere Schutzkappe	Tapa interior	
76-215	Stub	Ergot	Stutzen	Extremo	
76-216	Bearing	Roulement	Lager	Rolamiento	2
76-217	Dowel	Goujon	Passtift	Pasador	
76-240	†Sleeve	Douille	Büchse	Casquillo	
76-241	Washer	Rondelle	Scheibe	Arandela	
76-242	Nut	Ecrou	Mutter	Tuerca	
76-243	†Outer Cover	Couvercle extérieur	Aussen Schutzkappe	Tapa exterior	
76-252	Gasket	Joint	Dichtung	Empaquetadura	4
76-253	†Driven Gear	Engrenage entrainé	Getriebenes Zahnrad	Engranaje impulsado	6
76-320	Bolt	Boulon	Schraube	Tornillo	
76-328	Washer	Rondelle	Scheibe	Arandela	
76-329	Lockwasher	Rondelle frein	Sicherungsscheibe	Freno	
76-3037	Sprocket	Pignon à chaîne	Ritzel	Piñón	
76-3038	Nut	Ecrou	Mutter	Tuerca	
76-3040	Lockwasher	Rondelle frein	Sicherungsscheibe	Freno	
76-3106	Fulcrum Pin	Goupille de butée	Drehbolzen	Espiga	
76-3107	Lever	Levier	Hebel	Palanca	
76-3151	Plug	Bouchon	Stopfen	Tapon	
76-3310	†Clutch Centre	Moyeaux d'embrayage	Kupplungsnabe	Cubo de embrague	
76-3316	Spring Plate	Plaque à ressort	Federplatte	Placa de resorte	
76-3318	Pressure Plate	Disque extérieur d'embrayage	Aussere Kupplungsdruckplatte	Disco exterior del embrague	
76-3324	Driving Plate	Disque d'entraînement	Mitnehmerplatte	Placa de manda	3
76-3325	Lockwasher	Rondelle frein	Sicherungsscheibe	Freno	
76-3326	Spring	Ressort	Feder	Resorte	3
76-3329	Nut	Ecrou	Mutter	Tuerca	3
76-3334	Push Rod	Guide de culbuteur	Stösselstange	Varilla	2
76-3343	Driven Plate	Disque entrainé	Reibscheibe	Disco accionado	3
76-3345	†Clutch Housing	Boîte d'embrayage	Kupplungsgehäuse	Caja de embrague	
76-4206	Bush	Douille	Büchse	Casquillo	
76-4207	Sleeve	Douille	Büchse	Casquillo	
76-4211	Spacer Bush	Bague entretoise	Distanzbüchse	Anillo espaciador	
76-4213	Bolt	Boulon	Schraube	Tornillo	
76-4214	Cap	Chapeau	Abdeckkappe	Tapon	
76-4215	Peg	Ergot	Stift	Esparago	
76-7509	"O" Ring	Bague "O"	"O" Ring	Anillo "O"	2
76-7510	"O" Ring	Bague "O"	"O" Ring	Anillo "O"	5
76-7513	Screw	Vis	Schraube	Tornillo	
76-7514	Screw	Vis	Schraube	Tornillo	

20

OIL PUMP & CRANKCASE BREATHER 175 c.c., 250 c.c. (†250 c.c.)

Part No. No. de pièce Bestell-nr No. de parte	Description	Designation	Beschreibung	Descripción	Per Set Par jeu Pr. Satz Juego de
2-204	Bolt	Boulon	Schraube	Tornillo	
2-525	Washer	Rondelle	Scheibe	Arandela	
2-1096	Washer	Rondelle	Scheibe	Arandela	
2-2395	Nut	Ecrou	Mutter	Tuerca	
21-5103	Nut	Ecrou	Mutter	Tuerca	3
21-5663	Bolt	Boulon	Schraube	Tornillo	4
24-5160	Nut	Ecrou	Mutter	Tuerca	2
24-8784	Lockwasher	Rondelle frein	Sicherungsscheibe	Freno	3
29-541	Lockwasher	Rondelle frein	Sicherungsscheibe	Freno	
29-925	Woodruff Key	Clavette disque	Rundkeil	Chaveta Woodruff	
36-382	Lockwasher	Rondelle frein	Sicherungsscheibe	Freno	2
40-310	Screw	Vis	Schraube	Tornillo	
42-7539	Grommet	Rondelle capuchon	Tülle	Manguera	
64-6054	Bolt	Boulon	Schraube	Tornillo	2
65-2593	Ball	Bille	Kugel	Bola	2
66-7518	Washer	Rondelle	Scheibe	Arandela	2
76-40	Cap	Chapeau	Abdeckkappe	Tapon	
76-41	†Gasket	Joint	Dichtung	Empaquetadura	
76-246	†Filter	Filtre	Filter	Filtro	
76-255	†Plunger	Plongeur	Plunger	Buzo	
76-259	†Plug	Bouchon	Stopfen	Tapon	
76-260	†Ball Seating (top)	Siège pour bille (supérieure)	Kugelsitz (Oben)	Asiento para bola (sup.)	
76-262	†Bolt	Boulon	Schraube	Tornillo	
76-263	†Lockwasher	Rondelle frein	Sicherungsscheibe	Freno	
76-264	†Ball Seating (bottom)	Siège pour bille (inférieure)	Kugelsitz (Unten)	Asiento para bola (inf.)	
76-265	†Spring	Ressort	Feder	Resorte	
76-267	†Suction Pipe	Tuyauterie d'aspiration	Saugrohr	Caño de succión	
76-288	†Pillar Bolt	Boulon de colonne	Stehbolzen	Tirante	2
76-290	†Cam Bolt	Boulon de colonne	Nockenbolzen	Tornillo para leva	
76-293	†Washer	Rondelle	Scheibe	Arandela	2
76-295	†Distance Piece	Entretoise	Distanzrohr	Distanciador	3
76-296	†Stud	Goujon	Stehbolzen	Esparrago	3
76-298	Nut	Ecrou	Mutter	Tuerca	
76-299	Washer	Rondelle	Scheibe	Arandela	2
76-302	Bolt	Boulon	Schraube	Tornillo	
76-305	†Cover	Couvercle	Schutzkappe	Tapa	
76-311	Drain Plug	Bouchon de vidange d'huile	Ablassschraube	Tapón	2
76-2514	†Screw	Vis	Schraube	Tornillo	2
76-3039	Distance Piece	Entretoise	Distanzrohr	Distanciador	
76-4121	†Bracket	Support	Verstrebung	Soporte	
76-4210	Stub	Ergot	Stutzen	Extremo	
76-4216	Lockwasher	Rondelle frein	Sicherungsscheibe	Freno	2

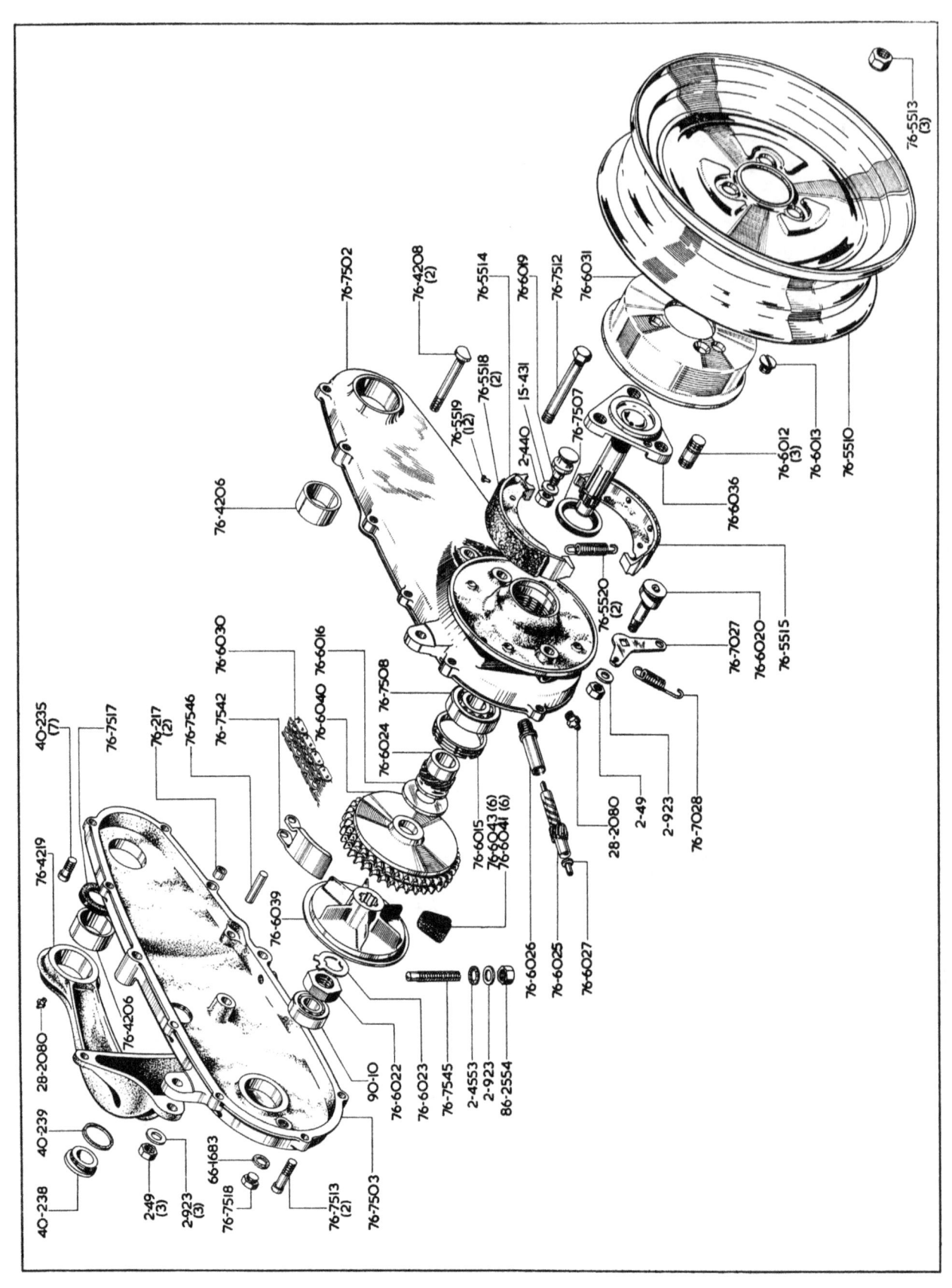

REAR WHEEL & REAR DRIVE 175 c.c., 250 c.c.

Part No. Bestell-nr No. de parte	Description	Designation	Beschreibung	Descripción	Per Set Par jeu Pr. Satz Juego de
2-49	Nut	Ecrou	Mutter	Tuerca	4
2-440	Nut	Ecrou	Mutter	Tuerca	5
2-923	Washer	Rondelle	Scheibe	Arandela	
2-4553	Sealing Washer	Joint d'étanchéité	Dichtung	Arandela de reten	2
15-431	Washer	Rondelle	Scheibe	Arandela	7
28-2080	Grease Nipple	Graisseur	Schmiernippel	Engrasador	
40-235	Screw	Vis	Schraube	Tornillo	
40-238	Cap	Chapeau	Abdeckkappe	Tapon	2
40-239	Sealing Ring	Bague d'étanchéité	Dichtring	Junta	
66-1683	Washer	Rondelle	Scheibe	Arandela	
76-217	Dowel	Goujon	Passtift	Pasador	2
76-4206	Bush	Douille	Büchse	Casquillo	
76-4208	Bolt	Boulon	Schraube	Tornillo	
76-4219	Bearing Arm	Support de palier	Lagerarm	Soporte de chumacera	
76-5510	Wheel	Roue	Rad	Rueda	
76-5513	Nut	Ecrou	Mutter	Tuerca	3
76-5514	Brake Shoe (leading)	Segment machoire de frein (avant)	Bremsbacke (Vorne)	Zapata (delantera)	
76-5515	Brake Shoe (trailing)	Segment machoire de frein (arrière)	Bremsbacke (Hintere)	Zapata (trasera)	
76-5518	Brake Lining	Garniture de frein	Bremsbelag	Guarnición	2
76-5519	Rivet	Rivet	Niete	Remache	12
76-5520	Spring	Ressort	Feder	Resorte	2
76-6012	Stud	Goujon	Stehbolzen	Esparago	2
76-6013	Screw	Vis	Schraube	Tornillo	3
76-6015	Retainer	Arrêtoir	Sicherung	Freno	
76-6016	Washer	Rondelle	Scheibe	Arandela	
76-6019	Pivot Pin	Axe	Bolzen	Eje	
76-6020	Brake Cam	Came de frein	Bremsnocke	Llave de freno	
76-6022	Nut	Ecrou	Mutter	Tuerca	
76-6023	Lockwasher	Rondelle frein	Sicherungsscheibe	Freno	
76-6024	Driving Gear	Engrenage d'entraînement	Antriebsrad	Engranaje de mando	
76-6025	Driven Gear	Engrenage entraîné	Getriebenes Zahnrad	Engranaje impulsado	
76-6026	Bush	Douille	Büchse	Casquillo	
76-6027	Thrust Pin	Support de ressort	Federstütze	Espiga de empuje	
76-6030	Chain	Chaîne	Kette	Cadena	
76-6031	Brake Drum	Tambour de frein	Bremstrommel	Tambor del freno	
76-6036	Shaft	Arbre	Welle	Arból	
76-6039	Cush Drive Spider	Brassure d'entraînement	Antriebsstern	Estrella de mando	
76-6040	Chain Wheel	Pignon de chaîne	Kettenrad	Piñón de cadena	
76-6041	Rubber Buffer	Caoutchouc butée	Gummipuffer	Tope de goma	6
76-6043	Rubber Buffer	Caoutchouc butée	Gummipuffer	Tope de goma	6
76-7027	Brake Cam Lever	Levier de came de frein	Bremsnockenhebel	Palanca de freno	
76-7028	Spring	Ressort	Feder	Resorte	
76-7502	Chain Case (inner)	Carter de chaîne (intérieur)	Kettenkasten (Innere)	Guardacadena (int.)	
76-7503	Chain Case (outer)	Carter de chaîne (extérieur)	Kettenkasten (Aussen)	Guardacadena (ext.)	
76-7507	Oil Seal	Joint d'huile	Simmering	Reten de aceite	
76-7508	Bearing	Roulement	Lager	Rolamiento	
76-7512	Bolt	Boulon	Schraube	Tornillo	2
76-7513	Screw	Vis	Schraube	Tornillo	
76-7517	Oil Seal	Joint d'huile	Simmering	Reten de aceite	
76-7518	Plug	Bouchon	Stopfen	Tapon	
76-7542	Chain Tensioner	Tendeur de chaîne	Ketten-Nachstelivorrichtung	Tensor de cadena	
76-7545	Adjuster Screw	Vis de réglage	Einstellschraube	Tornillo de ajuste	
76-7546	Pivot Pin	Axe	Bolzen	Eje	
86-2554	Nut	Ecrou	Mutter	Tuerca	
90-10	Bearing	Roulement	Lager	Rolamiento	

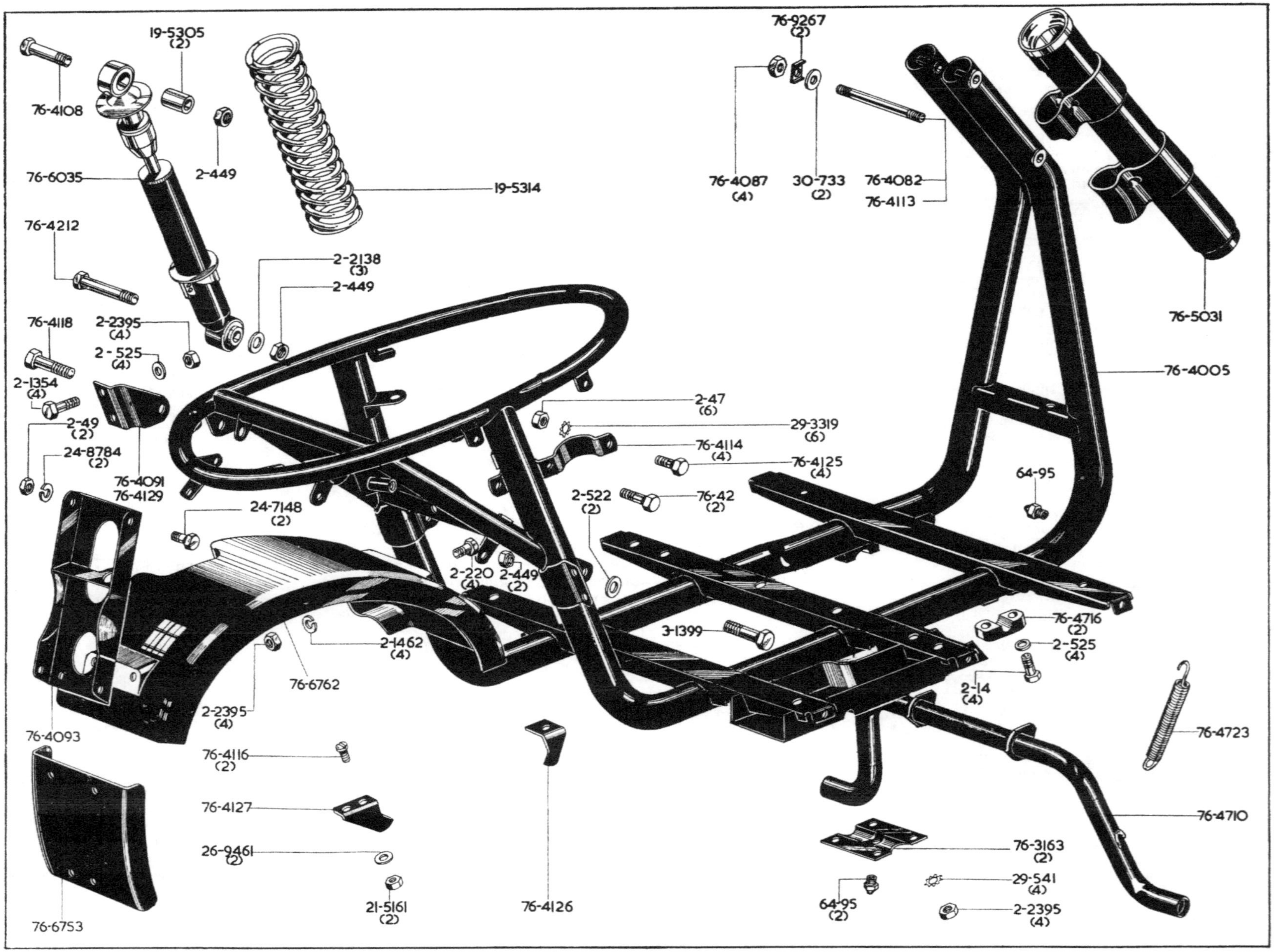
19-5305 (2)
76-4108
76-6035
2-449
19-5314
76-4212
2-2138 (3)
2-449
76-4118
2-2395 (4)
2-525 (4)
2-1354 (4)
2-49 (2)
24-8784 (2)
76-4091
76-4129
24-7148 (2)
76-9267 (2)
76-4087 (4)
30-733 (2)
76-4082
76-4113
76-5031
76-4005
2-47 (6)
29-3319 (6)
76-4114 (4)
76-4125 (4)
64-95
2-522 (2)
76-42 (2)
2-220 (4)
2-449 (2)
76-4716 (2)
2-525 (4)
3-1399
2-1462 (4)
2-14 (4)
76-6762
2-2395 (4)
76-4093
76-4723
76-4116 (2)
76-4127
76-4710
76-3163 (2)
26-9461 (2)
29-541 (4)
21-5161 (2)
76-4126
64-95 (2)
2-2395 (4)
76-6753

FRAME & SHOCK ABSORBER 175 c.c., 250 c.c.

Part No. / No. de pièce / Bestell-nr / No. de parte	Description	Designation	Beschreibung	Descripción	Per Set / Par jeu / Pr. Satz / Juego de
1-6033	Washer	Rondelle	Scheibe	Arandela	4
2-14	Bolt	Boulon	Schraube	Tornillo	4
2-47	Nut	Ecrou	Mutter	Tuerca	6
2-49	Nut	Ecrou	Mutter	Tuerca	2
2-220	Bolt	Boulon	Schraube	Tornillo	4
2-449	Nut	Ecrou	Mutter	Tuerca	4
2-522	Washer	Rondelle	Scheibe	Arandela	2
2-525	Washer	Rondelle	Scheibe	Arandela	8
2-1354	Bolt	Boulon	Schraube	Tornillo	4
2-1462	Lockwasher	Rondelle frein	Sicherungsscheibe	Freno	4
2-2138	Washer	Rondelle	Scheibe	Arandela	3
2-2395	Nut	Ecrou	Mutter	Tuerca	12
3-1399	Bolt	Boulon	Schraube	Tornillo	
19-5305	Bush	Douille	Büchse	Casquillo	2
19-5314	Spring	Ressort	Feder	Resorte	2
21-5161	Nut	Ecrou	Mutter	Tuerca	2
24-7148	Bolt	Boulon	Schraube	Tornillo	2
26-9461	Washer	Rondelle frein	Sicherungsscheibe	Freno	2
29-3319	Lockwasher	Rondelle frein	Sicherungsscheibe	Arandela	6
30-733	Washer	Rondelle	Scheibe	Arandela	2
64-95	Grease Nipple	Graisseur	Schmiernippel	Engrasador	3
76-42	Bolt	Boulon	Schraube	Tornillo	2
76-3163	Plate	Plaque	Scheibe	Placa	2
76-4005	Frame	Cadre	Rahmen	Cuadro	
76-4082	Stud	Goujon	Stehbolzen	Esparago	
76-4087	Nut	Ecrou	Mutter	Tuerca	
76-4091	Clip	Bride	Klammer	Grapa	4
76-4093	Bracket	Support	Verstrebung	Soporte	
76-4108	Bolt	Boulon	Schraube	Tornillo	
76-4113	Stud	Goujon	Stehbolzen	Esparago	
76-4114	Bracket	Support	Verstrebung	Soporte	
76-4116	Screw	Vis	Schraube	Tornillo	
76-4118	Bolt	Boulon	Schraube	Tornillo	
76-4125	Bolt	Boulon	Schraube	Tornillo	
76-4126	Bracket	Support	Verstrebung	Soporte	
76-4127	Bracket	Support	Verstrebung	Soporte	
76-4129	Clip	Bride	Klammer	Grapa	
76-4212	Bolt	Boulon	Schraube	Tornillo	
76-4710	Centre Stand	Béquille centrale	Mittelständer	Muleta	
76-4716	Pivot Block	Pivot de béquille	Ständerzapfen	Pivote para muleta	
76-4723	Spring	Ressort	Feder	Resorte	2
76-5031	Head Tube Complete	Tube de direction complet	Lenkerrohr Kompl.	Tubo para manillar completa	
76-6035	Shock Absorber	Amortisseur	Stossdämpfer	Amortiguador	
76-6753	Mudguard Extension	Prolongement de garde-boue	Verlangerungsstuck für Kotflügel	Extensión para guardabarro	
76-6762	Rear Guard	Garde-boue de roue ar	Hinterradschutzblech	Guardabarro tras.	
76-9267	Clip	Bride	Klammer	Grapa	2

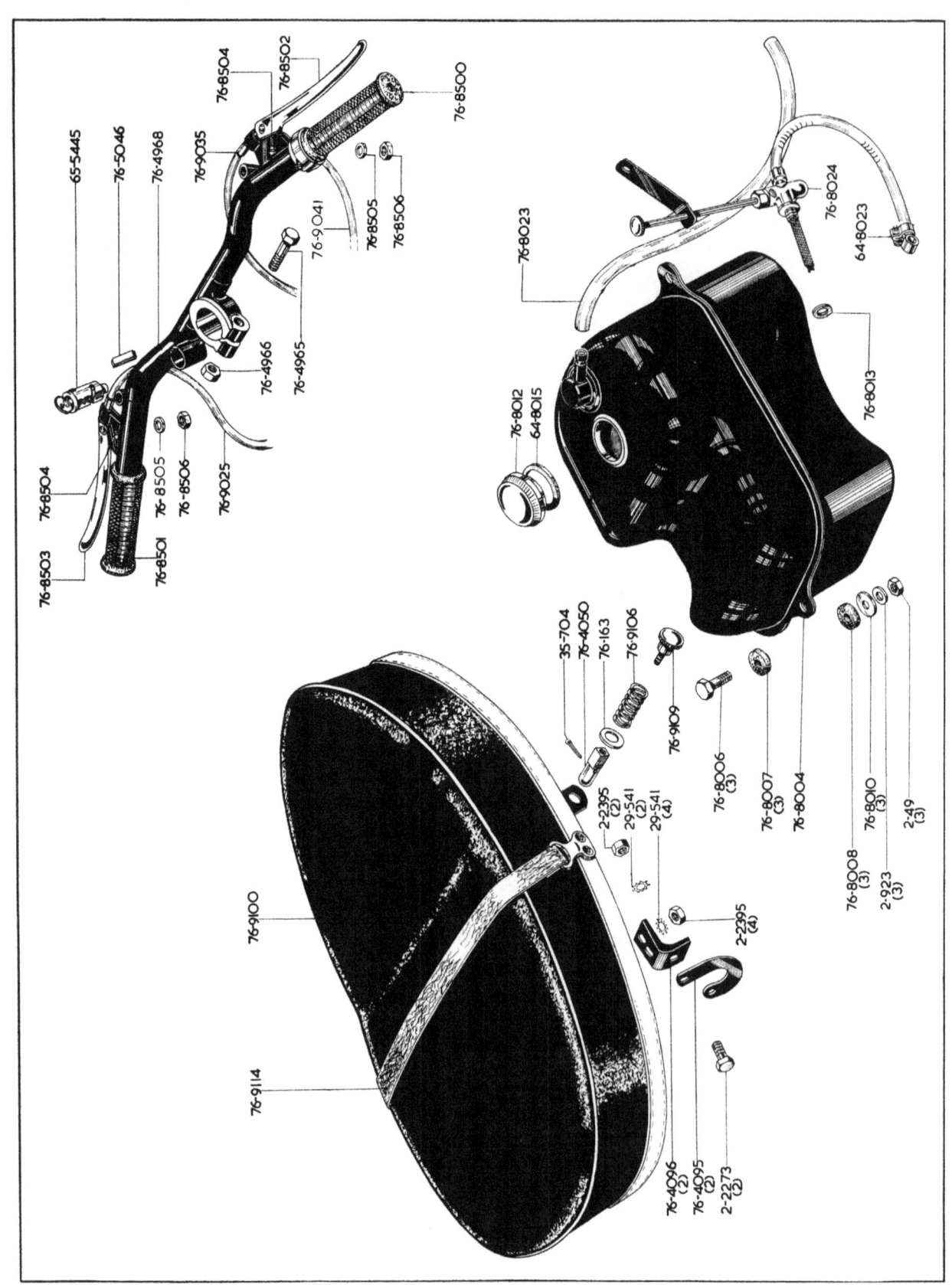

PETROL TANK & HANDLEBAR AND CONTROLS & DUAL SEAT 175 c.c., 250 c.c.

Part No. No. de pièce Bestell-nr No. de parte	Description	Designation	Beschreibung	Descripción	Per Set Par jeu Pr. Satz Juego de
2-49	Nut	Ecrou	Mutter	Tuerca	2
2-923	Washer	Rondelle	Scheibe	Arandela	3
2-2273	Bolt	Boulon	Schraube	Tornillo	3
2-2395	Nut	Ecrou	Mutter	Tuerca	6
29-541	Lockwasher	Rondelle frein	Sicherungsscheibe	Freno	6
35-704	Split Pin	Goupille fendue	Splint	Chaveta hendida	
64-8013	Sealing Washer	Joint d'étanchéité	Dichtung	Arandela de reten	
64-8015	Sealing Washer	Joint d'étanchéité	Dichtung	Arandela de reten	
64-8023	Clip	Bride	Klammer	Grapa	
65-5445	Lock and Key	Serrure et clef	Schloss mit Schlüssel	Cerradura y llave	
76-163	Washer	Rondelle	Scheibe	Arandela	
76-4050	Plunger	Plongeur	Plunger	Buzo	
76-4095	Hinge Pivot	Gond de porte	Turangel	Gozne	2
76-4096	Bracket	Support	Verstrebung	Soporte	2
76-4965	Bolt	Boulon	Schraube	Tornillo	
76-4966	Nut	Ecrou	Mutter	Tuerca	
76-4968	Handlebar	Guidon	Lenker	Manillar	
76-5046	Key	Clavette	Keil	Chaveta	
76-8004	Petrol Tank	Réservoir d'essence	Benzintank	Deposito de combustible	
76-8006	Bolt	Boulon	Schraube	Tornillo	3
76-8007	Rubber Pad (top)	Tampon caoutchouc (dessus)	Gummiauflage (Oben)	Cojin de goma (sup.)	3
76-8008	Rubber Pad (bottom)	Tampon caoutchouc (inférieure)	Gummiauflage (Unten)	Cojin de goma (inf.)	3
76-8010	Washer	Rondelle	Scheibe	Arandela	3
76-8012	Filler Cap	Bouchon de remplissage	Verschlusskappe	Tapa	
76-8013	Sealing Washer	Joint d'étanchéité	Dichtung	Arandela de reten	
76-8023	Breather Pipe	Tuyau d'aspiration	Schnüfferohr	Tubo del respirador	
76-8024	Petrol Pipe and Tap	Tuyauterie d'essence et robinet	Benzinleitung und Hahn	Caño de benzina con grifo	
76-8500	Throttle Twist Grip	Poignée tournante de commande des gaz.	Gasdrehgriff	Puño girante de acelerador	
76-8501	Rubber Grip	Poignée en caoutchouc	Gummigriff	Puño fijo de goma	
76-8502	Brake Lever	Levier de frein	Bremshebel	Palanca de freno	
76-8503	Clutch Lever	Levier d'embrayage	Kupplungshebel	Palanca del embrague	
76-8504	Fulcrum Pin	Goupille de butée	Drehbolzen	Espiga	2
76-8505	Washer	Rondelle	Scheibe	Arandela	2
76-8506	Nut	Ecrou	Mutter	Tuerca	2
76-9025	Clutch Cable	Câble de commande de l'embrayage	Kupplungskabel	Cable Bowden para embrague	
76-9035	Front Brake Cable	Câble de commande du frein avant	Vorderradbremskabel	Cable Bowden para acelerador	
76-9041	Throttle Cable	Commande des gaz	Gaszug	Cable Bowden para acelerador	
76-9100	Dual Seat	Sellie Double	Doppelsitz	Asiento doble	
76-9106	Spring	Ressort	Feder	Resorte	
76-9109	Button	Tirette	Knopf	Tirador	
76-9114	Lifting Handle	Poignée de levage	Griff zum Aufbocken	Puño elevadora	

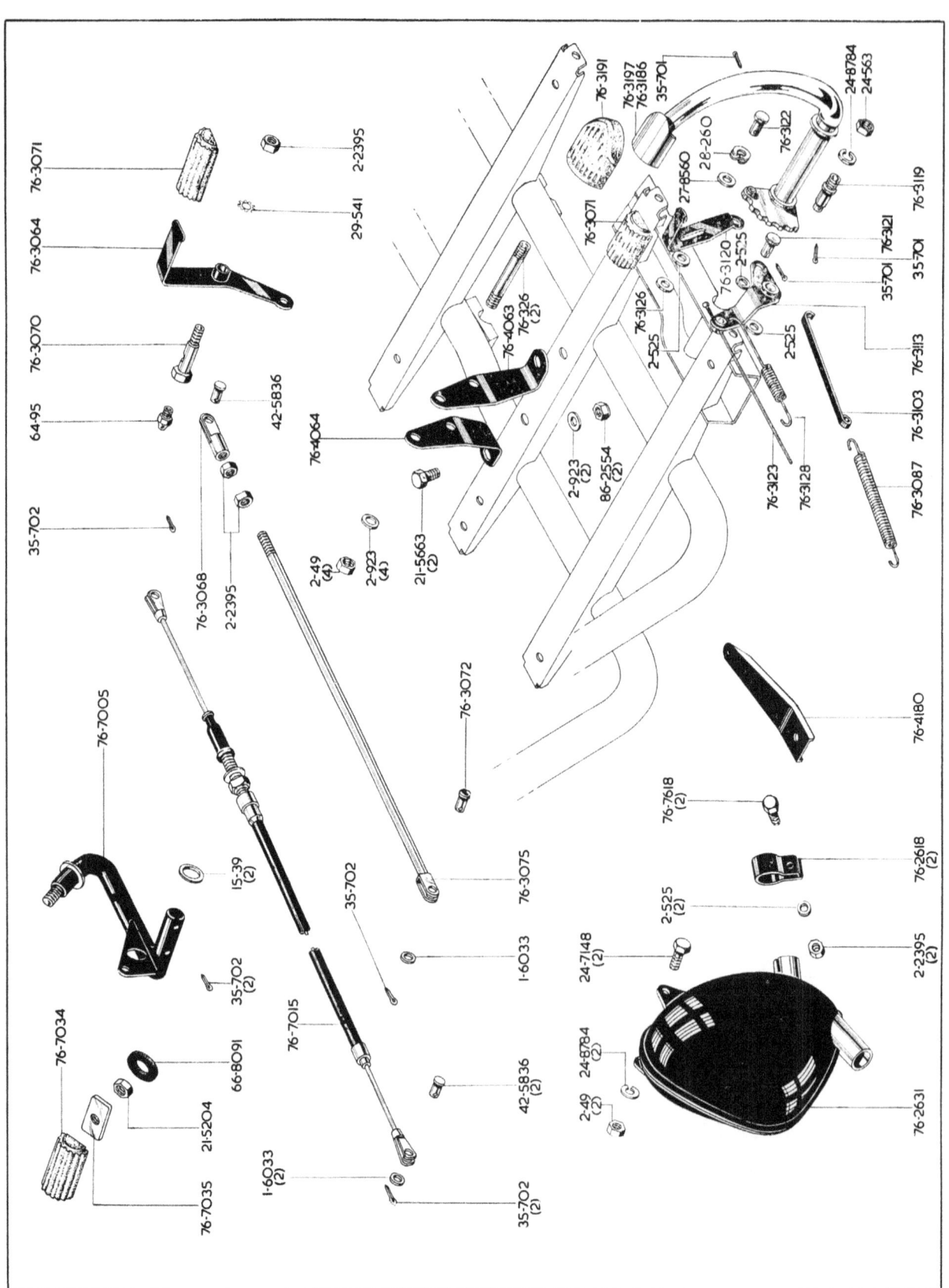

FOOT CONTROLS & ENGINE PLATES & SILENCER 175 c.c., 250 c.c. (*175 c.c. †250 c.c.)

Part No. / No. de pièce / Bestell-nr / No. de parte	Description	Designation	Beschreibung	Descripción	Per Set / Par jeu / Pr. Satz / Juego de
1-6033	Washer	Rondelle	Scheibe	Arandela	3
2-49	Nut	Ecrou	Mutter	Tuerca	6
2-525	Washer	Rondelle	Scheibe	Arandela	5
2-923	Washer	Rondelle	Scheibe	Arandela	6
2-2395	Nut	Ecrou	Mutter	Tuerca	5
15-39	Washer	Rondelle	Scheibe	Arandela	2
21-5204	Nut	Ecrou	Mutter	Tuerca	
21-5663	Bolt	Boulon	Schraube	Tornillo	2
24-563	Nut	Ecrou	Mutter	Tuerca	
24-7148	Bolt	Boulon	Schraube	Tornillo	2
24-8784	Lockwasher	Rondelle frein	Sicherungsscheibe	Freno	2
27-8560	Washer	Rondelle	Scheibe	Arandela	3
28-260	Lockwasher	Rondelle frein	Sicherungsscheibe	Freno	
29-541	Lockwasher	Rondelle frein	Sicherungsscheibe	Freno	
35-701	Split Pin	Goupille fendue	Splint	Chaveta hendida	3
35-702	Split Pin	Goupille fendue	Splint	Chaveta hendida	6
42-5336	Pivot Pin	Pivot	Drehzapfen	Eje	3
64-95	Grease Nipple	Graisseur	Schmiernippel	Engrasador	
66-8091	Rubber Buffer	Butée caoutchouc	Gummipuffer	Tope de goma	2
76-326	Stud	Goujon	Stehbolzen	Espárago	1
76-2618	Clip	Bride	Klammer	Grapa	2
76-2631	Silencer	Silencieux	Schalldämpfer	Silenciador	
76-3064	Lever	Levier	Hebel	Palanca	
76-3068	Coupling	Accouplement	Kuppeln	Acoplamiento	
76-3070	Pivot Pin	Boulon	Drehbolzen	Tornillo	2
76-3071	Rubber Pad	Tampon caoutchouc	Gummiauflage	Cojín de goma	
76-3072	Pivot Pin	Pivot	Drehzapfen	Eje	
76-3075	Rod	Tige	Stange	Varilla	
76-3087	Spring	Ressort	Feder	Resorte	
76-3103	Link	Maillon	Glied	Varilla	
76-3113	Lever	Levier	Hebel	Palanca	
76-3119	Spindle	Arbre	Welle	Arbol	
76-3120	Neutral Pedal	Pédale neutre	Nullfusshebel	Pedal neutro	
76-3121	Pivot Pin	Pivot	Drehzapfen	Eje	
76-3122	Pivot Pin	Pivot	Drehzapfen	Eje	
76-3123	Link Rod Complete	Tige d'accouplement (complet)	Kupplungstange (Kompl)	Varilla de acoplamiento (completa)	
76-3126	Distance Piece	Entretoise	Distanzrohr	Distanciador	
76-3128	Spring	Ressort	Feder	Resorte	
76-3186	*Starter Pedal	Pédale de kick	Starthebel	Arancador	
76-3191	Rubber Pad	Tampon caoutchouc	Gummiauflage	Cojín de goma	
76-3197	†Starter Pedal	Pédale de kick	Starthebel	Arancador	
76-4063	Engine Plate (R/H)	Plaque d'appui pour moteur (droite)	Motorabstützblech (Rechts)	Placa de apoyo del motor (derecho)	
76-4064	Engine Plate (L/H)	Plaque d'appui pour moteur (gauche).	Motorabstützblech (Links)	Placa de apoyo del motor (izq.)	
76-4180	*Bracket	Support	Verstrebung	Soporte	
76-7005	Brake Pedal	Pédale de frein	Fussbremshebel	Pedal de freno	
76-7015	Rear Brake Cable	Câble de commande du frein (arrière).	Seilzug für Hinterradbremse	Cable Bowden para freno trasera	
76-7034	Rubber Pad	Tampon caoutchouc	Gummiauflage	Cojín de goma	
76-7035	Pedal Pad	Tampon	Auflage	Cojín	
76-7618	Bolt	Boulon	Schraube	Tornillo	2
86-2554	Nut	Ecrou	Mutter	Tuerca	2

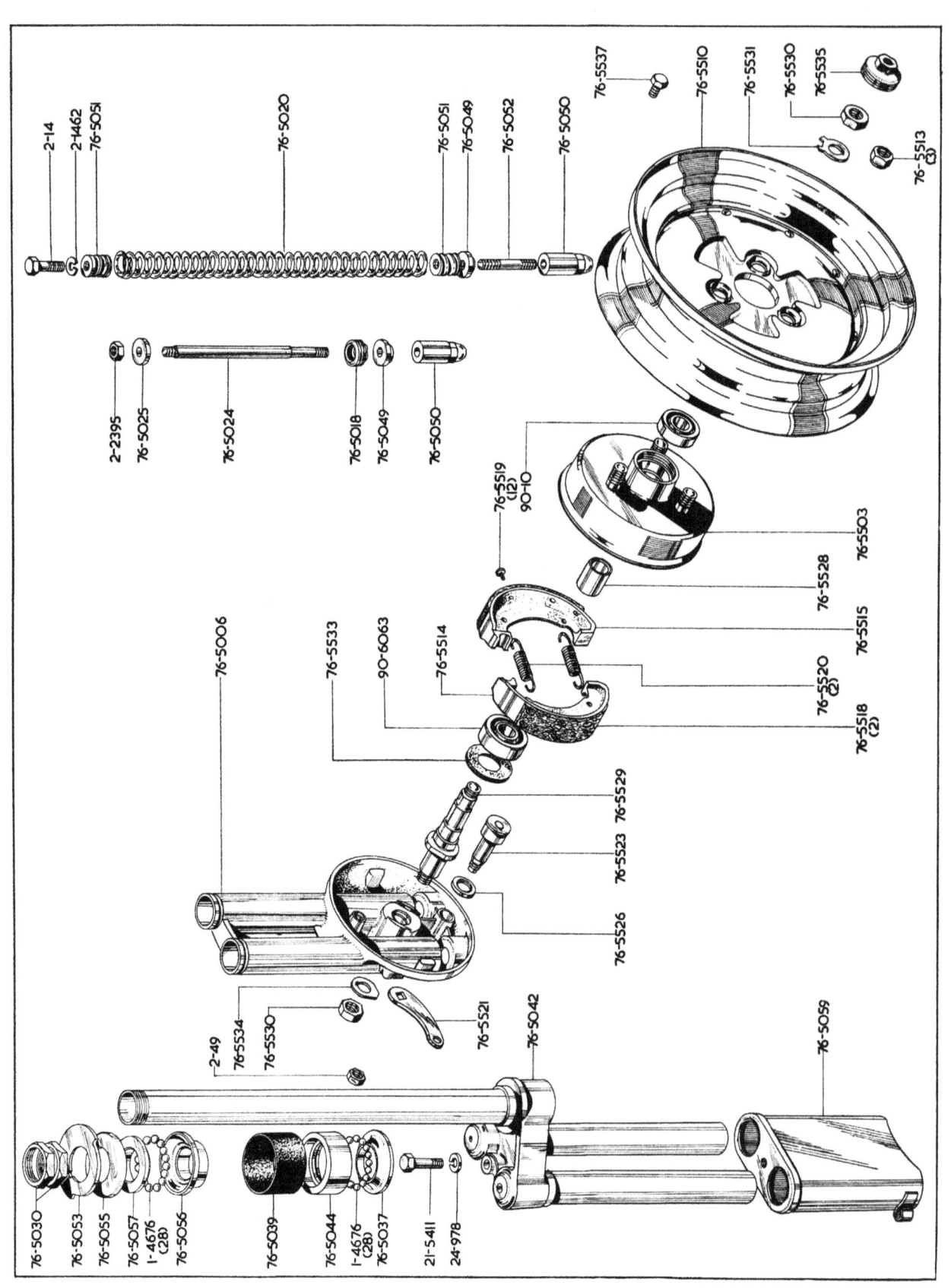

FRONT FORK & FRONT WHEEL 175 c.c., 250 c.c.

Part No. No. de pièce Bestell-nr No. de parte	Description	Designation	Beschreibung	Descripción	Per Set Par jeu Pr. Satz Juego de
1-4676	Ball	Bille	Kugel	Bola	56
2-14	Bolt	Boulon	Schraube	Tornillo	
2-49	Nut	Ecrou	Mutter	Tuerca	
2-1462	Washer	Rondelle	Scheibe	Arandela	
2-2395	Nut	Ecrou	Mutter	Tuerca	
21-5411	Bolt	Boulon	Schraube	Tornillo	
24-978	Lockwasher	Rondelle frein	Sicherungsscheibe	Freno	
76-5006	Lower Member	Partie inférieure	Unterglied	Parte inferior	
76-5018	Disc Valve	Soupape à disque	Scheibenventil	Valvula de disco	
76-5020	Spring	Ressort	Feder	Resorte	
76-5024	Rod	Tige	Stange	Varilla	
76-5025	Washer	Rondelle	Scheibe	Arandela	
76-5030	Nut	Ecrou	Mutter	Tuerca	
76-5037	Cone	Cone	Konus	Cona	
76-5039	Rubber Sleeve	Caoutchouc douille	Gummimuffe	Manguita de goma	
76-5042	Front Fork	Fourche av	Vordergabel	Horquilla delantera	
76-5044	Cup	Cuvette	Schale	Copa	
76-5049	Washer	Rondelle	Scheibe	Arandela	2
76-5050	Domed Nut	Ecrou borgne	Hutmutter	Tuerca abovedada	2
76-5051	Spring Anchorage	Ancrage de ressort	Federanker	Sujeción del resorte	2
76-5052	Stud	Goujon	Stehbolzen	Esparago	
76-5053	Stop Plate	Plaque d'arrêt	Anschlag	Placa limitadora	
76-5055	Cover	Couvercle	Schutzkappe	Tapa	
76-5056	Cup (top)	Cuvette (supérieure)	Schale (Oben)	Copa (sup.)	
76-5057	Cone (top)	Cone (supérieure)	Konus (Oben)	Cona (sup.)	
76-5059	Shroud	Fourreau	Hülse	Manguito	
76-5503	Brake Drum Complete	Tambour de frein complet	Bremstrommel Kompl.	Tambar del freno completa	
76-5510	Wheel	Roue	Rad	Rueda	
76-5513	Nut	Ecrou	Mutter	Tuerca	3
76-5514	Brake Shoe (leading)	Frein (avant)	Bremsbacke (Vorne)	Zapata (delantera)	2
76-5515	Brake Shoe (trailing)	Frein (arrière)	Bremsbacke (Hintere)	Zapata (trasera)	1
76-5518	Brake Lining	Garniture de frein	Bremsbelag	Guarnición	2
76-5519	Rivet	Rivet	Niet	Remache	12
76-5520	Spring	Ressort	Feder	Resorte	2
76-5521	Brake Cam Lever	Levier de came de frein	Bremsnockenghebel	Palanca de freno	
76-5523	Brake Cam	Came de frein	Bremsnocke	Llave de freno	
76-5526	Distance Piece	Entretoise	Distanzrohr	Distanciador	
76-5528	Distance Piece	Entretoise	Distanzrohr	Distanciador	
76-5529	Spindle	Arbre	Welle	Arbol	
76-5530	Nut	Ecrou	Mutter	Tuerca	2
76-5531	Lockwasher	Rondelle frein	Sicherungsscheibe	Freno	
76-5533	Oil Seal	Joint d'huile	Simmering	Reten de aceite	
76-5534	Washer	Rondelle	Scheibe	Arandela	
76-5535	Cap	Chapeau	Abdeckkappe	Tapon	
76-5537	Bolt	Boulon	Schraube	Tornillo	
90-10	Bearing	Roulement	Lager	Rolamiento	
90-6063	Bearing	Roulement	Lager	Rolamiento	

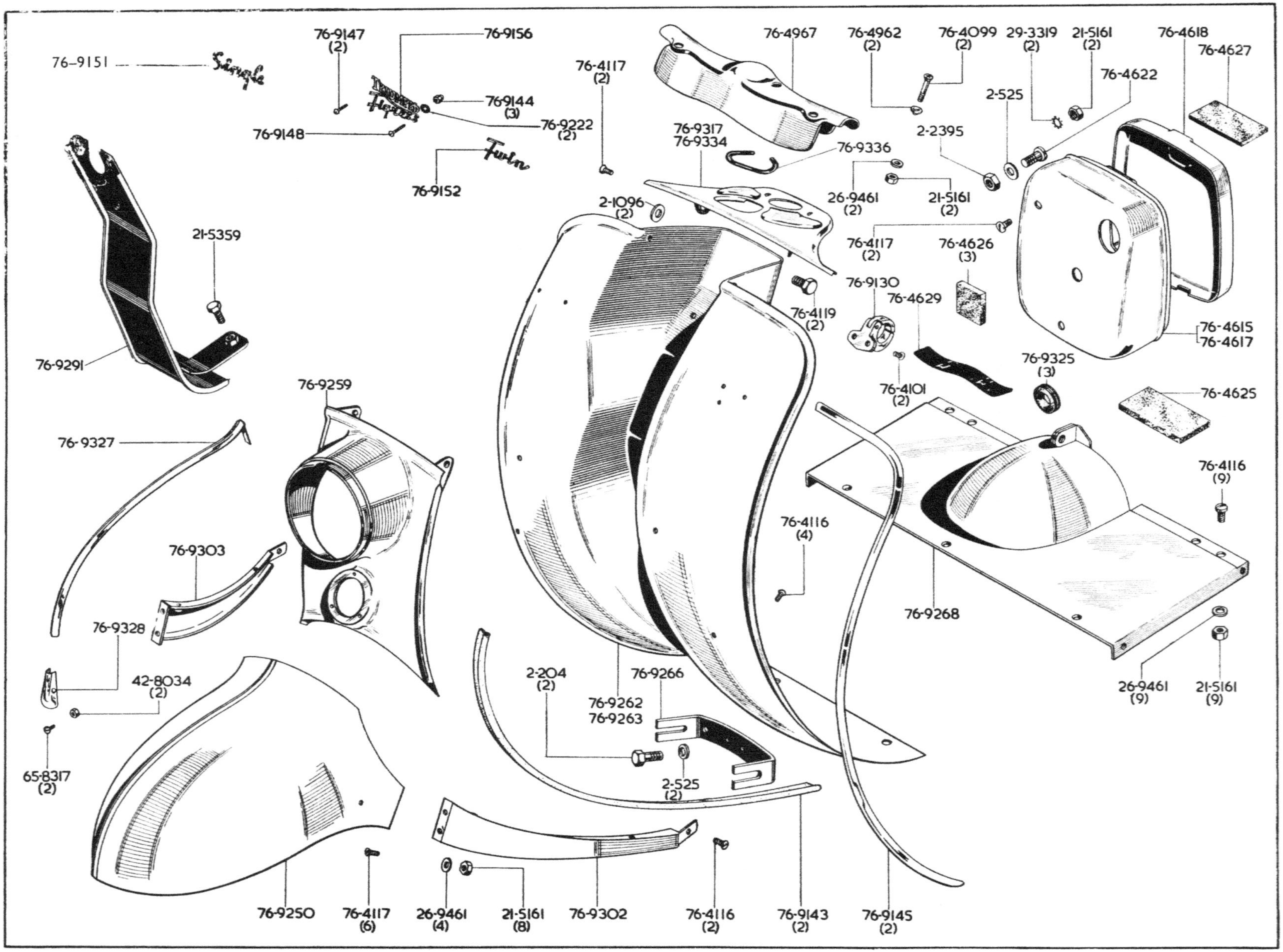
76-9151
Single
76-9147
(2)
76-9156
76-9144
(3)
76-9222
(2)
76-9148
Twin
76-9152
76-4117
(2)
76-4967
76-4962
(2)
76-4099
(2)
29-3319
(2)
21-5161
(2)
76-4618
76-4627
76-4622
2-525
2-2395
76-9317
76-9334
76-9336
26-9461
(2)
21-5161
(2)
2-1096
(2)
76-4117
(2)
76-4626
(3)
21-5359
76-9130
76-4629
76-4119
(2)
76-4615
76-4617
76-9325
(3)
76-9291
76-4101
(2)
76-9259
76-4625
76-9327
76-4116
(9)
76-4116
(4)
76-9303
76-9268
76-9328
42-8034
(2)
2-204
(2)
76-9266
76-9262
76-9263
26-9461
(9)
21-5161
(9)
65-8317
(2)
2-525
(2)
76-9250
76-4117
(6)
26-9461
(4)
21-5161
(8)
76-9302
76-4116
(2)
76-9143
(2)
76-9145
(2)

LEGSHIELD & FRONT GUARD & BATTERY BOX 175 c.c., 250 c.c. (†175 c.c. *250 c.c.)

Part No. / No. de pièce / Bestell-nr / No. de parte	Description	Designation	Beschreibung	Descripción	Per Set / Par jeu / Pr. Satz / Juego de
2-204	Bolt	Boulon	Schraube	Tornillo	2
2-525	Washer	Rondelle	Scheibe	Arandela	3
2-1096	Washer	Rondelle	Scheibe	Arandela	2
2-2395	Nut	Ecrou	Mutter	Tuerca	
21-5161	Nut	Ecrou	Mutter	Tuerca	21
21-5359	Bolt	Boulon	Schraube	Tornillo	
26-9461	Washer	Rondelle	Scheibe	Arandela	11
29-3319	Lockwasher	Rondelle frein	Sicherungsscheibe	Freno	2
42-8034	Nut	Ecrou	Mutter	Tuerca	2
65-8317	Screw	Vis	Schraube	Tornillo	2
76-4099	Screw	Vis	Schraube	Tornillo	2
76-4101	Screw	Vis	Schraube	Tornillo	2
76-4116	Screw	Vis	Schraube	Tornillo	15
76-4117	Screw	Vis	Schraube	Tornillo	10
76-4119	Bolt	Boulon	Schraube	Tornillo	2
76-4615	Battery Box (L/H) 12 v. — 6 v.	Boîte à batterie (gauche) 12 v. — 6 v.	Batteriekasten (Links) 12 v. — 6 v.	Caja de batería (izq.) 12 v. — 6 v.	
76-4617	Battery Box (R/H) 12 v.	Boîte à batterie (droite) 12 v.	Batteriekasten (Rechts) 12 v.	Caja de batería (der.) 12 v	
76-4618	Battery Lid	Couvercle de batterie	Batterie Deckel	Tapa de batería	
76-4622	Screw	Vis	Schraube	Tornillo	3
76-4625	Rubber Pad	Tampon caoutchouc	Gummiauflage	Cojín de goma	
76-4626	Rubber Pad	Tampon caoutchouc	Gummiauflage	Cojín de goma	
76-4627	Rubber Pad	Tampon caoutchouc	Gummiauflage	Cojín de goma	
76-4629	Rubber Pad	Tampon caoutchouc	Gummiauflage	Cojín de goma	
76-4962	Washer	Rondelle	Scheibe	Arandela	2
76-4967	Handlebar Cover	Capotage de guidon	Abdeckkappe für Lenker	Cubremanillar	
76-9130	Hook for Handbag	Crochet porte sac à main	Haken für Handtasche	Gancho para bolsa de mano	
76-9144	Nut	Ecrou	Mutter	Tuerca	3
76-9143	Rubber Moulding	Moulé caoutchouc	Profilgummi	Profil de goma	2
76-9145	Beading	Moulure	Zierleiste	Moldura	2
76-9147	Screw	Vis	Schraube	Tornillo	2
76-9148	Screw	Vis	Schraube	Tornillo	2
76-9151	Name Plate "Single"	Ecusson "Single"	Typenzeichen "Single"	Placa-marca "Single"	
76-9152	Name Plate "Twin"	Ecusson "Twin"	Typenzeichen "Twin"	Placa-marca "Twin"	
76-9156	Name Plate "Triumph Tigress"	Ecusson "Triumph Tigress"	Typenzeichen "Triumph Tigress"	Placa-marca "Triumph Tigress"	
76-9222	Washer	Rondelle	Scheibe	Arandela	2
76-9250	Front Guard	Garde-boue de roue av	Vorderradschutzblech	Guardabarro del.	
76-9259	Headlamp Cowling	Capotage de phare	Abdeckkappe für Scheinwerfer	Cubrefarol	
76-9262	Legshield (12 v.)	Protege-jambe (12 v.)	Beinschutz (12 v.)	Guardapiernas (12 v.)	
76-9263	Legshield (6 v.)	Protege-jambe (6 v.)	Beinschutz (6 v.)	Guardapiernas (6 v.)	
76-9268	Floor Panel	Panneau de plancher	Bodenplatte	Panel de piso	
76-9291	Splash Panel	Pare-gouttes	Schutzblech	Salpicadero	
76-9302	Mudguard Extension Piece (L/H)	Prolongement de garde-boue (gauche).	Verlangerungsstuck für Kotflügel (Links).	Extensión para guardabarro (izq.)	
76-9303	Mudguard Extension Piece (R/H)	Prolongement de garde-boue (droite).	Verlangerungsstuck für Kotflügel (Rechts).	Extensión para guardabarro (der.)	
76-9317	†Instrument Panel	Tableau de bord	Armaturebrett	Tablero de instrumentos	
76-9325	Grommet	Rondelle capuchon	Tülle	Manguera	3
76-9327	Beading	Moulure	Zierleiste	Moldura	
76-9334	*Instrument Panel	Tableau de bord	Armaturebrett	Tablero de instrumentos	
76-9336	Rubber Moulding	Moulé caoutchouc	Profilgummi	Profil de goma	

33

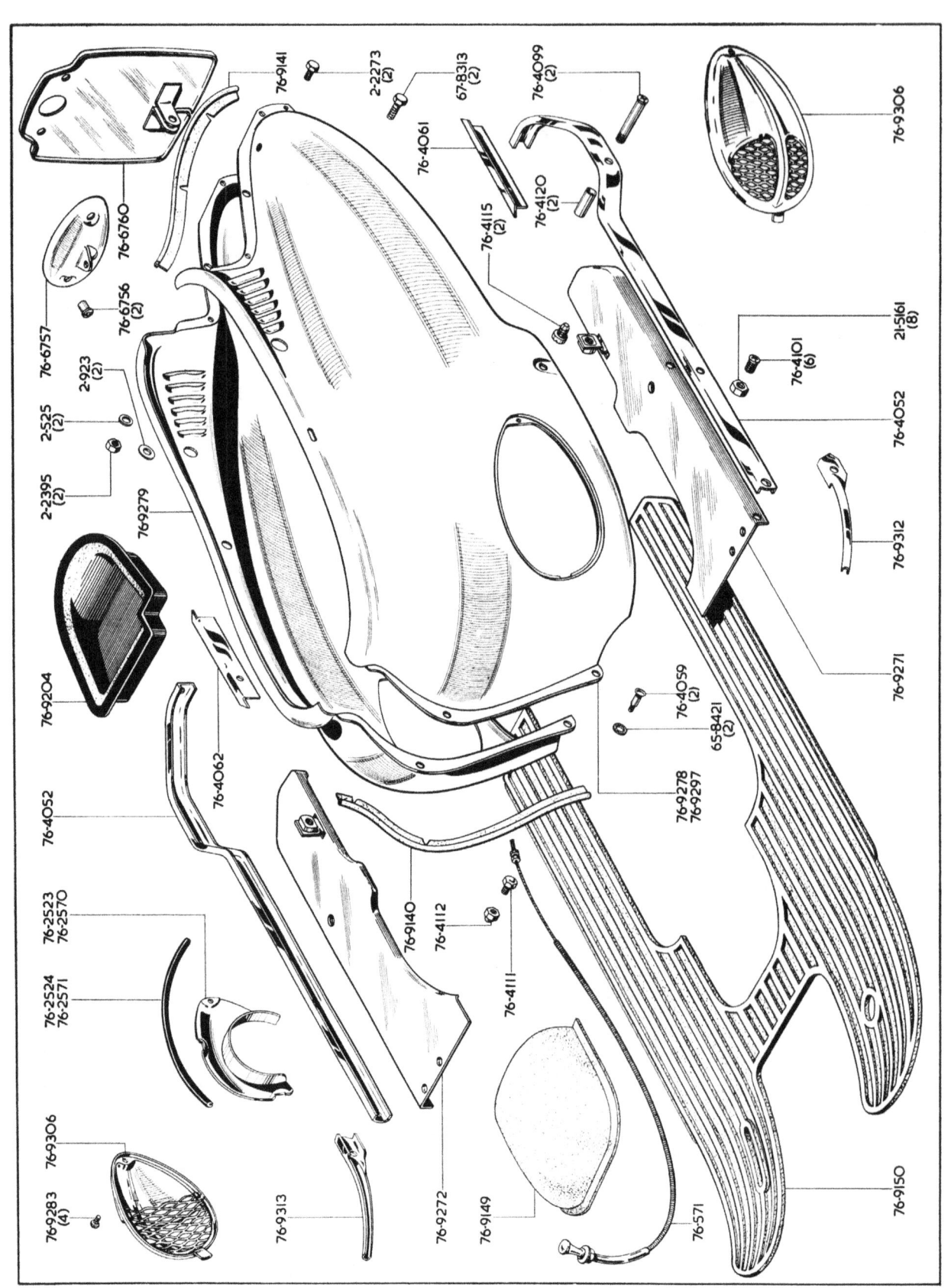

SIDE PANELS & FOOTBOARDS & NUMBER PLATE 175 c.c., 250 c.c. (†175 c.c. *250 c.c.)

Part No. / No. de pièce / Bestell-nr / No. de parte	Description	Designation	Beschreibung	Descripción	Per Set / Par jeu / Pr. Satz / Juego de
2-525	Washer	Rondelle	Scheibe	Arandela	2
2-923	Washer	Rondelle	Scheibe	Arandela	2
2-2273	Bolt	Boulon	Schraube	Tornillo	2
2-2395	Nut	Ecrou	Mutter	Tuerca	2
21-5161	Nut	Ecrou	Mutter	Tuerca	8
65-8421	Washer	Rondelle	Scheibe	Arandela	2
67-8313	Bolt	Boulon	Schraube	Tornillo	2
76-571	*Choke Control Cable	Cable de commande l'etrangleur	Drosselseilzug	Cable del estrangulador de aire	
76-2523	†Cover	Couvercle	Schutzkappe	Tapa	
76-2524	†Rubber Moulding	Moulé caoutchouc	Profilgummi	Modlura de goma	
76-2570	Cover	Couvercle	Schutzkappe	Tapa	
76-2571	Rubber Moulding	Moulé caoutchouc	Profilgummi	Moldura de goma	
76-4052	Beading	Moulure	Zierleiste	Moldura	2
76-4059	Screw	Vis	Schraube	Tornillo	2
76-4061	Edging Strip (L/H)	Encadrement profilé (gauche)	Profileinfassung (Links)	Cinta de arista (izq.)	
76-4062	Edging Strip (R/H)	Encadrement profilé (droite)	Profileinfassung (Rechts)	Cinta de arista (der.)	
76-4099	Screw	Vis	Schraube	Tornillo	2
76-4101	Screw	Vis	Schraube	Tornillo	6
76-4111	Bolt	Boulon	Schraube	Tornillo	
76-4112	Nut	Ecrou	Mutter	Tuerca	
76-4115	Screw	Vis	Schraube	Tornillo	2
76-4120	Spacer Bush	Bague entretoise	Distanzbüchse	Anillo espaciador	2
76-6756	Screw	Vis	Schraube	Tornillo	2
76-6757	Cover	Couvercle	Schutzkappe	Tapa	
76-6760	Number Plate	Plaque de police	Nummernschild	Chapa de patente	
76-9140	Rubber Moulding	Moulé caoutchouc	Profilgummi	Moldura de goma	
76-9141	Rubber Moulding	Moulé caoutchouc	Profilgummi	Moldura de goma	
76-9149	Rubber Moulding	Moulé caoutchouc	Profilgummi	Moldura de goma	
76-9150	Rubber Mat	Recouvrement caoutchouc	Gummibelag	Estera de goma	
76-9204	Tool Tray (rubber)	Compartiment pour outils (caoutchouc).	Werkzeugschachtel (Gummi.)	Bandeja de herramientas (goma)	
76-9271	Footrest (L/H)	Repose-pied (gauche)	Fussraste (Links)	Descansa-pie (izq.)	
76-9272	Footrest (R/H)	Repose-pied (droite)	Fussraste (Rechts)	Descansa-pie (der.)	
76-9278	†Side Panel (L/H)	Panneau lateral (gauche)	Seitenblech (Links)	Panel de lado (izq.)	
76-9279	Side Panel (R/H)	Panneau lateral (droite)	Seitenblech (Rechts)	Panel de lado (der.)	
76-9283	Screw	Vis	Schraube	Tornillo	4
76-9297	*Side Panel (L/H)	Panneau lateral (gauche)	Seitenblech (Links)	Panel de lado (izq.)	
76-9306	Grille Complete	Couvercle complet	Deckel Kompl.	Tapa completa	2
76-9312	Beading (L/H)	Moulure (gauche)	Zierleiste (Links)	Moldura (izq.)	
76-9313	Beading (R/H)	Moulure (droite)	Zierleiste (Rechts)	Moldura (der.)	

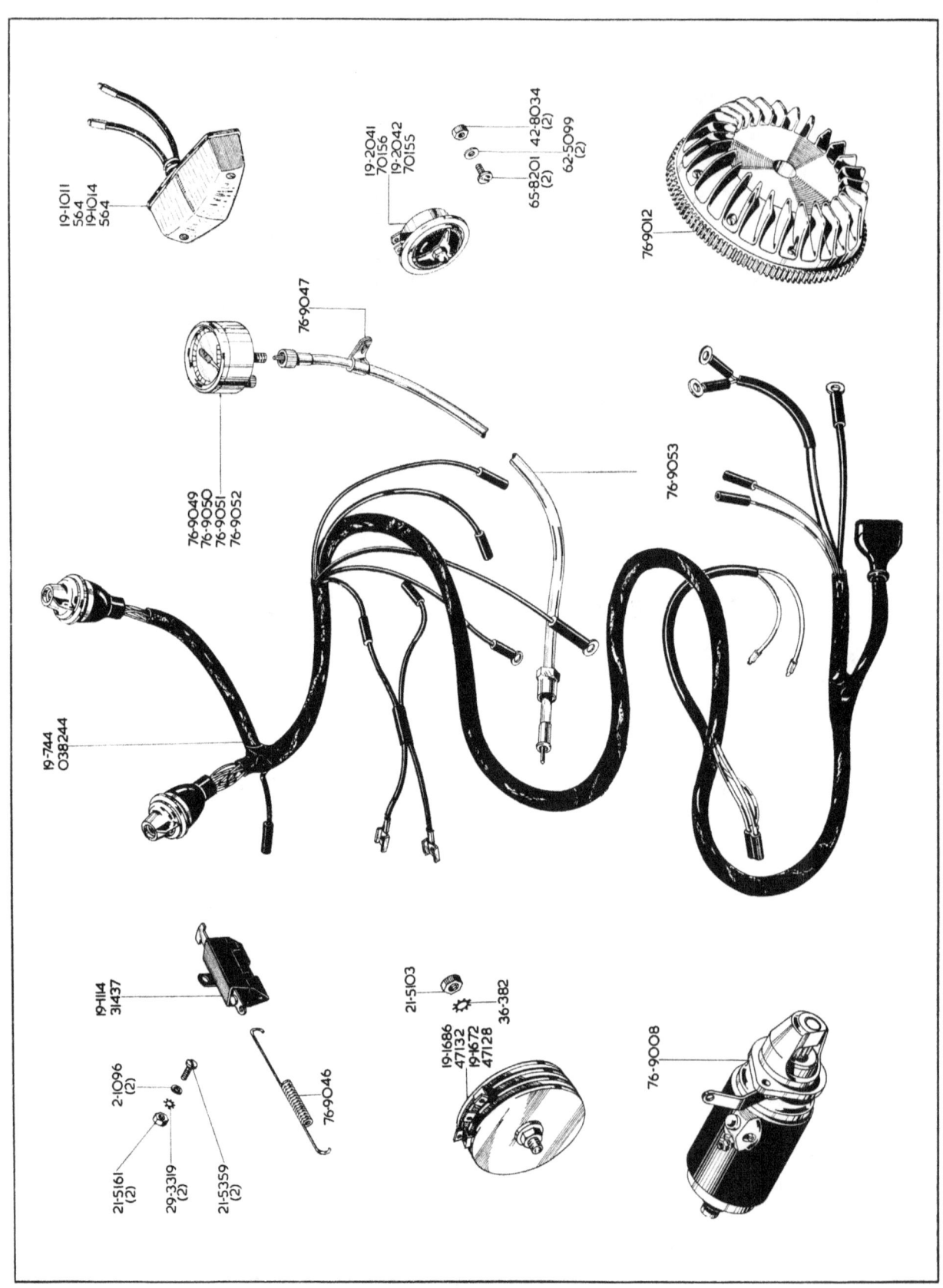

ELECTRICAL EQUIPMENT & SUNDRIES 250 c.c.

Part No. No. de pièce Bestell-nr No. de parte	Description	Designation	Beschreibung	Descripción	Makers No. No. du fabricant Nr-Hersteller No. fabricante
2-1096	Washer	Rondelle	Scheibe	Arandela	
19-744	Harness Complete	Faiseau de câbles complet	Kalbestrang Kompl.	Juego de cables completa	038244
19-1011	Rear Lamp (6 v.)	Feu rouge arrière (6 v.)	Schlusslicht (6 v.)	Luz roja trasera (6 v.)	564
19-1014	Rear Lamp (12 v.)	Feu rouge arrière (12 v.)	Schlusslicht (12 v.)	Luz roja trasera (12 v.)	564
19-1114	Stop Lamp Switch	Commutateur de lampe de stop	Stoplichtschalter	Interruptor para la luz "stop"	31437
19-1672	Rectifier (12 v.)	Redresseur (12 v.)	Gleichrichter (12 v.)	Rectificador (12 v.)	47128
19-1686	Rectifier (6 v.)	Redresseur (6 v.)	Gleichrichter (6 v.)	Rectificador (6 v.)	47132
19-2041	Horn (12 v.)	Avertisseur (12 v.)	Hupe (12 v.)	Bocina (12 v.)	70156
19-2042	Horn (6 v.)	Avertisseur (6 v.)	Hupe (6 v.)	Bocina (6 v.)	70155
21-5103	Nut	Ecrou	Mutter	Tuerca	
21-5161	Nut	Ecrou	Mutter	Tuerca	
21-5359	Screw	Vis	Schraube	Tornillo	
29-3319	Lockwasher	Rondelle frein	Sicherungsscheibe	Freno	
36-382	Lockwasher	Rondelle frein	Sicherungsscheibe	Freno	
42-8034	Nut	Ecrou	Mutter	Tuerca	
65-5099	Washer	Rondelle	Scheibe	Arandela	
65-8201	Screw	Vis	Schraube	Tornillo	
76-9008	Starter (12 v.)	Demarreur (12 v.)	Anlasser (12 v.)	Arancador (12 v.)	
76-9012	Generator (12 v.)	Génératrice (12 v.)	Generator (12 v.)	Generador (12 v.)	
76-9047	Clip	Bride	Klammer	Grapa	
76-9049	Speedo Head (6 v.) m.p.h.	Compteur de vitesses (6 v.) m.p.h.	Tachometer (6 v.) m.p.h.	Velocimetro (6 v.) m.p.h.	
76-9050	Speedo Head (6 v.) k.p.h.	Compteur de vitesses (6 v.) k.p.h.	Tachometer (6 v.) k.p.h.	Velocimetro (6 v.) k.p.h.	
76-9051	Speedo Head (12 v.) m.p.h.	Compteur de vitesses (12 v.) m.p.h.	Tachometer (12 v.) m.p.h.	Velocimetro (12 v.) m.p.h.	
76-9052	Speedo Head (12 v.) k.p.h.	Compteur de vitesses (12 v.) k.p.h.	Tachometer (12 v.) k.p.h.	Velocimetro (12 v.) k.p.h.	
76-9053	Speedo Cable	Câble de compteur	Tachometer Kabel	Arbol de transmisión del velocimetro.	

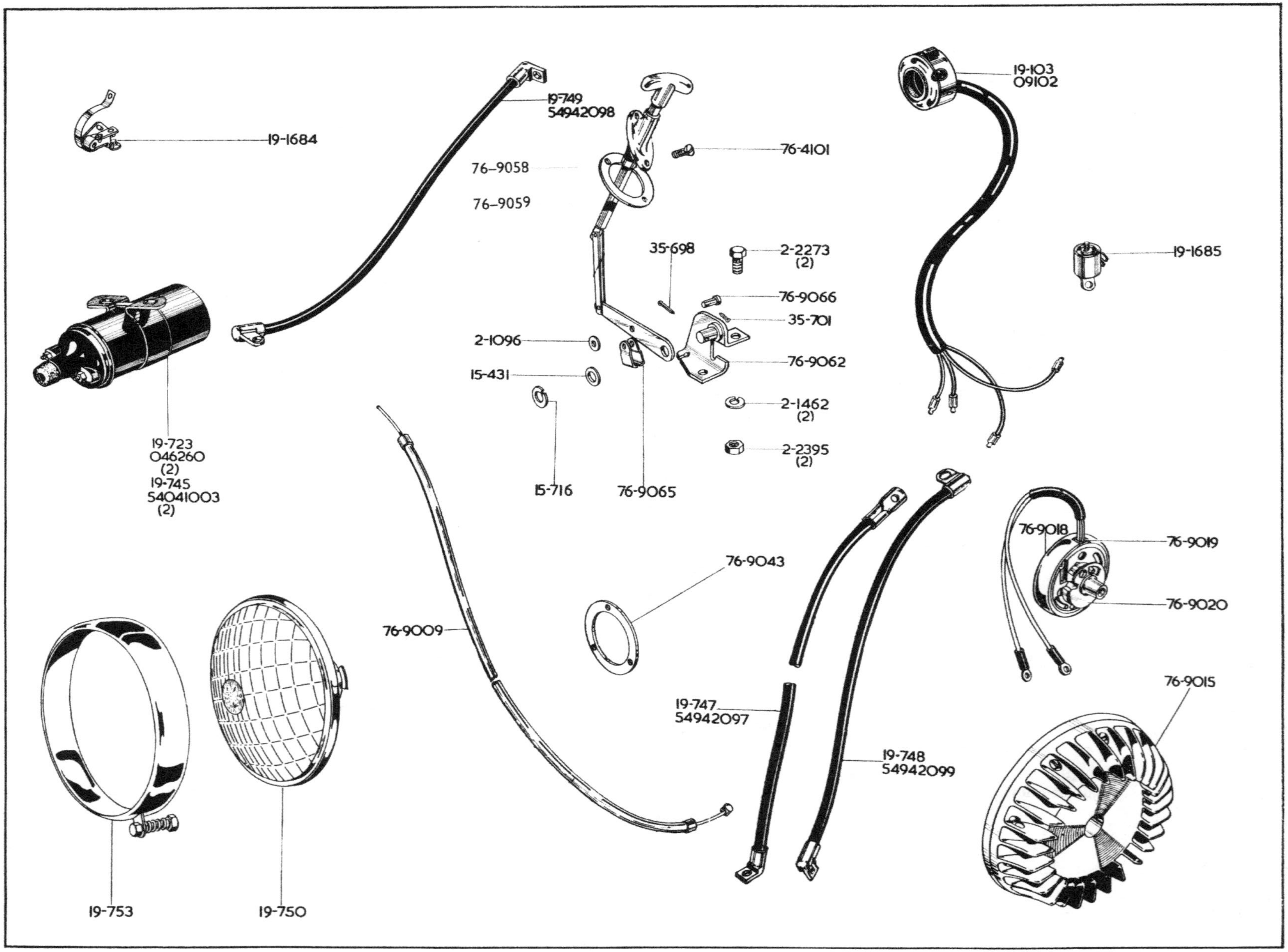
19-1684
19-749
54942098
76-9058
76-9059
76-4101
19-103
09102
19-1685
35-698
2-2273
(2)
76-9066
35-701
2-1096
15-431
76-9062
2-1462
(2)
2-2395
(2)
19-723
046260
(2)
19-745
54041003
(2)
15-716
76-9065
76-9018
76-9019
76-9020
76-9043
76-9009
76-9015
19-747
54942097
19-748
54942099
19-753
19-750

ELECTRICAL EQUIPMENT & SUNDRIES 250 c.c.

Part No. No. de pièce Bestell-nr No. de parte	Description	Designation	Beschreibung	Descripción	Makers No. No. du fabricant Nr.-Hersteller No. fabricante
2-1096	Washer	Rondelle	Scheibe	Arandela	
2-1462	Lockwasher	Rondelle frein	Sicherungsscheibe	Freno	
2-2273	Bolt	Boulon	Schraube	Tornillo	
2-2395	Nut	Ecrou	Mutter	Tuerca	
15-431	Washer	Rondelle	Scheibe	Arandela	
15-716	Lockwasher	Rondelle frein	Sicherungsscheibe	Freno	
19-103	Horn Push and Dipswitch	Avertisseur et inverseur code-phare.	Hupe und Abblendschalter	Bocina commutador de cruce	09102
19-723	Coil (6 v.)	Bobine (6 v.)	Spule (6 v.)	Bobina (6 v.)	046260
19-745	Coil (12 v.)	Bobine (12 v.)	Spule (12 v.)	Bobina (12 v.)	54041003
19-747	Starter Cable (positive) 12 v.	Câble du démarreur (positif) 12 v.	Anlasserkabel (Pos.) 12 v.	Cable del arancador (positivo) 12 v.	54942097
19-748	Starter Cable (negative) 12 v.	Câble du démarreur (negatif) 12 v.	Anlasserkabel (Neg.) 12 v.	Cable del arancador (negativo) 12v.	54942099
19-749	Battery Cable (12 v.)	Câble à la batterie (12 v.)	Batteriekabel (12 v.)	Cable de la bateria (12 v.)	54942098
19-750	Headlamp Unit	Phare complet	Scheinwerfer Kompl.	Faról completa	516728
19-753	Headlamp Rim	Portière de phare	Scheinwerferring	Anillo porta-cristal para faról	516723
19-1684	Contact Set (6/12 v.)	Jeu de vis platinées	Kontaktsatz	Juego de platinos	54410078
19-1685	Condenser (6/12 v.)	Condensateur (6/12 v.)	Kondensator (6/12 v.)	Condensador (6/12 v.)	425377
35-698	Split Pin	Goupille fendue	Splint	Chaveta hendida	
35-701	Split Pin	Goupille fendue	Splint	Chaveta hendida	
76-4101	Screw	Vis	Schraube	Tornillo	
76-9009	Starter Cable	Câble du démarreur	Anlasserkabel	Cable del arancador	
76-9015	Generator (6 v.)	Génératrice (6 v.)	Generator (6 v.)	Generador (6 v.)	
76-9018	Cover	Couvercle	Schutzkappe	Tapa	
76-9019	Grommet	Rondelle capuchon	Tülle	Manguera	
76-9020	Contact Breaker (6/12 v.)	Contacts du rupteur (6/12 v.)	Unterbrecher (6/12 v.)	Martillo del interruptor (6/12 v.)	
76-9043	Spacer Ring	Bague entretoise	Distanzring	Anillo espaciador	
76-9058	Locking Plate	Plaque de blocage	Sicherungsscheibe	Placa cerradora	
76-9059	Starter Complete	Démarreur complet	Anlasser Kompl.	Arancador completa	
76-9062	Bracket	Support	Verstrebung	Soporte	
76-9065	Clip	Bride	Klammer	Grapa	
76-9066	Pivot Pin	Axe	Drehzapfen	Eje	

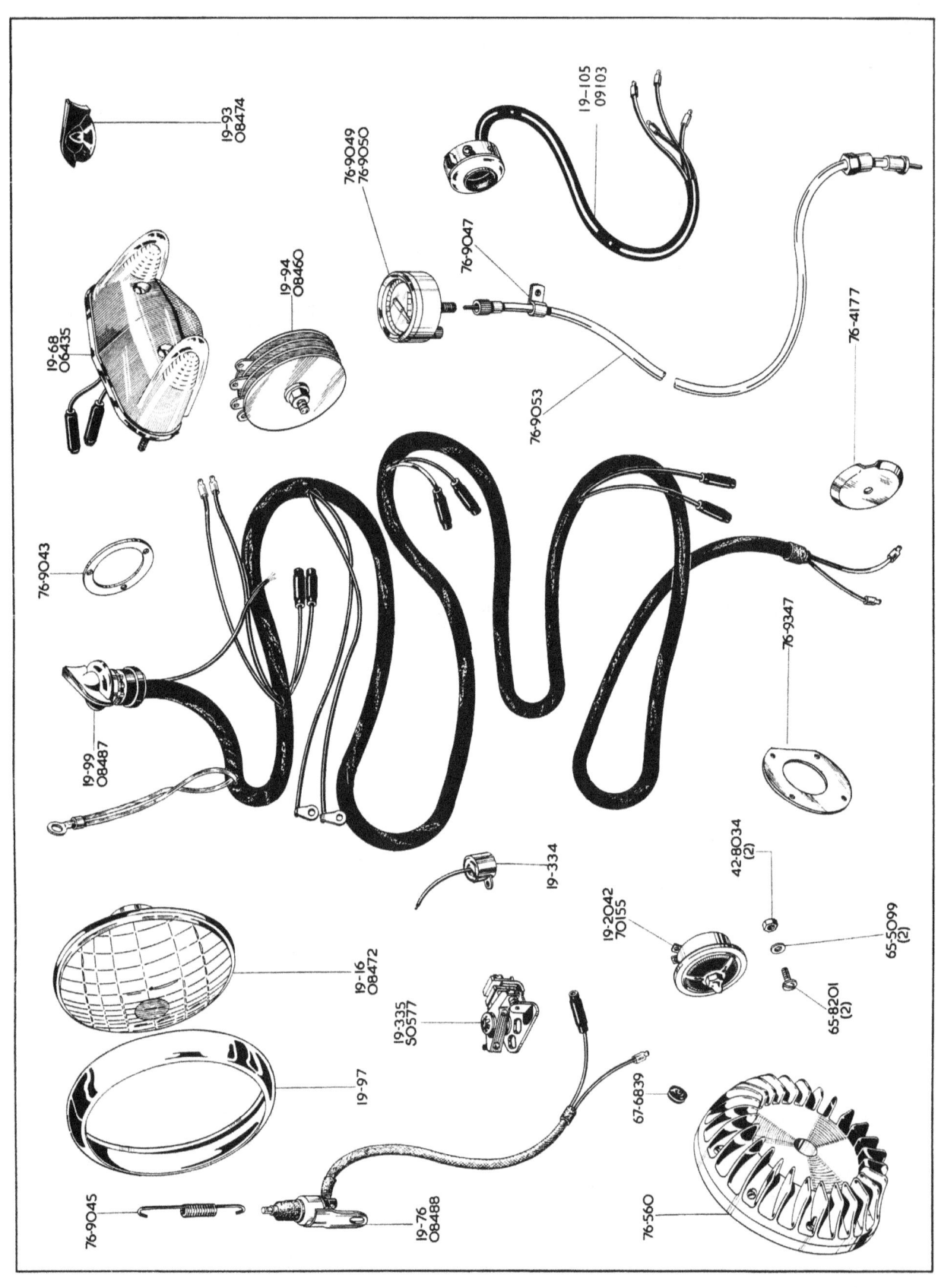

ELECTRICAL EQUIPMENT & SUNDRIES 175 c.c.

Part No. No. de pièce Bestell-nr No. de parte	Description	Designation	Beschreibung	Descripción	Makers No. No. du fabricant Nr-Hersteller No. fabricante
19-16	Headlamp Unit	Phare complet	Scheinwerfer Kompl.	Faról completa	08472
19-68	Rear Lamp	Feu rouge arrière	Schlusslicht	Luz roja trasera	06435
19-76	Stop Lamp Switch	Commutateur de lampe de stop	Stoplichtschalter	Interruptor para la luz "stop"	08488
19-93	Switch	Interrupteur	Schalter	Interruptor	08474
19-94	Rectifier	Redresseur	Gleichrichter	Rectificador	08460
19-97	Headlamp Rim	Portière de phare	Scheinwerferring	Anillo porta-cristal para faról	
19-99	Harness Complete	Faisceau de câbles complet	Kabelstrang Kompl.	Juego de cables completa	08487
19-105	Horn Push and Dipswitch	Avertisseur et inverseur code-phare	Hupe und Abblendschalter	Bocina y commutador de cruce	09103
19-334	Condenser	Condensateur	Kondensator	Condensador	
19-335	Contact Set	Jeu de vis plantinées	Kontartsatz	Juego de platinos	S0577
19-2042	Horn	Avertisseur	Hupe	Bocina	70155
42-8034	Nut	Ecrou	Mutter	Tuerca	
65-5009	Washer	Rondelle	Scheibe	Arandela	
65-8201	Screw	Vis	Schraube	Tornillo	
67-6839	Grommet	Rondelle capuchon	Tülle	Manguera	
76-560	Generator	Génératrice	Generator	Generador	
76-4177	Cover	Couvercle	Schutzkappe	Tapa	
76-9043	Spacer Ring	Bague entretoise	Distanzring	Anillo espaciador	
76-9045	Spring	Ressort	Feder	Resorte	
76-9047	Clip	Bride	Klammer	Grapa	
76-9049	Speedo Head (m.p.h.)	Compteur de vitesses (m.p.h.)	Tachometer (m.p.h.)	Velocimetro (m.p.h.)	
76-9050	Speedo Head (k.p.h.)	Compteur de vitesses (k.p.h.)	Tachometer (k.p.h.)	Velocimetro (k.p.h.)	
76-9053	Speedo Cable	Câble de compteur	Tachometer Kabel	Arbol de transmisión del velocimetro.	
76-9347	Cover	Couvercle	Schutzkappe	Tapa	

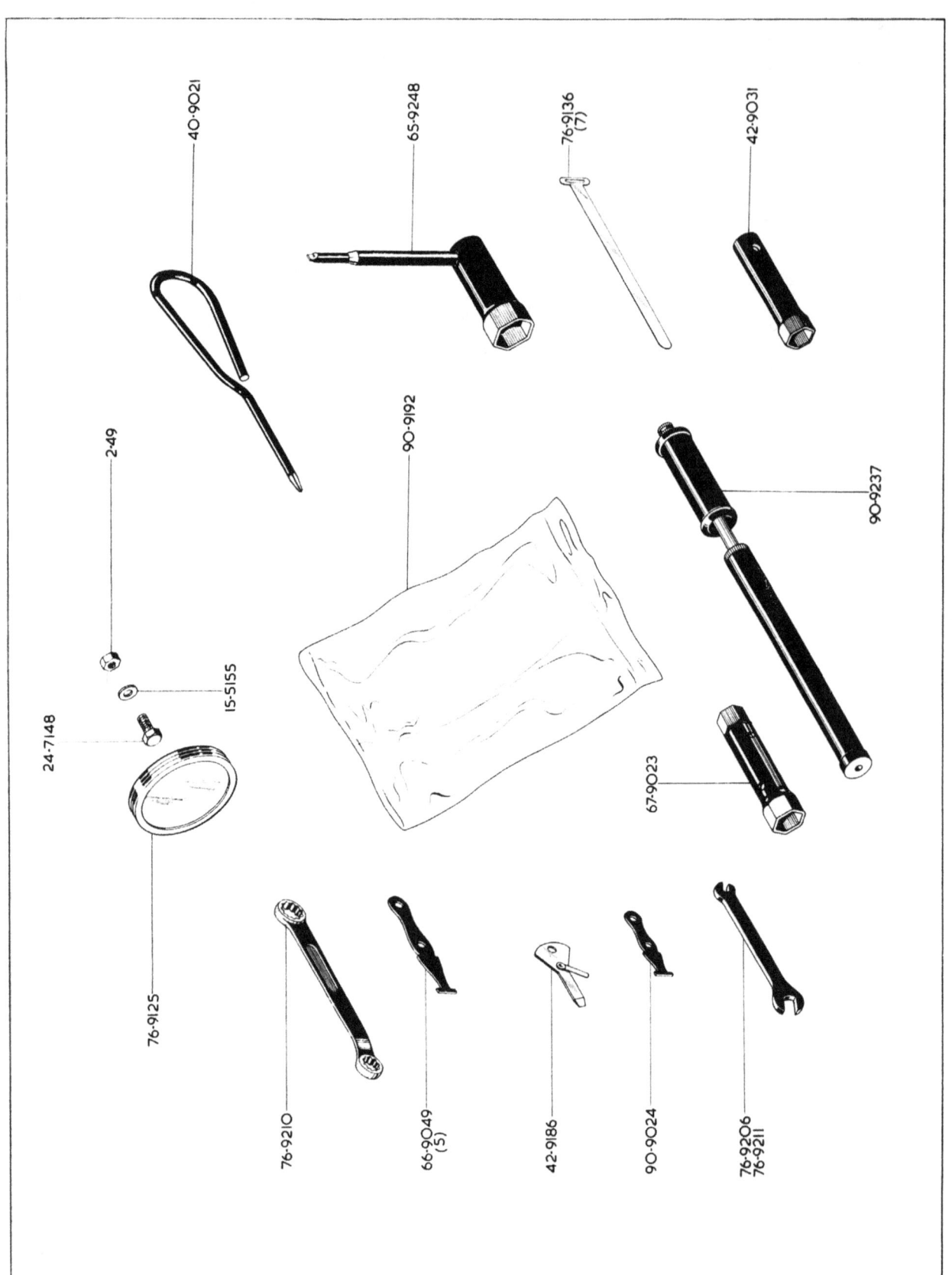

TOOLS 175 c.c., 250 c.c. (*175 c.c. †250 c.c.)

Part No. No. de pièce Bestell-nr No. de parte	Description	Designation	Beschreibung	Descripción	Per Set Par jeu Pr. Satz Juego de
2-49	Nut	Ecrou	Mutter	Tuerca	
15-5155	Washer	Rondelle	Scheibe	Arandela	
24-7148	Bolt	Boulon	Schraube	Tornillo	
40-9021	Screwdriver	Tournevis	Schraubenzieher	Destornillador	
42-9031	Box Spanner	Clé à douille	Steckschlüssel	Llave de tubo	
42-9186	†Feeler Gauge	Cale d'épaisseur	Spion	Calibrador de cinta	
65-9248	*Box Spanner	Clé à douille	Steckschlüssel	Llave de tubo	
66-9049	Rubber Strap	Bande caoutchouc	Gummiband	Cinta de goma	5
67-9023	*Box Spanner	Clé à douille	Steckschlüssel	Llave de tubo	
76-9125	Licence Holder	Porte permet	Licenzhalter	Portalicencia	
76-9136	Clip	Bride	Klammer	Grapa	7
76-9206	†Double Ended Spanner	Clé à fourche double	Doppelschraubenschlüssel	Llave de dos bocas	
76-9209	†Tool Kit Complete	Outillage complet	Werkzeug Kompl	Herramientos completa	
76-9210	†Ring Spanner	Clé annulaire	Ringschlüssel	Llave anular	
76-9211	*Double Ended Spanner	Clé à fourche double	Doppelschraubenschlüssel	Llave de dos bocas	
76-9223	*Tool Kit Complete	Outillage complet	Werkzeug Kompl	Herramientos completa	
90-9024	Rubber Strap	Bande caoutchouc	Gummiband	Cinta de goma	
90-9192	Tool Bag	Trousse à outils	Werkzeughülle	Bolsa de herramientos	
90-9237	Inflator	Pompe à air	Luftpumpe	Bomba de aire	

43

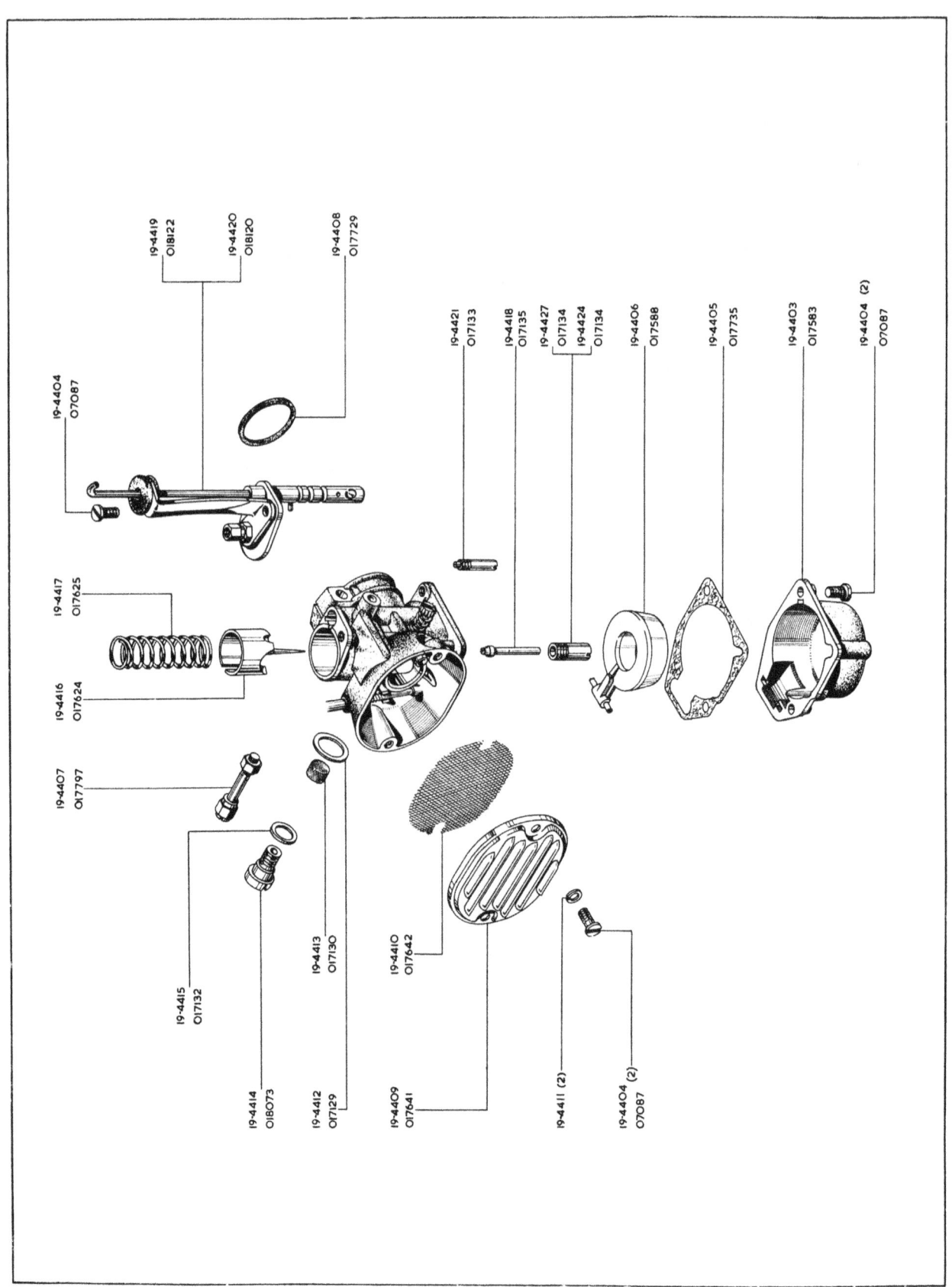

CARBURETTERS 250 c.c.

Part No. No. de pièce Bestell-nr No. de parte	Description	Designation	Beschreibung	Descripción	Per Set Par jeu Pr. Satz Juego de
19-4403	Float Chamber	Cuve du flotteur	Schwimmergehäuse	Cámara del flotador	
19-4404	Screw	Vis	Schraube	Tornillo	5
19-4405	Gasket	Joint	Dichtung	Empaquetadura	
19-4406	Float	Flotteur	Schwimmer	Flotador	
19-4407	Screw and Nut	Vis et ecrou	Schraube und Mutter	Tornillo y tuerca	
19-4408	"O" Ring	Bague "O"	"O" Ring	Anillo "O"	
19-4409	Cover	Couvercle	Schutzkappe	Tapa	
19-4410	Filter Gauze	Gaze du filtre	Filtergaze	Gasa de filtro	
19-4411	Lockwasher	Rondelle frein	Sicherungsscheibe	Freno	2
19-4412	Sealing Washer	Joint d'étanchéité	Dichtung	Arandela de reten	
19-4413	Filter Gauze	Gaze du filtre	Filtergaze	Gasa de filtro	
19-4414	Screw	Vis	Schraube	Tornillo	
19-4415	Sealing Washer	Joint d'étanchéité	Dichtung	Arandela de reten	
19-4416	Throttle Slide	Boisseau des gaz	Gassschieber	Corredera de aceleración	
19-4417	Spring	Ressort	Feder	Resorte	
19-4418	Emulsifying Tube	Tube d'émulsion	Emulgierrohrchen	Tubo emulsivo	
19-4419	Starting Slide	Volet d'air	Startschieber	Corredera de aranque	
19-4421	Slow Running Jet	Gicleur de ralenti	Leerlaufdüse	Surtidor piloto	
19-4427	Main Jet	Gicleur principal	Hauptdüse	Surtidor principal	
76-57	Carburetter	Carburateur	Vergaser	Carburador	
76-9041	Throttle Cable	Commande des gaz	Gaszug	Cable bowden para acelerador	

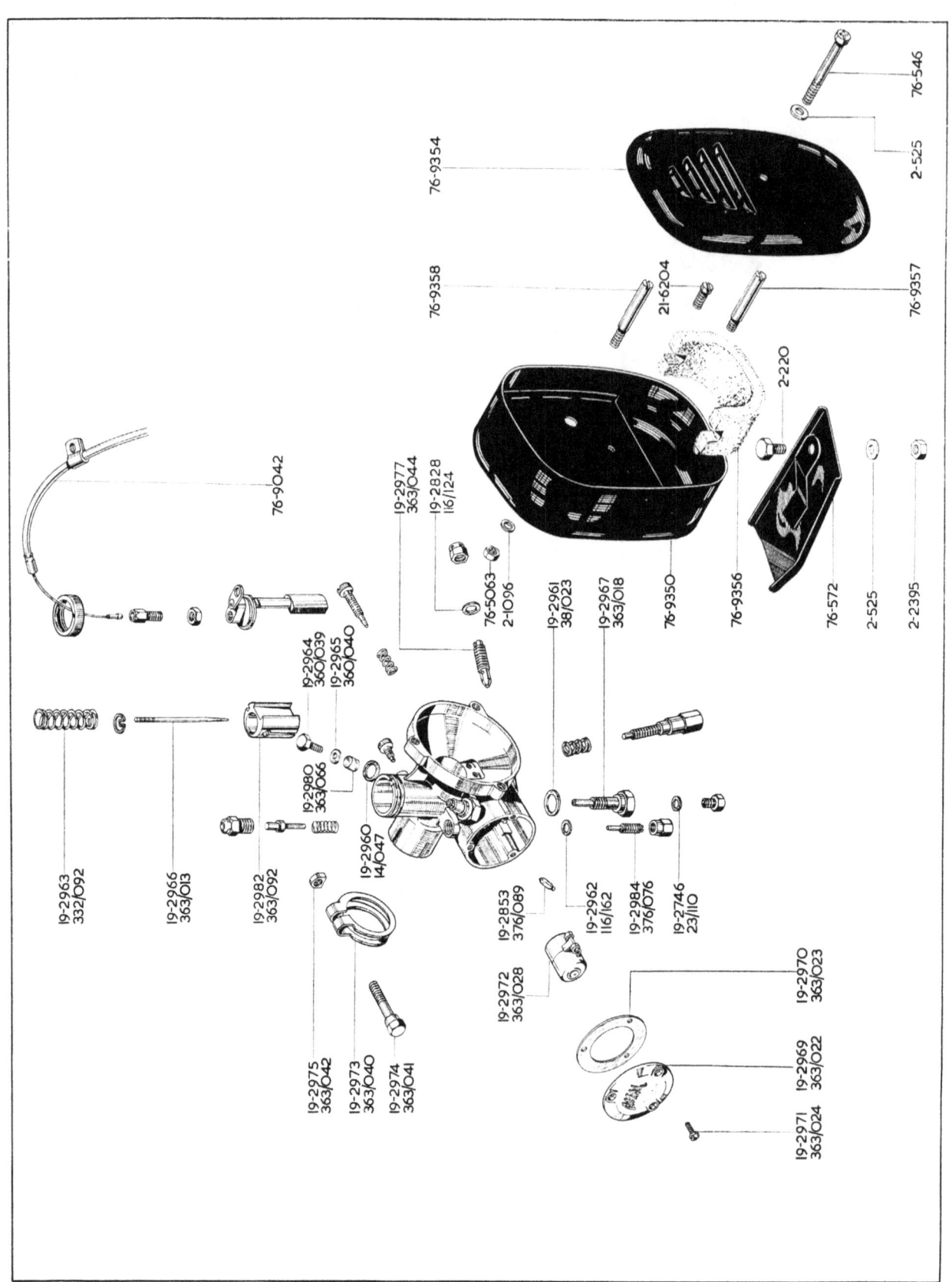

CARBURETTERS & AIR FILTER 175 c.c.

Part No. No. de pièce Bestell-nr No. de parte	Description	Designation	Beschreibung	Descripción	Makers No. No. du fabricant Nr-Hersteller No. fabricante
2-220	Bolt	Boulon	Schraube	Tornillo	
2-525	Washer	Rondelle	Scheibe	Arandela	
2-1096	Washer	Rondelle	Scheibe	Arandela	
2-2395	Nut	Ecrou	Mutter	Tuerca	
19-2746	Sealing Washer	Joint d'étanchéité	Dichtung	Arandela de reten	23/110
19-2828	Sealing Washer	Joint d'étanchéité	Dichtung	Arandela de reten	116/124
19-2853	Needle	Aiguille	Nadel	Aguja	376/089
19-2960	Sealing Washer	Joint d'étanchéité	Dichtung	Arandela de reten	14/047
19-2961	Sealing Washer	Joint d'étanchéité	Dichtung	Arandela de reten	38/023
19-2962	Sealing Washer	Joint d'étanchéité	Dichtung	Arandela de reten	116/162
19-2963	Spring	Ressort	Feder	Resorte	332/092
19-2964	Bolt	Boulon	Schraube	Tornillo	360/039
19-2965	Sealing Washer	Joint d'étanchéité	Dichtung	Arandela de reten	360/040
19-2966	Jet Needle	Aiguille	Düsennadel	Aguja del acelerador	363/013
19-2967	Needle Jet	Gicleur d'aiguille	Nadeldüse	Surtidor de aguja	363/018
19-2969	Cover	Couvercle	Schutzkappe	Tapa	363/022
19-2970	Gasket	Joint	Dichtung	Empaquetadura	363/023
19-2971	Screw	Vis	Schraube	Tornillo	363/024
19-2972	Float	Flotteur	Schwimmer	Flotador	363/028
19-2973	Clip	Bride	Klammer	Grapa	363/040
19-2974	Bolt	Boulon	Schraube	Tornillo	363/041
19-2975	Nut	Ecrou	Mutter	Tuerca	363/042
19-2977	Main Jet	Gicleur principal	Hauptdüse	Surtidor principal	363/044
19-2980	Filter Gauze	Gaze du filtre	Filtergaze	Gasa de filtro	363/066
19-2982	Throttle Slide	Boisseau des gaz	Gasschieber	Corredera de aceleración	363/092
19-2984	Pilot Jet	Gicleur du dispositif de ralenti	Leerlaufdüse	Surtidor piloto	376/076
21-6204	Screw	Vis	Schraube	Tornillo	
76-546	Screw	Vis	Schraube	Tornillo	
76-570	Carburetter	Carburateur	Vergaser	Carburador	
76-572	Carburetter Drip Tray	Attrapé couttes pour carburateur	Tropfbrett für Vergaser	Cubeta de escurrir para carburador	
76-5063	Nut	Ecrou	Mutter	Tuerca	
76-9042	Throttle Cable	Commande des gaz	Gaszug	Cable Bowden para acelerado	
76-9349	Air Filter Complete	Filtre à air complet	Luftfilter Komp.	Filtro de aire completa	
76-9350	Air Cleaner Housing	Logement de l'epurateur d'air	Gerüst für Luftreiniger	Alojamiento del limpiador de aire	
76-9345	Cover	Couvercle	Schutzkappe	Tapa	
76-9356	Filter	Filtre	Filter	Filtro	
76-9357	Screw	Vis	Schraube	Tornillo	
76-9358	Screw	Vis	Schraube	Tornillo	

ELECTRICAL EQUIPMENT
EQUIPEMENT ELECTRIQUE
ELEKTRISCHE AUSRUSTUNG
EQUIPO ELECTRICO

JOSEPH LUCAS LTD., GREAT KING STREET, BIRMINGHAM, ENGLAND.

THE WIPAC GROUP, BLETCHLEY, ENGLAND.

SPARK PLUGS
BOUGIES
ZUNDKERZEN
BUJIAS

CHAMPION SPARKING PLUG CO. LTD., FELTHAM, MIDDLESEX, ENGLAND.

SPEEDOMETERS
COMPTEURS DE VITESSES
TACHOMETER
VELOCIMETROS

SMITH'S MOTOR ACCESSORIES, CRICKLEWOOD WORKS, LONDON, ENGLAND.

CARBURETTERS
CARBURATEURS
VERGASER
CARBURADORES

AMAL LTD., HOLFORD ROAD, WITTON, BIRMINGHAM 6, ENGLAND.
ZENITH CARBURETTER CO. LTD., HONEYPOT LANE, STANMORE, MIDDLESEX, ENGLAND.

48

ADDENDUM

The following pages are from the archive of a US distributor for Triumph motorcycles & scooters

These are copies of original UK factory communications and are somewhat rare.

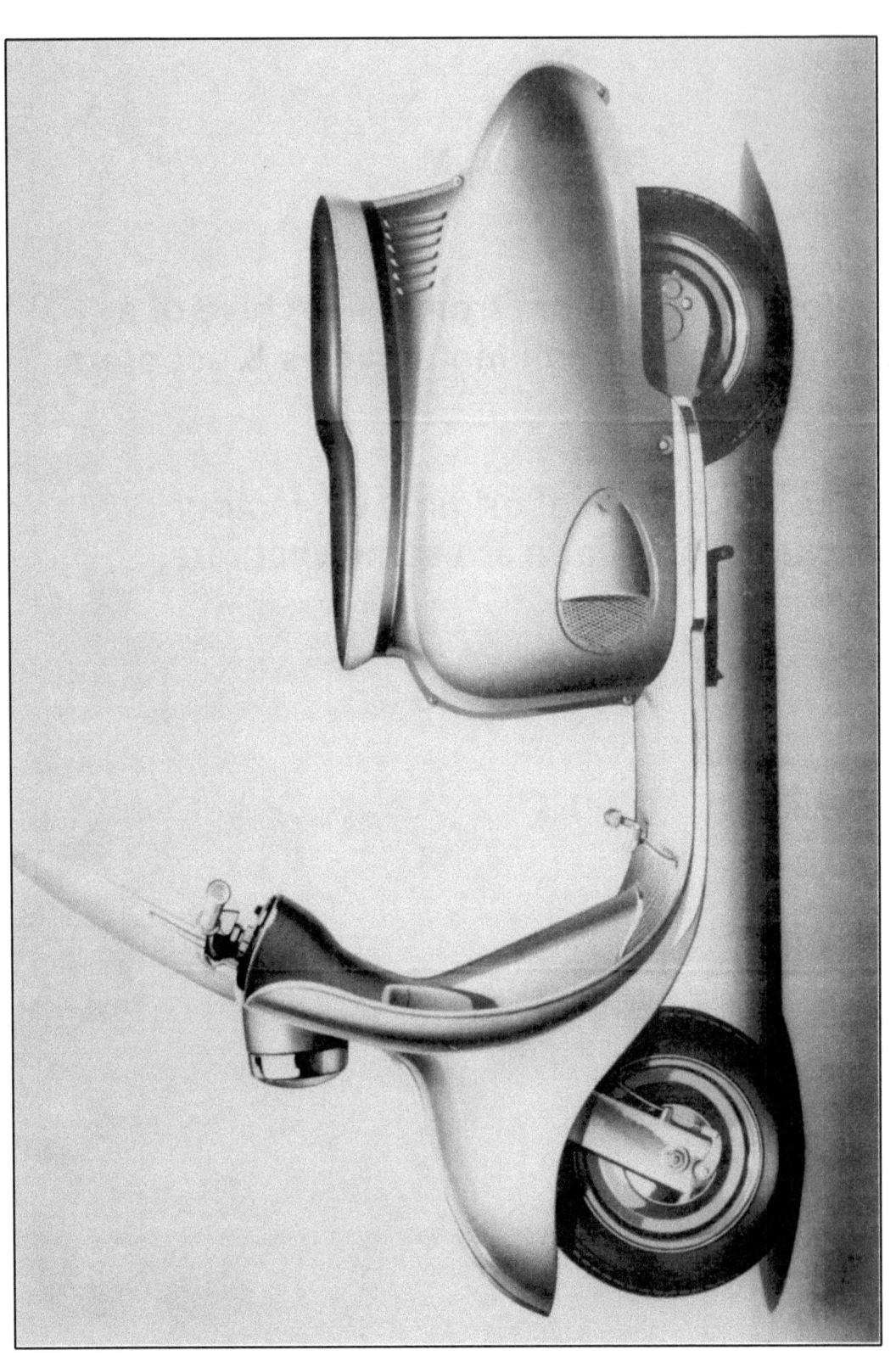

THE NEW TRIUMPH SCOOTER TO BE PRODUCED WITH ALTERNATIVE POWER PLANTS. Triumph's new Scooter which was designed by MR. EDWARD TURNER, will be powered by a 250 c.c. OHV VERTICAL TWIN engine capable of serious touring yet flexible and extremely ECONOMICAL TO OPERATE. The alternate power unit is a 175 c.c. single cylinder two stroke. Road tests reveal for the four-stroke a GASOLINE CONSUMPTION rate of 140 MPG at 35 MPH. The transmission is by engine shaft clutch gear drive to a four-speed gearbox and finally by chain in a cast chain bath which forms an arm carrying the rear wheel. The Triumph Scooter is light in weight and extremely EASY TO OPERATE.

The TRIUMPH *Corporation* TOWSON, BALTIMORE 4, MARYLAND, U. S. A.

December 9, 1959

Wiring Code for 19-744 Scooter Harness and Switches (2) Assembly

Lighting Switch	Color of Wire
Terminal # 1	Red
# 2	Brown w/blue tracer
# 3	Blue
# 4	Not used
# 5	Black
# 6	Metal link to # 5
# 7	Green w/black tracer
# 8	Brown w/green tracer
#10	Brown w/blue tracer - metal link to #2 terminal
#11	Brown w/green tracer - metal link to #8 terminal

Ignition Switch

#12	Brown w/blue tracer
#12	Brown w/blue tracer - metal link between (2) #12 terminal
#13	Brown w/lavender tracer
#13	Metal link to other terminal #13
#14	White
#15	Black w/white tracer
#16	Green w/yellow tracer
#17	Metal link to #16 terminal
#18	Black
#19	White - metal link to terminal #14

ZENITH CARBURETTERS
SPARE PARTS SCHEDULE

Model	Carburetter	Zenith Ref. †
B2, B2S TW2, TW2S	**17 MXZ**	C.10

† (Stamped on carburetter body)

1959 B.S.A. "Sunbeam"
Motor Scooter
Models B2 and B2S, 249 c.c. 2 cyls. 4 stroke o.h.v.

1959 TRIUMPH "Tigress"
Motor Scooter
Models TW2 and TW2S, 249 c.c. 2 cyls. 4 stroke o.h.v.

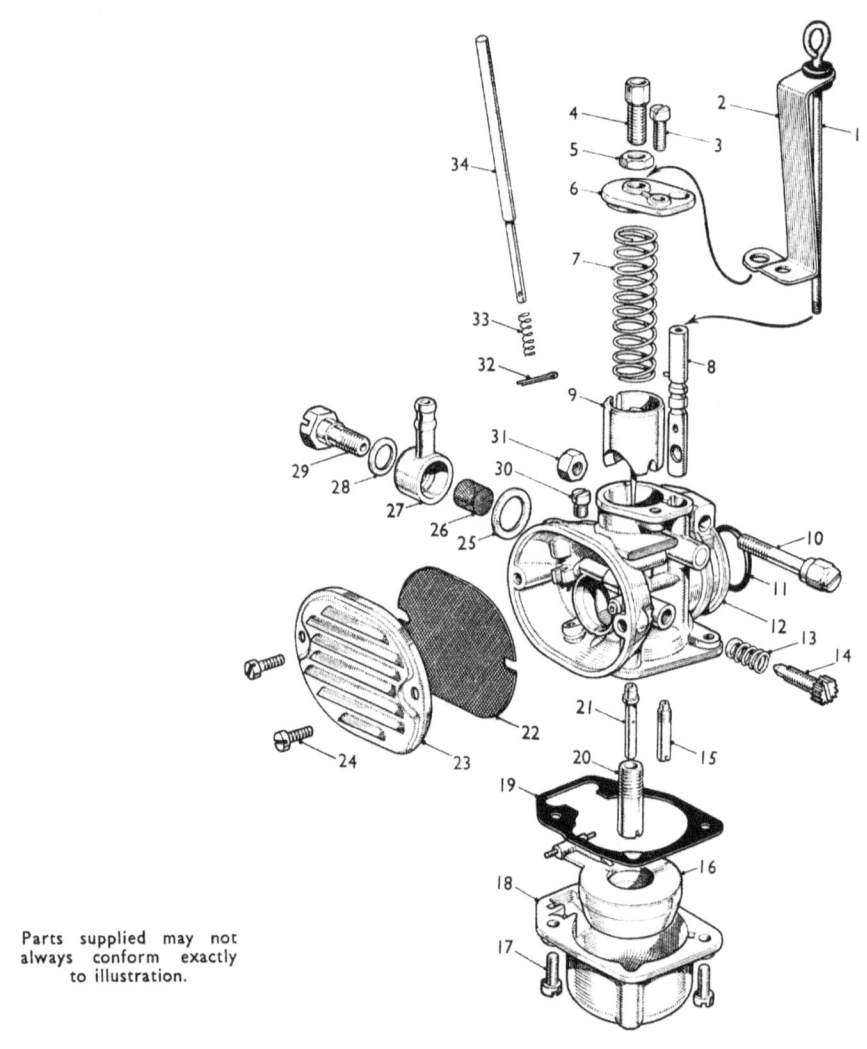

Parts supplied may not always conform exactly to illustration.

STANDARD SETTING:

Carb. Ref.	Main Jet	Emulsion Tube	Slow-running Jet	Starter Slide
C.10	82	017135	40	200 (starter outlet) (slow-running outlet undrilled)

SPARE PARTS SCHEDULE (for carb. ref. C.10)

Ref.	Description	Part No.	Price Each	Bin No.	Ref.	Description	Part No.	Price Each	Bin No.
1	Control rod for starter slide	018111	1/3		19	Gasket (carburetter body/bowl)	017735	4d.	
2	Bracket for do.	018121	3/-		20	Main jet*	017134	2/6	
3	Screw fixing cover plate	07087	2d.		21	Emulsion tube*	017135	2/-	
4	Cable adjuster	017988	1/3		22	Gauze for air intake	017642	2/-	
5	Locknut for do.	017464	4d.		23	Cover for do.	017641	3/-	
6	Cover plate	017581	3/-		24	Screw fixing cover (2 off)	07087	2d.	
7	Spring for main slide	017625	8d.		25	Washer for filter elbow	017129	1d.	
8	Starter slide*	018122	4/-		26	Filter gauze	017130	1/-	
9	Main slide and needle assembly	017624	6/6		27	Filter elbow	017128	1/-	
10	Clamping screw (includes item 31)	017797	1/3		28	Washer for filter plug	017132	1d.	
11	"O" Sealing ring	017729	9d.		29	Filter plug	018063	1/-	
12	Carburetter body (not available as a separate part)				30	Plugging screw	017619	3d.	
13	Spring for throttle adjustment screw	017156	9d.		31	Nut for clamping screw (see item 10)			
14	Throttle adjustment screw	017144	1/-			Control cable assembly (not shown)	018097	2/6	
15	Slow-running jet*	017133	1/6			Carburetter assembled complete with cable (Home market only)	C.10	£4-7-6	
16	Float	017588	6/-			IMPORTANT: Items marked * are variables; state size required.			
17	Screw fixing carburetter bowl (2 off)	07087	2d.			Prices subject to alteration without notice.			
18	Carburetter bowl	017583	7/6						

All spare part prices are subject to 25% increase.

NOTES:

Brief details of carburetters :—

Bore and type	...	17 MXZ :-17 m/m. (0·669″), horizontal
Engine connection	...	25·4 m/m. (1″) bore, 17·5 m/m. ($\frac{11}{16}$″) deep
Throttle	...	Slide type, for cable control; opens vertically
Strangler	...	None fitted
Fuel inlet connection	...	For $\frac{3}{16}$″ bore flexible pipe
Overall length	...	65·5 m/m. ($2\frac{9}{16}$″)

FOR SERVICE INFORMATION ON THIS CARBURETTER
REFER TO BULLETIN SB.206

Zenith Carburetters are fitted as standard equipment to many well-known cars, trucks and engines.

Service sheets similar to this are available to cover numerous applications, and will be sent on request if the make, model and year of vehicle or engine are given.

May we send you details of our

CARBURETTER REPLACEMENT SCHEME

FUEL FILTERS

SPARES SERVICE BOXES

MASTER CARBURETTERS, Etc.

Issued by THE ZENITH CARBURETTER CO. LTD.
HONEYPOT LANE, STANMORE, MIDDLESEX.
Telegrams: Zenicarbur, Norphone, London.   Telephone: WORdsworth 4343 (12 lines)

Printed in England

KNOW YOUR ENGINE

No. 1: The Triumph 250 c.c. Twin

THE Triumph 249 c.c. vertical-twin four-speed engine unit, cut-away to show the push-rod-operated o.h.v. mechanism with its unusual rocker arrangement; the primary gear drive with overhung clutch, and final duplex-chain transmission enclosed within a light-alloy case that forms the rear swinging-fork structure. Note the sturdy outrigger member, providing a wide, forked pivot, co-axial with the gear mainshaft, so providing constant centres for the chain drive irrespective of the arcwise movement of the pivot arm.

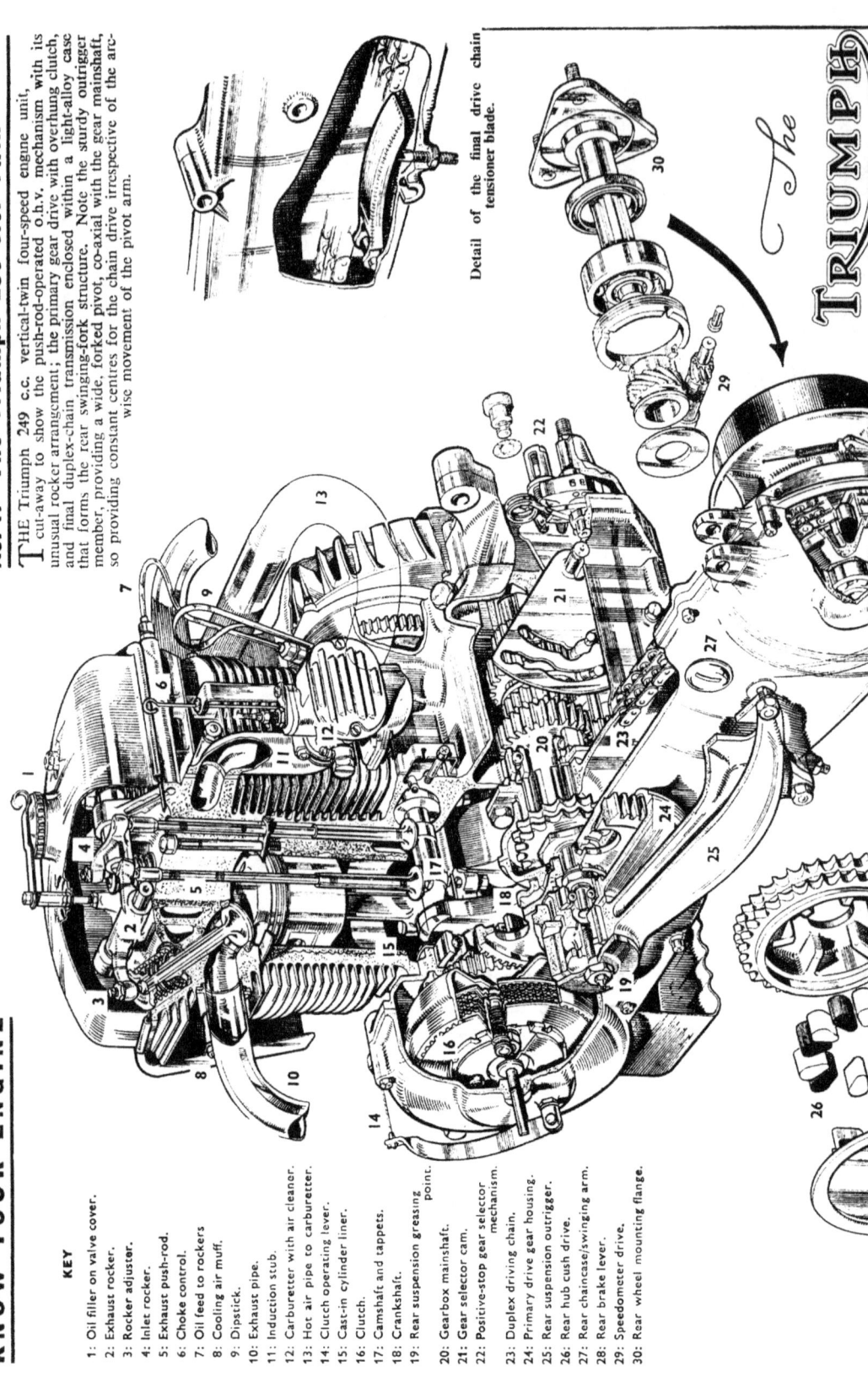

Detail of the final drive chain tensioner blade.

KEY
1: Oil filler on valve cover.
2: Exhaust rocker.
3: Rocker adjuster.
4: Inlet rocker.
5: Exhaust push-rod.
6: Choke control.
7: Oil feed to rockers
8: Cooling air muff.
9: Dipstick.
10: Exhaust pipe.
11: Induction stub.
12: Carburetter with air cleaner.
13: Hot air pipe to carburetter.
14: Clutch operating lever.
15: Cast-in cylinder liner.
16: Clutch.
17: Camshaft and tappets.
18: Crankshaft.
19: Rear suspension greasing point.
20: Gearbox mainshaft.
21: Gear selector cam.
22: Positive-stop gear selector mechanism.
23: Duplex driving chain.
24: Primary drive gear housing.
25: Rear suspension outrigger.
26: Rear hub cush drive.
27: Rear chaincase/swinging arm.
28: Rear brake lever.
29: Speedometer drive.
30: Rear wheel mounting flange.

The TRIUMPH Corporation
TOWSON, BALTIMORE 4, MARYLAND

Reprinted from MOTOR CYCLING with SCOOTER WEEKLY   December 10, 1959

ALTERATIONS TO TIGRESS SCOOTERS, MODELS TW2 and TW2S, SINCE JANUARY 1959.

Position of speedometer cable altered to eliminate acute bend.

Improved material for pedal rubbers.

Improved clutch with gear cut driving teeth.

Modification to primary drive lubrication and cover flanges widened.

Stouter gear operating rod.

Improved gear operating lever and nut.

Longer carburettor manifold.

Improved accessibility of gearbox filler plug.

Improved material for rocker cover gasket.

Improved rear brake operating lever with longer cable and adjuster.

Increased diameter of rocker cover washers to prevent distortion of cover.

Rubber beading added to steering stem hole in instrument panel to prevent cables chafing.

Kickstart lever changed to one piece forging with new rubber.

Alteration to location for fork top cover.

Thickness of camshaft pinion webb increased.

Depth of keyway in primary driven gear altered, thickness of webb and diameter of boss increased.

Improved starter control on 12v model.

Modified carburettor providing float 'tickler' and adjustable air bleed. Emulsion tube bore altered.

Spring clip added to rocker cover to retain oil filler cap.

Grease nipple added to front fork bottom member.

Offside rear engine fixing lug changed to ¼" clip.

Nyloc nuts fitted to front engine bolts.

Neutral finder adjuster pivot and bolt altered to ensure trapping link rod.

Rubber grommet added to inner cover to provide seal for flywheel generator.

Keeper plate replacing plunger pin to control position of plunger in gearchange quadrant.

New pattern twist-grip rubber.

Air ducting modified to enclose modified exhaust pipes: carburettor and coils re-positioned.

Outside choke control mounted on legshield.

Re-designed centre stand with rubber feet.

DECEMBER, 1960.

PARTS SERVICE BULLETIN

No. 14.

SUPERSEDED PARTS.

Below is a list of superseded parts. The new spares number should always be used when re-ordering.

OLD PART NO.	DESCRIPTION.	NEW SPARES NO.
61-3613	Generator rotor extractor tool	82961-5002
76-3611	Clutch housing & primary gear	94376-3345
	Use with clutch driven plate.	91976-3343
76-3043	Cam plate and quadrant complete	95376-3167
76-4961	Handlebar cover screw.	90376-4099
76-9048	Speedometer cable.	84276-9053
	Use with clip.	90676-9047
76-9165	Wheel disc screw circlip.	90676-9225
76-9255	Front mudguard bezel.	91176-9328
76-9256	" " combing.	91776-9327
76-9300	" " extension piece.	92276-9302
76-9301	" " " "	92276-9303
19-98	Head lamp lens.	19-61
61-5002	Flywheel extractor tool.	82761-5040
76-35	D/S inner cover stud.	90676-44
76-36	D/S inner/outer cover stud.	90676-43
76-37	" " " " " (long).	90676-39
76-100	Rocker cover stud spacing washer.	402 2-6537
	Use with steel washer	90176-101
	and fibre washer	90176-102
76-2550	Cooling fan inner cover.	94176-2575.
	Use with rubber grommet.	91276-2577
76-2617	Exhaust pipe flange gasket.	90676-2650
76-3109	Layshaft first gear.	94076-3207
76-3140	Gear lever.	91676-3206
76-3160	Kickstart lever.	94476-3197.
	Use with rubber.	91276-3191
76-3186	Kickstart lever.	94476-3197.
	Use with chain	91776-3211.
	and rubber.	91276-3191
76-4082	Head lug stud	91076-4138

a Dealer Service

C/R. A.B.

Continued.. .. ....

FROM TRIUMPH ENGINEERING CO. LTD.,
SCOOTER DIVISION, WAVERLEY WORKS, BIRMINGHAM 10

SCOOTER PARTS SERVICE BULLETIN NO.14. (CONT.2.)

OLD PART NO.	DESCRIPTION.	NEW SPARES NO.
76-4113	Head lug stud.	91076-4471
76-4115	Screw.	90776-4134
76-4119	Instrument panel & nacelle screw.	90476-543
76-4710	Centre stand.	93976-4725
76-4968	Handlebar.	95876-4950
76-7015	Rear brake cable.	93276-7038
	Use with lever.	91676-7037
76-7027	Rear brake lever.	91676-7037
	Use with cable.	93276-7038
76-8014	Petrol tap and pipe.	93976-9024
76-9000	Electric starter knob.	92976-9074
	Use with body	91876-9076
	washer	10176-158
	nut	90376-242
76-9283	Side grille fixing screw.	402 1-4606
76-9278	Body panel left-hand.	97576-9404
76-9279	Body panel right-hand.	97576-9405
76-9297	Body panel left-hand.	97576-9404
76-307	Rocker oil feed pipe.	92676-364
76-344	Primary oil feed pipe.	91876-366
76-273	Dipstick.	91476-318
76-3321	Clutch driven plate.	91976-3343
	Use with clutch housing.	94376-3345
76-2761	Exhaust pipe clip (bottom).	41442-2861
76-2781	Exhaust pipe clip (top).	41442-2860
76-9045	Stop light switch spring.	91276-9044
76-230	Camshaft.	95476-334
	Use with oil pump eccentric.	92076-232
76-4972	Speaker mounting bracket.	91276-4976
76-8500	Throttle twist grip.	83076-8511
	Use with rubber.	81276-8509
	and dummy grip.	81276-8510
76-8501	Dummy grip.	81276-8510
	Use with throttle twist grip rubber.	81176-8509
76-8508	Throttle twist grip rubber.	81176-8509
	Use with dummy grip.	81276-8510
76-3106	Clutch lever fulcrum.	91676-3185
76-3107	Clutch lever.	91676-3185
76-3019	Mainshaft complete.	96676-3174
76-9033	Clutch cable.	92576-9025
	Use with protective spring.	91076-9031
76-9262	Legshield 12 volt.	97476-9377
76-9263	Legshield 6 volt.	97476-9378

Continued......

SCOOTER PARTS SERVICE BULLETIN NO.14. (CONT.3.)

Petrol Tap Plunger.

The petrol tap plunger is now available as a separate part. The spares number is 19-5342.

Front Fork Lubrication.

We recommend Jetlube AP-1 for Scooter front forks. This is available in half pound tubes, spares number 81800-7005

B.S.A. 250c.c. SCOOTER.

DETAILED PROCEDURE FOR MODIFYING PRIMARY TRANSMISSION.

PARTS REQUIRED.

- 1. 76-3345 Clutch Housing.
- 3. 76-3343 Driven Plates.
- 1. 64-3227 Clutch Push Rod 'O' Ring.
- 1. 76-243 Clutch Primary Cover.
- 1. 76-335 Camshaft Eccentric.
- 1. 76-309 Oil Pipe Adaptor (5/16").
- 2. 66-7510 Fibre Washers.
- 1. 76-3140 Gear Operating Lever.
- 1. 76-3075 Gear Operating Rod.
- 1. 76-56 Carburetter Gasket.
- 2. 76-2617 Exhaust Pipe Sealing Washers.
- 1. 76-7517 Mainshaft Oil Seal.
- 1. 76-3310 Clutch Centre.
- 1 set 76-3326 Clutch Springs.
- 1. 76-351 Inner Primary Cover.
- 1. 76-252 Primary Cover Gasket.
- 1. 76-344 Oil Pipe.
- 1. 76-346 Oil Pipe Adaptor (1/4").
- 1. 76-7510 'O' Ring.
- 1. 76-3184 Nut.
- 1. 76-49 Manifold.
- 1. 19-4408 Carburetter 'O' Ring.
- 1. 76-213 Crankshaft Oil Seal.
- 1. 76-291 C/B Shaft Oil Seal.

REMOVING AUTOMOTIVE UNIT FROM FRAME.

1. Break rear lamp connections and remove rear number plate.
2. Remove dual seat and side valances.
3. Drain off oil from engine, primary drive and gearbox.
4. Raise rear wheel clear of ground or work trestle and remove wheel.
5. Dis-connect spark plug leads and remove air ducting from around cylinder head together with cool air pipe.
6. Un-hook kickstart chain tensioner from R/H exhaust pipe, slacken off exhaust pipe-to-silencer clips and remove exhaust pipes.
7. Dis-connect speedometer drive from rear hub. Dis-connect rear brake cable from cam lever.
8. Dis-connect L.T. wires from top of ignition coils.
9. Remove clutch cable from clutch lever on primary drive case.
10. Dis-connect petrol pipe at carburetter end. Remove petrol tap bracket from rocker cover stud. Remove carburetter and manifold.
11. Remove nut securing gear-shift lever to quadrant shaft on gearbox and remove lever.
12. Depress kickstart lever, remove spring link connecting chain to lever.
13. Dis-connect rectifier earth lead from gearbox outer cover.
    Remove curved bearing support arm from left side of machine (3 nuts at the rear and hollow bolt at front with grease nipple).
    Remove large, pegged steel washer.
14. Dis-connect lower end of rear suspension damper.
15. Remove rear mudguard (two ¼" nuts and bolts at front and two at rear carrying silencer and petrol tank support bracket).
16. Remove two ⅜" nuts from bolts attaching automotive unit to rear vertical frame tubes. On left hand tube remove quarter clip secured by two ¼" bolts.
17. Drive ⅜" bolts practically through but still allow them to support engine.
18. Remove front engine plates by unscrewing nuts from two crankcase studs and remove two 5/16" nuts and bolts securing 'L' shaped engine plates to frame cross member. Slide plates off studs and leave unit supported only at rear.
19. Dis-connect generator cables by breaking connections beneath floorboards.
20. Drive out two rear retaining bolts, tilt unit forward to clear lugs then tilt to left and lift out.

DISMANTLING THE UNIT.

1. Clean down unit.
2. Remove contact breaker cover.
3. Remove C/B plate, held by 2 hexagons.
4. Remove advance and retard mechanism held by one central bolt. (Extractor 61-5005).
5. Remove outer primary cover.
6. Remove clutch springs and spring plate but then replace one spring and nut, so keeping clutch together to hold primary driven gear when unscrewing nut. Flatten tab washer and unscrew driven gear nut.
7. Flatten clutch nut tab washer and remove nut.
8. Remove clutch centre (Extractor 61-5007).
9. Remove driven gear (Extractor 61-5025) and key from shaft.
10. Remove clutch bearing from engine mainshaft; Remove C/B drive shaft.
11. Remove inner primary cover (6 nuts and washers).
12. Remove generator cover (4 screws).
13. Remove generator flywheel (Extractor 61-5002). Crankshaft can be held by tool made from old clutch centre or use service tool 61-5022.
14. Remove stator plate.
15. Remove nut securing kickstart sprocket and jerk sprocket off shaft taper. (Remove key and place to one side).
16. Remove gearbox outer cover followed by selector quadrant. Remove all Phillips screws holding inner gearbox/timing cover, not forgetting 2 behind selector quadrant.
17. Centralise camplate (2nd gear position or approximate) and withdraw inner cover complete with gear cluster, and mainshaft thrust washer.
18. Flatten camshaft pinion tab washer and, holding crankshaft, remove camshaft nut and pinion (Extractor 61-5025).
19. Remove brass camshaft retaining plate (2 screws). Remove oil pump drive link held to pump plunger by screw and tab washer and take off camshaft eccentric.

REASSEMBLING WITH NEW PARTS.

1. Fit new camshaft eccentric with side marked "O" outwards.
2. Replace oil pump drive link, screw and tab washer.
3. Replace camshaft retaining plate (2 screws).
4. Replace camshaft pinion (key will have remained in position on shaft lining up timing marks on camshaft and mainshaft pinion. Fit tab washer and nut.
5. Ensure that upper front engine stud is in position in crankcase.
6. Fit new primary inner cover, ensuring that rubber 'O' ring is in position on outer chaincase. Jointing compound should be applied to joint between crankcase and cover.
7. Clean off old jointing compound from gearbox inner cover and apply fresh. Replace complete gear cluster with cover, not forgetting mainshaft thrust washer. Replace and tighten retaining screws, not forgetting 2 in gearbox portion of cover.
8. Replace selector quadrant followed by gearbox outer cover, using jointing compound.

9. **Place K/S return spring over K/S spindle with long end dropping down,** engage sprocket over keyway, fit washer and nut ensuring key in position.

10. Engage short end of return spring in hole at back of sprocket, then with a long hooked piece of wire over long end of spring, swing round clockwise to place end of spring behind gearbox cover.

11. Replace stator, not forgetting 3 distance pieces on studs and pull generator lead through hole to avoid fouling flywheel.

12. **Replace flywheel and nut.** Do not overtighten, for preference employ torque wrench at 25 - 30 lb.ft.

13. Replace generator cover.

14. Fit primary driven gear key to gearbox mainshaft carefully to avoid dropping into chaincase. Replace pinion, tab washer and nut. Do not tighten fully until clutch is assembled.

15. Fit new clutch bearing and housing. Replace clutch centre thrust washer with chamfer outwards, assemble plates on clutch centre and fit to mainshaft. (They can be held together by one spring and nut temporarily). Replace clutch nut and lockwasher, followed by springs, nuts and spring plate.

16. Tighten driven pinion nut and bend over tab washer.

17. Replace C/B drive shaft <u>minus</u> 'O' ring.

18. Fit clutch push-rod complete with 'O' ring to new outer cover, apply new gasket to cover with jointing compound both sides. Fit cover and screws.

19. Fit oil return pipe and unions between cylinder head and top of outer cover with fibre washer beneath each union.

20. Put left hand side cylinder on T.D.C. compression stroke, rotate engine backwards through 5° (half distance between 2 vanes on cooling fan, remembering it is a backward running engine).

21. Ensure that advance and retard mechanism is free, then fit A/R assembly to drive shaft so that flat on cam is at approximately 6 o'clock position. Lightly screw in retaining screw.

22. Fit contact breaker plate, condensor with black and white lead to left hand side. Rotate plate and ensure that both sets points open .015".

23. Move C/B plate until bottom set joints just breaking. If movement insufficient, cam must be re-positioned.

24. Tighten cam on to shaft with screw.

25. Fit hexagons to hold C/B plate.

26. Check A/R unit operation and re-check timing.

27. Replace C/B cover.

<u>RE-FITTING AUTOMOTIVE UNIT.</u>

1. Put front engine studs in position, pick up unit and holding tilted slightly to left, pass rear drive through vertical frame members.

2. Bring unit upright and slide into position so that the two crankcase lugs slide into mounting brackets on vertical frame pillars.

3. Fit rear mounting bolts through lugs on frame and on crankcase. Place $\frac{1}{4}$" clip over bolt on R/H side and fit two $\frac{1}{4}$" bolts and nuts.

4. Slide 'L' shaped front engine plates over front studs with feet of plates turned outwards. Fit washers and nuts to studs but do not tighten.

5. Replace bolts through frame cross member and tighten securely. Tighten nuts on crankcase studs.

6. Replace curved bearing support arm. Three long bolts at rear pass through from rear of chaincase. Two bolts have flats on heads engaging in flats in chaincase, middle bolt has hexagon head.

7. Replace large washer on front end of bearing arm, engaging over dowel pin and re-fit hollow bolt with grease nipple.

8. Re-connect speedo drive cable and rear brake cable.

9. Re-connect L.T. leads to coils, longer head to R/H coil.

10. Re-fit rear mudguard. Two $\frac{1}{4}$" bolts and nuts on frame cross member and two at rear on bracket carrying petrol tank and silencer.

11. Connect K/S chain to pedal with spring link.

12. Replace gearshift lever over spindle on gearbox and fit new shouldered nut, tightening securely.

13. Fit new type gear control rod between gearshift lever and pedal. Adjust length of rod so that gearshift pedal is in centre of footboard slot thus giving sufficient movement both for and aft to select gears.

14. Fit new modified manifold to carburetter, then to cylinder head.

15. Fit petrol pipe to carburetter. Replace petrol tap support bracket on rocker cover stud.

16. Refit exhaust pipes to cylinder head and tighten exhaust pipe/silencer clips.

17. Fit air ducting around cylinder head.

18. Replace H/T leads on spark plugs.

19. Fit clutch cable to lever on primary drive cover.

20. Re-connect generator leads beneath footboards.

21. Re-connect rectifier earth lead to gearbox outer cover.

22. Put $\frac{1}{4}$ pint oil in gearbox and primary drive case and $2\frac{1}{2}$ pints in engine.

23. Re-fit body panels and dual seat.

24. Re-fit rear number plate and re-make rear lamp connections.

VELOCEPRESS MANUALS – MOTORCYCLE BY MAKE

AJS 1932-1948 SINGLES & TWINS 250cc THRU 1000cc (BOOK OF)
AJS 1945-1960 SINGLES 350cc & 500cc MODELS 16 & 18 (BOOK OF)
AJS 1955-1965 SINGLES 350cc & 500cc (BOOK OF)
ARIEL UP TO 1932 (BOOK OF)
ARIEL 1932-1939 PREWAR MODELS (BOOK OF)
ARIEL 1933-1951 (WORKSHOP MANUAL)
ARIEL 1939-1960 4 STROKE SINGLES (BOOK OF)
ARIEL 1958-1964 LEADER & ARROW (BOOK OF)
BMW R26 R27 (1956-1967) FACTORY WORKSHOP MANUAL
BMW R50 R50S R60 R69S (1955-1969) FACTORY WORKSHOP MANUAL
BRIDGESTONE 90 SERIES FACTORY WSM & PARTS CATALOGUE
BRIDGESTONE 175 SERIES FACTORY WSM & PARTS CATALOGUE
BRIDGESTONE 350 SERIES FACTORY WSM & PARTS CATALOGUES
BSA SUNBEAM SCOOTER WORKSHOP MANUAL 1959-1965
BSA SERVICE SHEETS MASTER CATALOGUE ALL MODELS 1945-1967
BSA BANTAM D1 TO D7 1948-1966 FACTORY SERVICE SHEETS MANUAL
BSA BANTAM ALL MODELS FROM 1948 ONWARDS (BOOK OF)
BSA SINGLES & V-TWINS UP TO 1927 (BOOK OF)
BSA SINGLES & V-TWINS UP TO 1930 (BOOK OF)
BSA SINGLES & V-TWINS UP TO 1935 (BOOK OF)
BSA SINGLES & V-TWINS 1936-1939 (BOOK OF)
BSA C10, C11 & C12 1945-1958 FACTORY SERVICE SHEETS MANUAL
BSA OHV & SV SINGLES 250-600cc 1945-1959 (BOOK OF)
BSA C15 & B40 1958-1967 FACTORY SERVICE SHEETS MANUAL
BSA OHV & SV SINGLES 250cc (ONLY) 1954-1970 (BOOK OF)
BSA B31, B32, B33 & B34 1945-60 FACTORY SERVICE SHEETS MANUAL
BSA OHV SINGLES 350 & 500cc 1955-1967 (BOOK OF)
BSA M20, M21 & M33 1945-1963 FACTORY SERVICE SHEETS MANUAL
BSA TWINS A7 & A10 1948-1962 FACTORY SERVICE SHEETS MANUAL
BSA TWINS A7 & A10 1948-1962 (BOOK OF)
BSA TWINS A50 & A65 1962-1965 FACTORY WORKSHOP MANUAL
BSA TWINS A50 & A65 1962-1969 (SECOND BOOK OF)
DOUGLAS 1929-1939 PREWAR ALL MODELS (BOOK OF)
DOUGLAS 1948-1957 POSTWAR ALL MODELS FACTORY SHOP MANUAL
DUCATI 160cc, 250cc & 350cc OHC MODELS FACTORY SHOP MANUAL
HONDA 50 ALL MODELS UP TO 1970 INC MONKEY & TRAIL (BOOK OF)
HONDA 90 ALL MODELS UP TO 1966 (BOOK OF)
HONDA 125-150cc TWINS C/CS/CB/CA FACTORY WORKSHOP MANUAL
HONDA 250-305 TWINS C/CS/CB FACTORY WORKSHOP MANUAL
HONDA 450 CB/CL 1965-1974 K0 TO K7 WORKSHOP MANUAL
HONDA C100 SUPER CUB FACTORY WORKSHOP MANUAL
HONDA C110 SPORT CUB 1962-1969 FACTORY WORKSHOP MANUAL
HONDA TWINS & SINGLES 50cc THRU 305cc 1960-1966 (BOOK OF)
HONDA TWINS ALL MODELS 125cc THRU 450cc UP TO 1968 (BOOK OF)
INDIAN PONYBIKE, BOY RACER & PAPOOSE ILL PARTS LIST & SALES LIT
J.A.P. ENGINES 1927-1952 & MOTORCYCLES 1934-1952 (BOOK OF)
LAMBRETTA 1947-1957 ALL 125 & 150cc MODELS (BOOK OF)
LAMBRETTA 1957-1970 LI & TV MODELS (SECOND BOOK OF)
MATCHLESS 1931-1939 ALL MODELS 250cc THRU 990cc (BOOK OF)
MATCHLESS 1945-1956 350 & 500cc SINGLES (BOOK OF)
MATCHLESS 1955-1966 350 & 500cc SINGLES (BOOK OF)
NEW IMPERIAL ALL SV & OHV FROM 1935 ONWARDS (BOOK OF)
NORTON 1932-1939 PREWAR MODELS (BOOK OF)
NORTON 1932-1947 (BOOK OF)
NORTON 1938-1956 (BOOK OF)
NORTON 1955-1963 MODELS 19, 50 & ES2 (BOOK OF)
NORTON 1955-1965 DOMINATOR TWINS (BOOK OF)
NORTON 1960-1970 TWIN CYLINDER FACTORY WORKSHOP MANUAL
NORTON 1970-1975 COMMANDO FACTORY WORKSHOP MANUAL
NORTON 1975-1978 MK 3 COMMANDO FACTORY WORKSHOP MANUAL
NSU PRIMA 1956-1964 ALL MODELS (BOOK OF)
NSU QUICKLY 1953-1963 ALL MODELS (BOOK OF)
PANTHER 1932-1958 LIGHTWEIGHT MODELS 250 & 350cc (BOOK OF)
PANTHER 1938-1966 HEAVYWEIGHT MODELS 600 & 650cc (BOOK OF)
RALEIGH MOPEDS 1960-1969 (BOOK OF)
RALEIGH MOTORCYCLES 1919-1933 (BOOK OF)
ROYAL ENFIELD 1934-1946 SINGLES & V TWINS (BOOK OF)
ROYAL ENFIELD 1937-1953 SINGLES & V TWINS (BOOK OF)
ROYAL ENFIELD 1946-1962 SINGLES (BOOK OF)
ROYAL ENFIELD 1958-1966 250cc & 350cc SINGLES (SECOND BOOK OF)
ROYAL ENFIELD 736cc INTERCEPTOR FACTORY WORKSHOP MANUAL
RUDGE 1933-1939 (BOOK OF)
SUNBEAM 1928-1939 (BOOK OF)
SUNBEAM 1946-1957 S7 & S8 (BOOK OF)
SUZUKI 50cc & 80cc UP TO 1966 (BOOK OF)
SUZUKI T10 1963-1967 FACTORY WORKSHOP MANUAL
SUZUKI T20 & T200 1965-1969 FACTORY WORKSHOP MANUAL
SUZUKI TWINS 1962 ONWARDS 125-500cc WORKSHOP MANUAL
TRIUMPH TIGRESS SCOOTER WORKSHOP MANUAL 1959-1965
TRIUMPH 1935-1939 PREWAR MODELS (BOOK OF)
TRIUMPH 1935-1949 (BOOK OF)
TRIUMPH 1937-1951 (WORKSHOP MANUAL)
TRIUMPH 1945-1955 FACTORY WORKSHOP MANUAL
TRIUMPH 1945-1958 TWINS (BOOK OF)
TRIUMPH 1956-1969 TWINS (BOOK OF)
VELOCETTE 1925-1970 ALL SINGLES & TWINS (BOOK OF)
VESPA 1951-1961 (BOOK OF)
VESPA 1955-1963 125 & 150cc & GS MODELS (SECOND BOOK OF)
VESPA 1955-1968 GS & SS (BOOK OF)
VESPA 1963-1972 90, 125 & 150cc (THIRD BOOK OF)
VILLIERS ENGINE UP TO 1959 INC. 3 WHEELERS (BOOK OF)
VILLIERS ENGINE UP TO 1969 (BOOK OF)
VINCENT 1935-1955 (WORKSHOP MANUAL)
YAMAHA 1961-1967 YA5 & YA6 (WORKSHOP MANUAL & ILL PARTS LIST)
YAMAHA 1971-1972 JT1& JT2 (WORKSHOP MANUAL & ILL PARTS LIST)

VELOCEPRESS TECHNICAL BOOKS – MOTORCYCLE

1930'S BRITISH MOTORCYCLE CARBS & ELEC COMPONENTS (BOOK OF)
1930'S BRITISH MOTORCYCLE ENGINES (OVERHAUL & MAINTENANCE)
1930'S BRITISH MOTORCYCLE GEARBOXES & CLUTCHES (BOOK OF)
CATALOG OF BRITISH MOTORCYCLES (1951 MODELS)
CYCLEMOTOR (BOOK OF)
LUCAS ELECTRONICS BRITISH M/CYCLES REPAIR & PARTS (1950-1977)
MOTORCYCLE ENGINEERING (P.E. Irving)
MOTORCYCLE ROAD TESTS 1949-1953 (Motor Cycle Magazine UK)
SPEED AND HOW TO OBTAIN IT (Motor Cycle Magazine UK)
TUNING FOR SPEED (P.E. Irving)

VELOCEPRESS MANUALS - THREE WHEELER'S

BMW ISETTA FACTORY WORKSHOP MANUAL
BSA THREE WHEELER (BOOK OF)
VINTAGE MORGAN THREE WHEELER (BOOK OF)

VELOCEPRESS MANUALS – AUTOMOBILE BY MAKE

ALFA ROMEO GIULIA WORKSHOP MANUAL 1300 TO 2000cc 1962-1975
ALFA ROMEO GIULIA TECH MANUAL CARBURETED CARS FROM 1962
ALFA ROMEO GIULIA TECH MANUAL FUEL INJECTED CARS FROM 1969
ALFA ROMEO GIULIETTA & GIULIA 750 & 101 SERIES 1955-1965 WSM
AUSTIN-HEALEY SPRITE & MG MIDGET WORKSHOP MANUAL 1958-1971
BMW 600 LIMOUSINE FACTORY WORKSHOP MANUAL
BMW 600 LIMOUSINE OWNERS HAND BOOK & SERVICE MANUAL
BMW 2000 & 2002 1966-1976 WORKSHOP MANUAL
CORVAIR 1960-1969 WORKSHOP MANUAL
CORVETTE V8 1955-1962 WORKSHOP MANUAL
FIAT 500 FACTORY WORKSHOP MANUAL 1957-1973
FIAT 600, 600D & MULTIPLA FACTORY WORKSHOP MANUAL 1955-1969
JAGUAR E-TYPE 3.8 & 4.2 SERIES 1 & 2 WORKSHOP MANUAL
JAGUAR MK 7, 8, 9 & XK120, 140, 150 WORKSHOP MANUAL 1948-1961
METROPOLITAN FACTORY WORKSHOP MANUAL
MGA & MGB OWNERS HANDBOOK & WORKSHOP MANUAL
MG MIDGET TC, TD, TF & TF1500 WORKSHOP MANUAL
PORSCHE 356 1948-1965 WORKSHOP MANUAL
PORSCHE 911 2.0, 2.2, 2.4 LITRE 1964-1973 WORKSHOP MANUAL
PORSCHE 911 2.7, 3.0, 3.2 LITRE 1973-1989 WORKSHOP MANUAL
PORSCHE 912 WORKSHOP MANUAL
TRIUMPH TR2, TR3, TR4 1953-1965 WORKSHOP MANUAL
VOLKSWAGEN TRANSPORTER, TRUCKS & WAGONS 1950-1979 WSM
VOLVO 1944-1968 ALL MODELS WORKSHOP MANUAL

VELOCEPRESS TECHNICAL BOOKS - AUTOMOBILE

FERRARI 250/GT SERVICE AND MAINTENANCE
FERRARI GUIDE TO PERFORMANCE
FERRARI OWNER'S HANDBOOK
FERRARI TUNING TIPS & MAINTENANCE TECHNIQUES
HOW TO BUILD A FIBERGLASS CAR
HOW TO BUILD A RACING CAR
HOW TO RESTORE THE MODEL 'A' FORD
MASERATI OWNER'S HANDBOOK
OBERT'S FIAT GUIDE
PERFORMANCE TUNING THE SUNBEAM TIGER
SOUPING THE VOLKSWAGEN
SOLEX CARBURETORS (EMPHASIS ON UK & EU AUTOMOBILES)
SU CARBURETORS (EMPHASIS ON UK AUTOMOBILES)
WEBER CARBURETORS (EMPHASIS ON ALFA & FIAT)

VELOCEPRESS BOOKS & GUIDES - AUTOMOBILE

ABARTH BUYERS GUIDE
COMPLETE CATALOG OF JAPANESE MOTOR VEHICLES
FERRARI 308 SERIES BUYER'S AND OWNER'S GUIDE
FERRARI BERLINETTA LUSSO
FERRARI BROCHURES AND SALES LITERATURE 1946-1967
FERRARI BROCHURES AND SALES LITERATURE 1968-1989
FERRARI SERIAL NUMBERS PART I - ODD NUMBERS TO 21399
FERRARI SERIAL NUMBERS PART II - EVEN NUMBERS TO 1050
FERRARI SPYDER CALIFORNIA
HENRY'S FABULOUS MODEL "A" FORD
MASERATI BROCHURES AND SALES LITERATURE

VELOCEPRESS BOOKS – RACING

CARRERA PANAMERICANA - MEXICAN ROAD RACE (BOOK OF)
DIALED IN - THE JAN OPPERMAN STORY
IF HEMINGWAY HAD WRITTEN A RACING NOVEL
VEDA ORR'S NEW REVISED HOT ROD PICTORIAL

AUTOBOOKS WORKSHOP MANUALS & BROOKLANDS ROAD TEST PORTFOLIOS

FOR A COMPLETE LISTING OF THE AUTOBOOKS & BROOKLANDS TITLES
THAT WE CURRENTLY HAVE AVAILABLE, PLEASE VISIT OUR WEBSITE.
www.VelocePress.com

Please check our website:

www.VelocePress.com

for a complete
up-to-date list of
available titles

www.ingramcontent.com/pod-product-compliance
Lightning Source LLC
Chambersburg PA
CBHW080433230426
43662CB00015B/2264